Week St. Mary Village

a community at large

Old College - built 1506

David M Martin

© 2007

First Published 2007

Published by
David Martin
27 St. Andrew's Road
Stratton
Bude
Cornwall
EX23 9AG

ISBN 978-0-9557219-0-8

Printed and bound by
Lazarus Press
Unit 7 Caddsdown Business Park
Bideford
Devon
EX39 3DX

www.lazaruspress.com

Cover picture by John Lynch

Dedication

To my Mother, who died so young, missing out on the pleasures that our families would have given her; also to Janet, a sister we never knew yet cannot help but wonder what contribution to life she would have made.

✝

Pauline Norah Martin
23.3.29 - 22.12.78

Janet Martin
3.5.52 - 5.5.52

Foreword

The problem with history is that it involves our yesterdays; and all of our yesterdays accumulate at an alarming rate without our really noticing. In other words, history just keeps on happening. And so we are indeed blessed that down the ages, and particularly here in venerable St. Mary's Wyke, many daily happenings have been recorded without premeditation through letters, diaries, summaries of events and other similar means. When combined with deeds, wills, transactions, parish records, illustrations and other "scraps of the past" they begin to form a latent and sometimes vast storehouse of interesting information that is waiting to be collected into a "history." This "collecting" is frequently the work of a writer-browser who skilfully seeks out and compiles a chronological account of the noteworthy and of the interesting that is both entertaining and useful; useful because some of the randomness and mystery have been removed from a finite segment of the history of people and place.

The motivation for the production of a new "history" is usually in the form of some personal interest kindled in the mind of the potential author or some event that points to a need for a unique compilation of facts. But for our author, David Martin, this stream of evocative mental images, complemented by a fascinating historic background, has been engendered by far more than that. His absorbing account of our village life has been written by one for whom, by his own admission, "Week St. Mary is the only place I call home." Subsequently, it is this creator's personal knowledge and experience that lends the book its air of authenticity and which provides the reader with a unique view of a Cornish "community at large".

Canon Rob Dickenson
Week St. Mary Rectory

Acknowledgements

To compile a book such as this would be impossible without the help of a large number of people. I shall be eternally grateful to the following who have contributed so much.

Contributors:

Abbott, Adrian
Abbott, Martin
Anston-Race, Donna & John
Baker, Glennys
Barriball, Pat
Booker, Bob & Lesley
Casey, Peter
Cauldwell, Marguerite
Cobbledick, Linda & Roy
Coles, David & Sheila
Colwill, Den
Colwill, Walter & Rita
Crocker-White, Brenda
Davies, Len
Denton, Beryl
Dickenson, Canon Rob
Goodman, Audrey
Gubbin, Peter
Henchley, Malcolm
Hoppé, Susannah
Hutchings, Keith & Enid
Johns MBE, Bob
Johns, Pat
Kamm, Damian
Kinsman, Dorcas & Arthur
Lynch, John
Martyn, Arthur & Ruth
Matthews, Joan
Medland, Mary
Middleton, Alan

Orchard, Den & Joyce
Parnell, Alfred
Parnell, Les & Doris
Paynter, Joseph
Perry, Monica
Petherick, Valerie
Pooley, Brenda
Pooley, Leo
Poulton, Gillian
Risdon, Reg & Lorna
Roberts, Jeff
Rogers, Gordon
Shipton, Jo
Skinner, Glynn
Swayne, Margaret
Tarrant, Audrey
Turner, Jeanette
Ward, John
Wise, Mrs
Young, Bill

Organisations:

Cornish & Devon Post
Cornwall Record Office
Landmark Trust
Launceston Museum
WSM Parish Council
WSM Parish Hall Committee
WSM Women's Institute

Special mention must be made of my sister, Linda Cobbledick, who has helped so much in the gathering of information, my wife Jean who has had to bear the constant pressure of helping to compile the information, and Jane Toplis for her proof-reading skills. Thank you all so much.

Contents

Introduction

It would be unusual to mention magpies and technology in the same sentence but those two words depict two of my main characteristics. It all started in 1983 when I rode my motorcycle to Exeter to purchase one of the latest home computers - Clive Sinclair's ZX-81. It was an eventful purchase on that extremely hot afternoon. Arriving at the car park I parked my Honda CX500 motorcycle and, accompanied by my wife, went off to Dixons to spend my money.

For such a small device it certainly came in a big box! We returned to the car park and saw to my horror that our motorcycle had fallen over onto the adjacent Cortina saloon. Because of the incredible weather the recently laid tarmac had softened allowing the footrest to sink. I was later told by the Cortina's owner that the surface was originally very uneven, with deep potholes, and 'they' levelled it with tarmac which meant that in some places it was several inches deep.

My motorcycle was fitted with a full-fairing and the weight of the machine hitting the Cortina caused the fairing to shift slightly, enough to prevent the handlebars from turning! My, did I sweat, trying to undo the clamps and shift the fairing back into line.

Eventually we managed to get on our way homeward but not before I left our telephone number on the parking ticket which I carefully placed onto the side window of the car - something for which the car-owner was really grateful.

The ZX-81 was the starting point for me, followed in turn by the Spectrum, the QL and the first model with its own screen, a TRS-80 (albeit only a green display!), before moving onto the Amstrad range of computers. The fascination of computers and what can be achieved is now almost a fact of modern life - nearly every device has some form of microchip built into it controlling another aspect of modern life!

Magpies! Like so many people the craving to collect and store is my other weakness. It is not necessarily a form of greed - a 'must have' no matter what - but almost an addiction to hang onto an earlier memory - this form as opposed to hanging onto something because, "...I might need it one day!"

With development of the Internet came the desire to have a web site of some worth. As Week St. Mary is the family 'home' it was obvious that the village should have a 'website' where all aspects of the village - its history, modern events, useful information, etc - could be found.

At this point that I must publicly acknowledge the fantastic support, of both the website and this book, given by my sister Linda Cobbledick. She is a co-owner of the website, helping to share the cost of the non-profit-making venture, and a staunch helper in the enormous task of researching material for this book.

During the course of compiling information about the village's long history it soon became apparent that both the quantity and quality of information was more appropriate in writing a book than filling endless web pages.

Week St. Mary is the only place I call 'home'. As a family we all grew up here, went to school here and stayed until employment beckoned elsewhere. Our Mother and a sister we never knew lie in the churchyard and we still support the village in many ways.

There are bound to be stories, rumours, unconfirmed facts or tales of old that have not come to light by the time this book reaches the publisher but I hope that the story so far will become my permanent contribution to the village I know and love, and I thank all of the contributors so very much for all their memories, photographs and documents - thank you everyone - all I have done is put it all together!

David M Martin - 2007

Week St. Mary

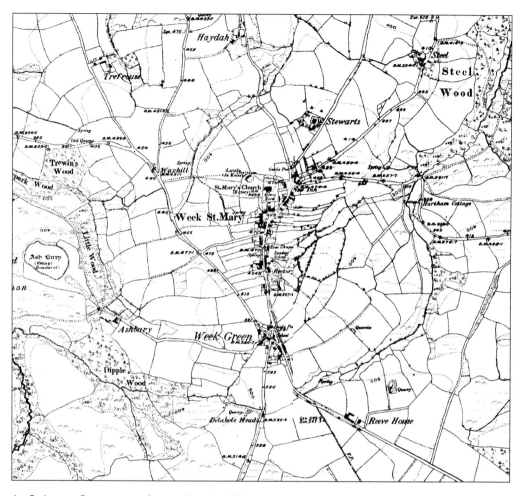

An Ordnance Survey map of approximately 1890 showing the extent of Week St. Mary village. The strip fields (burgage plots) can be clearly seen either side of the main thoroughfare through the village.

In this extract of a map of Cornwall by John Seller, 1694, Week St. Mary is known only by the name of 'Wike'.

It is interesting to note the spellings of some of the placenames, particularly 'Poffyll'; at least visitors to our shores might have pronounced it correctly, rather than attempting the current spelling of 'Poughill'. On a map dated 1701 it was spelt 'Pughill', with the modern-day version appearing on a map dated 1808. Equally, 'Wike' became 'S.Maryweek' in 1701 and just 'Week' on the 1808 map.

Bude did not appear on maps until much later - 'Stratton' was the main town of that area, probably dating back to Roman times.

'Week St. Mary was a town
When Launceston was a fuzzy down'

Just after the beginning

It is hard to imagine how a village happens; first one house, then another and it slowly grows until a community is formed with all the facilities necessary to allow it to survive. No one can be absolutely sure where the first building appeared or indeed, why here at all. Geography often forms a reason for the existence of an inn or place of business, such as on a crossroads, or nearby a river crossing, adding to the desire for new residents to put down their roots.

Week St. Mary (St. Mary's village) was originally a settlement on the frontiers separating the early Saxon invaders from the old Celtic inhabitants. The frontier ran southwest from Bude between the village and the coast. The deep valleys and tumbled hills made a natural boundary, further defended by such camps as Ashbury and Whalesborough.

Situated just a few miles inland from the Atlantic coastline, the settlement has grown from humble beginnings into a substantial thriving community. It is firmly planted in Cornwall albeit only a mile or so from the Devon border.

The present change in social structures has resulted in a gradual decline of village commercialism, across the land, falling victim to the modern supermarket and the ever-growing on-line business activity through the Internet. During the past 50 years we have seen the loss of the village blacksmith, carpenters, tailors, garage, filling pumps, grocery shops and general stores, but more on that later.

The village is mentioned in the Domesday Book, compiled in 1086 under instructions from William the Conqueror. It contains records of over 13,000 settlements. The extract for Week St. Mary appears alongside its 'English' translation.[1]

The same Richard holds WEEK ST MARY. Cola held it TRE and it paid geld for half a hide. Yet there is 1 hide. [There is] land for 8 ploughs. There are 3 ploughs, and 4 slaves and 6 villans and 10 bordars, and 2 acres of woodland, and pasture 1 league long and as much broad. Formerly 20s; now it is worth 30s. The same man holds PENHALLYM. Erneis held it TRE and it paid geld for half a hide. Yet there are 1 & ½ hides. [There is] land for 10 ploughs. There are 6 ploughs, and 6 slaves and 8 villans and 22 bordars, and 6 acres of woodland. [There is] pasture 1 league long and as much broad. Formerly 40s; now it is worth 30s. The same man holds DOWNINNEY. Maeligrle-Sveinn held it TRE and it paid geld for 1 hide. Yet there are 2 hides. There is land for 12 ploughs. There are 10 ploughs, and 10 slaves and 10 villans and 20 bordars. [There is] pasture 1 league long and as much broad.

[1]*A translation from the Doomsday Book for Week St. Mary, formerly known as 'Wich'*

Although difficult to grasp at first it is still noticeable that it mentions quite a bit of ground and a number of people - this shows that the village has already grown to some substance by this period in our history.

Week St. Mary is thus recorded in the Domesday Book as the small settlement of 'Wich' and this manor was granted to Richard Fitz Turold, steward of the Earl of Cornwall, Robert of Mortain, a half brother of William I. The settlement had a recorded occupancy of about six villagers and ten smallholders.

This period of our history was apparently quite a bloody one; the military conquest of England by William, duke of Normandy (later William I), was mainly through his victory over Harold II at the Battle of Hastings. Edward the Confessor had designated William as his successor in 1051, so when Harold, duke of Wessex, was crowned king of England in 1066 instead, William assembled an invasion force of some 5,000 knights.[2]

After defeating Harold's army near Hastings on October 14 and advancing to London, he was crowned king in Westminster Abbey on Christmas Day, 1066. Native revolts continued until 1071, notably in Northumbria. The Norman Conquest brought great social and political changes to England, linking the country more closely with Western Europe and replacing the old English aristocracy with a Norman aristocracy. The English language was subjected to a long period of influence by Anglo-French, which remained in literary and courtly use until the reign of Edward III and in legal reporting until the 17th century.

> **1215**: Magna Carta - Magna Carta was originally written because of disagreements between Pope Innocent III, King John and his English barons about the rights of the King. Magna Carta required the king to renounce certain rights, respect certain legal procedures and accept that the will of the king could be bound by the law. It explicitly protected certain rights of the King's subjects - whether free or unfree - most notably the right of Habeas Corpus. Many clauses were renewed throughout the Middle Ages, and further during the Tudor and Stuart periods, and the 17th and 18th centuries. By the early 19th century most clauses in their original form had been repealed from English law.

Week St. Mary was allegedly a small, typical medieval market town which served the surrounding countryside; generally of up to half a day's walk away. This ancient borough is noted for the arrangement of 'strip fields' (burgage stitches) radiating outwards from the church and castle. Whilst other examples of strip fields can be found nearby at Forrabury they do not follow the same layout.

It seems probable that for centuries it was a place of some importance in the surrounding countryside. A few fields westward of the present village and church is a flat-topped circular hill known as Ashbury: it is now a field, but all round it can be seen the earth-works which surrounded a prehistoric fortified "bury" ("burgh" or "borough").

Later came the Normans to settle in a hostile country. Anyone coming from the coast, who has seen Week St. Mary church tower persistently pushing itself into view, can imagine a Norman Baron finding hereabouts a good place on which to build his castle. This is what certainly happened. The field adjoining the Churchyard on the west is still known as "Castle Ditch," and in it is a large mound, which marks the site of an old building, and which from its shape tells us that it was a Norman Castle. Under the shelter of this castle we may suppose was built the Church of "Our Lady of Week" on the same site as the present Church.

The Castle, together with the Manor and Borough of Week, belonged in 1085 to the powerful Baron Fitz Turold, Lord of Cardinham. A member of his house settled here, and about 1171, Osbert, Prior of Tywardreath, with eight of his monks, witnessed a deed by which Walter de Wick and Aliz, daughter of Richard de Wick, granted to the Priory the right of the advowson[3] 'in the Church of the Blessed Virgin Mary of Wick'. It is plain therefore that the family called "de Wick" took its name from Wick St. Mary.

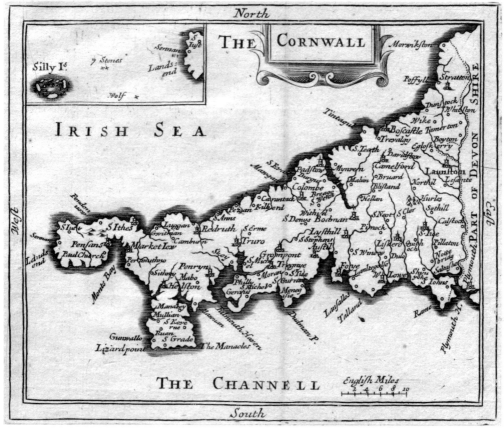

[4]Map of Cornwall 1694

The monks of Tywardreath did not long retain the patronage, for at an early date the manor of Week came into the possession of the Blanchminster family. Ralph de Blanchminster, of whom there is a monumental effigy in armour in Stratton Church, died in 1348.

That Week St. Mary was still considered a place of some importance may be inferred from the following story:

Richard Buvyle, Rector of the neighbouring parish of Whitstone, died in 1358, slain either by his own hand or by some enemy. He was doubtless buried at cross roads. Rumour had it that he was a saint, and some remarkable cures having taken place at his grave, the body was translated to Whitstone Church. Meanwhile the "cult" of this new saint had taken hold of all North Cornwall and Devonshire. Bands of people kept nightly vigils at the first place of his burial, saying prayers for his soul. These, with the friends who brought them victuals, turned the place into a regular fair, resulting in such behaviour that Bishop Grandisson felt bound to interfere. He ordered the "cultus" to cease until due enquiry into the alleged cures had been made. In 1361, a jury consisting of three vicars, three curates and six laymen was specially summoned at Week St. Mary for the purpose, and they sent to the Bishop a certificate of ten cures performed on five men and five women. After this the matter seems to have died a natural death, for we hear no more about it.

A writer in 1799 says: "The Churchtown is in all ancient records called the Borough of Week St. Mary, and the occupiers of certain fields are still called Burgage holders. The custom of electing a mayor is still kept up, but his office is merely nominal."

Papers in the possession of the late Col. I'ans show that certain families held different estates by lease, which were tributary to the Crown; and in particular the honour and fee of Week St. Mary was a part of the inheritance of the Duchy of Cornwall. Edward III created the Duchy in 1337 for maintenance of his eldest son, then aged 7 years. Christopher Pollard, Esq., after having granted leases of several burgage tenements, sold the fee to Prince Charles, afterwards Charles I, in a warrant dated February, 1616, and addressed to the free tenants of the Manor of Swannacott and Week St. Mary. In 1637 an order was issued for the steward and bailiff of Week St. Mary to appear "within goat skin mantles" and account before the court. (Further examples of this account to the Duke of Cornwall appear later in this book).

The descendants of the Blanchminsters and their connections including such famous names as Tresillian, Granville, Earl of Bath, Carteret, continued to be patrons of the Living of Week St. Mary until 1786, when, by agreement with the Master and Fellows of Sidney Sussex College, Cambridge, Lord Carteret exchanged it for that of Wilshampstead, which was close to his family seat near Bedford.

Following on from the Domesday reference the manor of Week St. Mary was held by the De Wyke family, then, during the 13th century the village passed to the Blanchminster family. The seaside town of Bude, just seven miles northwest of Week St. Mary still has a number of properties owned by the Blanchminster Trust.[5]

The major components of the ancient borough are the church, 'castle' and the market site. The ruins of this castle located in the field adjoining the church and locally named Castle Ditch, would almost certainly have been of wooden construction. Nothing but distinct mounds are visible suggesting ancient ramparts although there is no evidence that the castle played host to any attacks! The earthworks represent a 11th or 12th century castle and reportedly it would have failed to gain any significance past the 14th or 15th centuries.

The church stands on the site of an earlier Norman church - the 99ft tower stands high and mighty and can be seen from so many vantage points of the surrounding countryside. Whilst mostly of 15th century construction there is evidence of 13th and 14th century work.

With the church and market area paired together at the northern end of the village it shows the strength and importance of each to the community both in the past and more recent centuries. The relatively recent demise of the cattle market has not detracted from the main Square being the natural assembly point for many village functions.

Lower Square 1905

Described in 1820, Week St. Mary, or St. Mary - Week, situated in the Hundred of Stratton and Deanery of Trigg-Major, just seven miles south of Stratton; about ten miles north-west of Launceston, which is the post-office town; and ten west of Holsworthy in Devonshire. The principal villages in this parish, exclusively of the church-town, are Bakesdown, Lower Exe, Kitsham and Week Orchard. These names are now only classed as 'areas' lying within the parish boundary.

The manor of Week St. Mary belonged at an early period to the Blanchminsters, from whom it passed to the Coleshills. In the process of time, the manorial rights were transferred from Week St. Mary to Swannacott; for in 1620 we find that Sir Warwick Hele held the manor of Swannacott, and Week St. Mary Burgh, as parcel of the same. The manor of Swannacott, including Week St. Mary, is now (written in 1820) the property of the Right Honourable Lord de Dunstanville, by inheritance from the Heles.

The surrounding properties in the parish include the manor of Marrais, or East-Orchard-Marrais and Marham Church, which belonged to the ancient Marrais family whose heirs married an ancestor of the Rolle family. Subsequent sales now finds Marhayes as a private dwelling. A licence for a private chapel was granted to the Lord of Marhays and in 1727 the estate of Marhays was responsible for the upkeep of an altar in the south aisle of the church.

The English Civil War: (1642-1649)

During the Civil War Cornwall was staunchly Royalist. However, in 1643 the Parliamentarian army advanced across the Tamar and set up their headquarters at Stratton.

The Royalist commander, Sir Ralph Hopton, gathered his forces together to attack them. On Saturday 13th May his army quartered at North Petherwin, in good spirits despite a lack of provisions. Because of a skirmish with a troop of enemy cavalry the Royalists got no further on May 14th than Week St. Mary, where they decided to camp for the night.

In Hopton's own words: "Noe sooner were they come into Mary-Weeke but were presently entertained with a fresh allarum from the Enemy, who found them in so good a posture that they dar'd not make any further attempt upon them there. The Cornish army stoode upon their guard all that night likewise, still in very great want of provisions, their owne stores onely affording a bisquett to a man, and the place so poore, that it was not able to supply them in any considerable proporcion."

Next day they advanced to Stratton, where on Tuesday 16th May they defeated the Roundheads at Stamford Hill, the first major battle of the war. After parading through the town of Bude, this battle is re-enacted by the Sealed Knot Society annually, attracting many visitors.

Above and right:

A typical English Civil War re-enactment by The Sealed Knot.

Founded by Brigadier Peter Young D.S.O., M.C., F.H., in 1968. Within two years the membership topped 1,000 and a second, Parliamentarian, Army was formed within the Society.

Old Documents

There has recently been a very interesting "find" of documents relating to St. Gennys' parish and some other places in Cornwall. These documents were found in an old box on an estate in Sussex this year by a Mr. Batchelor, who is a direct descendant of General Batchelor, who purchased the manor of Crackington in 1889 at a price of £15,000.

No one can say now why these documents were not handed over when the General sold the manor some years later to the late William James Harris, but it is a great piece of good fortune that they have at last come to light. It happened that Mr. Batchelor's son visited St. Gennys recently, knowing that much of the parish had once belonged to his ancestor, the General. He also acquired a copy of Mr. Roger Parnall's history of St. Gennys, and contacted the author when he had found the old box at his home containing the documents. More than twenty old deeds and documents were in the box, mostly in good condition, and dating from 1565 to about the year 1800. Six documents are dated prior to 1600 and four more prior to 1628. Some are written in Latin, and others in medieval script. The earliest deed relates to Tremoutha (described in the deed as Lemouth), comprising a dwelling house, garden, orchard, 30 acres of arable land, 12 acres of meadow, 10 of pasture, 10 of wood and 20 of heath. This document shows that at that time Richard Roscarrock was interested in the ownership of the property. His family came from Roscarrock in St. Endellion parish.

The second document in date is even more interesting - dated 28th March 1566, and made between the famous Richard Grenville of Stowe and George Rolle, of Marhayes, in Week St. Mary. It relates to the sale to George Rolle of Grenville's half share of the Manor of Crackington, which he and Rolle had jointly purchased in 1563 from Henry, Earl of Huntingdon.

The third deed dated 7th June, 1589, records a release of Tremoutha and a tenement in Week St. Mary by John Roscarrock to George Rolle and bears the signature of John Roscarrock in great clarity and beauty. Little did he think as he signed in 1589 that we should be admiring the quality of his script nearly 400 years later!

The fourth deed dated in 1589 relates to the acquisition by George Rolle and his wife Margaret of a house, two gardens and 182 acres in Trehole and Hillparks, St Gennys. The last two of the XVI Century deeds relate to the sale on the 20th June, 1589, by John Roscarrock, Esquire, to George Rolle of Marrays, gent; and Andrew Rolle, his son and heir apparent, of all the lands in St. Gennys and Poundstock which came to John Roscarrock through Thomas Roscarrock his father. These lands included Tregoale alias Tregawle, Mellooke and Penwarne. Tregole, of course, is in Poundstock, Mellooke should need no explanation and Penwarne is now part of Trelay in St. Gennys.

Vanished Names - Four more deeds represent the years from 1602 to 1627. In a deed dated 30th March 1602, George Rolle, then described as of East Orchard, Marreys (Marhayes in Week Saint Mary parish), released to his son and heir Andrew Rolle all his rights in Penwarden and Penwarden Wood in St. Gennys.

17

You will not find the name Penwarden on any current map today, but it forms part of the farm known as Trelay in St. Gennys.

It should be noted that despite the above entry, referring to the date of 30th March 1602, the following is recorded on George Roll(e)'s headstone in Week St. Mary churchyard, by way of the inscription: 'Here lieth the body of GEORGE ROLL, ESQUIER who died the 10th day of February In Regni Elizabeth Anno Domini 1602'

On 20th June, 1603, Andrew Rolle of East Orchard, son and heir of George Rolle (then described as deceased), granted to Henry Rolle, of Stevenstone in Devon and Robert Rolle, of Ghanton, in Devon, Esquires, his manors of East Orchard, Marrayes and Crackington.

On 20th September, 1615, Walter Hickeman, of Kew, Surrey, Esquire, sold to Robert Hooper, of St. Gennys, Yeoman, a fourth part of Tecliffe, alias Cliffe, West Tresmoren and Penkey, St. Gennys. Those, who like interpreting place-names will instantly recognise Cleave, as it is called today. The price was £53. The last of the XVII century deeds is a lease dated 1st February, 1627, made between Andrew Rolle and Thomas Bray, of St. Gennys (described as a husbands man), of five fields known as Hill Downe Park, with the meadow and garden adjoining in St. Gennys, lately held by Edward Rawle. The letting was for 99 years on the lives of Thomas Bray, the tenant, and of Peter and Edward, the sons of Thomas Hallett, of St, Gennys, Yeoman. That was in 1615. It is interesting to recall, as evidence of the manner in which Christian names are handed down in families, that there was a Thomas Hallett living at St. Gennys in the present century. The Halletts were always said to have been men of some substance in St. Gennys. The description "Yeoman" in 1615 and the place-names "Hallett's Shute" and "Hallett's Lane" confirm this.

The only other deed in the box was of much later date. On 15th February 1811, the Right Honourable John Lord Rolle, of Stevenstone, Devon, leased to Stephen Smeeth (another good old St. Gennys and North Cornwall name), described as of St. Gennys husbandman, two waste plots adjoining the road leading from Wainhouse Corner in Jacobstow to Sparrett (Tresparrett) Posts in St. Gennys. This was a lease for 99 years on the lives of the tenant and his children Mary and Loveday, then aged 5 and 3 respectively.

The remaining documents in the chest consisted of three identical copies of a Rental and Valuation of the Manor of Crackington, un-dated but circa 1800, and two further copies with information as to existing lives on which the various tenancies depended.

Other interesting papers in the collection include a list of lands in the County of Cornwall referring to property in Stratton, Launcells and Week St. Mary, and also to Hartland and Horwood in Devon.

Lastly, and perhaps surprisingly, there were five letters dated between February 1712 and June 1713 from John Buller, of Morval, near Looe, relating to family matters and thought to have been sent to Sir John Coryton.

Through the generosity of Mr. Batchelor, all these invaluable documents have been donated to the County Museum (the Royal Institution of Cornwall) at Truro. ∎

The Blacksmith's shop was demolished and the junction widened as the level of traffic increased

Now Box Tree Cottage, this photograph shows it as two cottages with adjoining barn, all thatched

Hayescott and Manciple House on the left with Lantern Cottage and Church Cottage on the right

Clifton Tenement, Glanville House and Treetops facing the village green

An outing, ready to depart from the Square, circa 1924

View past New College towards Manciple House, circa 1914

21

The un-made Square showing the original Post Office and shop

Mr. William Higgins standing in the doorway of his shop

'Sea View' - Granny Pooley's shop doorway on the left and the house entrance on the right

Higgins' shop on the right and latterly Ridgman's, with the petrol pumps, just visible on the left

The original row of cottages leading towards Kilbroney, Week Green. The building in the distance is the cottage depicted below beside the entrance to Kilbroney

The view towards Week Green seen upon entering the village from the south

Thomasine Bonaventure

Much has been written of this woman. Many of the stories that have been passed down through the generations dwell on the romantic element of the story whilst others pooh-pooh the whole story giving it a totally different slant. The Dictionary of National Biography has registered a version in that it seems that some of the tales about her early life are incorrect and she belonged to the gentry and was not a poor shepherd's daughter.

One of the best 'popular' versions is that of the following, from "A Romance of Week St. Mary"[6]

In the year 1463, in the reign of King Edward IV, a London merchant, accompanied by his serving man, was crossing the moors to the south of Wyke St. Mary, and, seeking shelter for the night, met a maiden looking after a few sheep. This event was in the general area of Greenamoor[d1]. At the stranger's request she took him to her father's humble home, and there the wayfarer stayed that night. Next morning Richard Burnsby, for such was his name, having been greatly impressed by their daughter's wit and beauty, asked the parents if he might take her to London to assist his wife. So Thomasine Bonaventure set off, travelling pillion behind her master's servant, and in a fortnight's time was riding through the streets of London town, which one day were to ring with the praises of this unknown village maid. After Thomasine had spent a few years as a capable and faithful serving maid, her mistress died, and she consented to become the wife of her master. Three years afterwards her husband died of the plague, leaving to his wife - a young and beautiful widow - the whole of his property. In one of her letters she announces her husband's death and gives the Reeve of Week St. Mary ten marks "to the intent that he shall cause skilful masons to build a bridge at the Ford of Green-a-more, yea, and with stout stonework well laid, and see that they do no harm to that tree which standeth fast by the brook, neither dispoyle they the rushes and plants that grow thereby: for there did I pass many goodly hours when I was a small mayde, and there did I first see the face of a faithful friend."

An old chronicler says: "Her dower, together with her youth and beauty, procured her to the cognizance of divers well-deserving men, who thereupon made addresses of marriage to her, but none of them obtained her affection, but only Henry Gall of St. Lawrence, Milk Street, an eminent and wealthy citizen, and a merchant adventurer."

Soon after their marriage we find that "twenty acres of woodland copse in the neighbourhood were bought and conveyed by the gracious lady Dame Thomasine Gall to feofees and trustmen, for the perpetual use of the poor of Week St. Mary, for fewel to be hewn in pieces once a year and finally and equally divided, for evermore on the vigil of St. Thomas the Twin."

After five years Henry Gall died, leaving his wife a great fortune, and it is written, "The fame of the virtue, wealth and beauty of the said Thomasine spread itself over the City of London, so that persons of the greatest magnitude of wealth and dignity there courted her, Among the rest it was the fortune of John Percyval, Esquire, goldsmith and userer (that is to say, banker) to prevail upon her to become his wife." He was very wealthy and of high repute, alderman of his ward and of noble character. Their wedding, about the year 1480, was made a kind of public festival. As a wedding gift of remembrance to her old home she directed that "a firm and stedfast road should be laid down with stones, at her sole cost, along the midst of Green-a moor, and fit for man and beast to travel on with their lawful occasions from Lanstephadon (Launceston) to the sea."

At another time she gave forty marks towards the building of a tower for St. Stephen's Church, above the causeway of Dunheved, and it was her wish "that they should carry their pinnacles so high that they might be seen from Swannacote Cross, by the moor, to the intent that they who do behold it from the Burgage Mound may remember the poor mayde who is now a wedded dame of London Citie."

In 1486 John Percyval became Sheriff of London, and in 1498 Lord Mayor, and was knighted by the King.

A letter written at this time to her mother reads:

"Sweet mother, thy daughter hath seen the face of the King. We were bydden to a banket at the royal palace, and Sir John and I could not choose but go. There was such a blaze of lords and ladies in silks and samite and jewels of gold, that it was like the citie of New Jerusalem in the Scriptures, and thy maid Thomasine was arrayed so fine that they brought up the saying that I was dressed like an altar. When we were led into the chamber where His Highness stood, the King did kiss me on the cheek as the manner is, and he seemed gentle and kind. But then he did turn to my good lord and husband, and say, with a look stern and stark enow, 'Ha, Sir John! See to it that thy fair dame be liege and true, for she comes of the burly Cornish stock, and they be ever rebels in blood and bone. Even now they be one and all for that knave Warbeck, who is among them in the West.' You will guess, dear mother, how my heart did beat. But withall the King did drink to me at the banket and merrily did call 'Health to our Lady Mayoress Dame Thomasine Percyval, which now feedeth her flock in the Citie of London.' And thereat they did laugh and fleer and shout, and there was flashing of tankards and jingling of cups all down the Hall."

After twenty-five years of married life, Sir John died in 1504, and Thomasine, who lived for another thirty-five years, "employed the residue of her life to works no less bountiful than charitable - namely, repairing highways, feeding and apparelling the poor, etc." In her will, dated 1512, she makes her cousin, John Dinham, residuary legatee and leaves £20 to her brother, John Bonaventer.

She died in 1539 at the age of eighty-nine. Stratton Church accounts show that on the day on which she was to be "remembered" prayer was to be made for the repose of her soul and two shillings and two pence[d2] paid to the priests for bread and ale.

Both she and her husband were very loyal to their native places. He, amidst many duties, endowed Macclesfield, near which he was born, with a free grammar school, "because there were few schoolmasters in that country, and the children, for lack of teaching, fell to idleness and consequently live dissolutely all their days."

In 1506 she began to make arrangements for her own grammar school, in Week St. Mary, and the foundation deed of 10th July mirrored that of her late husband's school in Macclesfield, in providing for board and education to be given free of charge by a graduate of Oxford or Cambridge. The endowment, comprising lands in Devon purchased by Thomasine from Sir John Lisle, was to be placed in the hands of nineteen feoffees[d3] on her death. These arrangements were largely complete by February 1508 when Thomasine made the first of her two wills, in which she gave property to the Merchant Taylors' Company to augment the chantry, founded by her late husband in St Mary Woolnoth, which was administered by the company. Later that year she acquired a royal licence enabling her to found a chantry in the church at Week St. Mary, and soon afterwards the first master of the school was appointed. She died before October 1512 and left the final arrangements for the school in the hands of her cousin, John Dinham.

Her will, dated 26th March 1512, included a large number of cash bequests to servants, friends, and her remaining family in Cornwall, as well as money for charitable works. She also established numerous post-obit arrangements in London and Cornwall through her bequests to churches and religious houses. In a codicil dated 10th April she made over more lands in Devon to the trustees of her school. She was buried alongside her third husband in the church of St Mary Woolnoth in London.[7]

At Week St. Mary Dame Percyval's chantry and college, or grammar school, of which there are some picturesque remains, include a recessed doorway with carved tympanum, a piece of battlemented wall, a well, and the steps leading up to the top of the wall, where the college bell was hung.

It has been thought that the chantry and college were abolished under the Chantry Act of 1545, and that the connection of the school with the Chantry of St. John in the Church gave the pretext for this action. Carew says: "In Thomasine Bonaventer's grammar school divers of the best gentlemen's sons of Devon and Cornwall had been virtuously trained up in both kinds of divine and humane learning under one Cholwill, an honest and religious teacher; which caused the neighbours so much the rather and the more to rewe that a petty smacke only of popery opened the gap for the suppression of the whole by the statute made in Edward VI's reign touching the suppression of Chanterie."

The fact however seems to be that when the Commissioners came to Week St. Mary to inspect the chantry, the school was already in decay. This is confirmed by the following extract from the report of the Trustees of the Launceston Charities in 1859: "Among the records at the Record Office, London, are certain Certificates of the Commissioners appointed in the reign of King Henry the Eighth and King Edward 6th to take the surveys of all Chantries, Colleges, and Free Chapels in the County of Cornwall, and that by a Certificate made in or about the 27th year of the reign of King Henry 8th it appears that a Chantry then existed in the parish of Week St. Mary in the

Re-enactment of the story of Thomasine Bonaventure, circa 1950

Thomasine Bonaventure depicted leaving the village for London

County of Cornwall on the foundation of Dame Thomasine Percival, wife of Sir John Percival, Knight, to find a priest for ever not only to pray for her soul within the Parish of Week St. Mary, but also that the said priest should teach children freely in a school founded by the said Dame Percival not far from the said Parish Church, and he to receive for his yearly stipend a salary of £12 and 6 shillings to be levied of the lands given amongst other uses to that intent and purpose: to find a manciple or usher also to instruct and teach children under the said schoolmaster, and he to have for the maintenance of his living yearly 26 shillings and 8 pence. To give to the Laundress to wash the clothes of the Schoolmaster and Principal for her reward yearly 13 shillings and 4 pence and the remainder of the said lands and possessions belonging to the said Chantry the Trustees willed should be expended in the keeping of an obit yearly (18th April, see Tywardreath Obituary) for her within the Parish Church aforesaid."

"From a similar certificate of certain other Commissioners appointed in the second year of King Edward VI (1548) and by a memorandum thereto, it was noted that the Borough of Launceston was a very meet place to establish a learned man to preach and set forth the word of God to the people and also to teach children in their grammar and other necessary knowledge, and that whereas the said school at Week St. Mary was then in decay, the said Borough of Launceston was a very meet place to have the foundation of the said school removed unto."

"By the ninth and tenth certificates of the said Commissioners issued some time in the reign of King Edward VI, it appears that the said Chantry of Week St. Mary was removed to Launceston, and that the schoolmaster, usher and laundress of the said school of Week St. Mary were to continue their services at their accustomed wages (amounting together to £17 13s 3d) at Launceston."

It was Horwell Grammar School[d4], as it was called, in Launceston, that benefited by the action of the Commissioners, so that "Dame Percyval's" Charity was not misappropriated by the Crown, but passed from her beloved Week St. Mary to Lanstephadon, which she also loved.

Thomasine Bonaventure's Will

Purchased from Sotheby's Sale (Lot 25) 10th July 1972 after a decision of the Reviewing Committee on the Export of Works of Art on 13th October 1972 prevented its export to the purchaser (Mr. H. P. Kraus of Liechenstein and New York). Purchased with grant of £125 from the Friends of the National Libraries. Total cost £190. Received 16th November 1972.

Deed of endowment and foundation of a chantry and obit and a grammar school; by Thomasine Percyvale of London, widow, formerly wife of Sir John Percyvale, Kt., formerly Mayor of the City of London.

(Recital: Thomasine P. bought from Sir John Lisle of Throkliston, Hants., Kt. The manor of Sympston [Simpson in Holsworthy] with 2 messuages, 2 tofts, 150 acres of land, 20 acres of meadow, 80 acres of pasture, 20 acres of wood in Down, Westlake, Burescote [Burscott in Holsworthy], Holdesworthy [Holsworthy] Estelake and Yeoldelond [Yellowland alias Youldon in Holsworthy], Devon. By recovery, fine, and releases John Bonaventure, Esq.,

Nicholas Dynham, gent. And John Snawe seised of property to use of Thomasine and to her will. Value of property in Devon £12 4s 6d. Recital of lack of teachers and priests in Week St. Mary).

Trustees of recital to convey property (above) to John Trevilian, Kt., and his firstborn son John Trevilian; Thomas Graynefeld, Kt., and his firstborn son, Roger Graynefeld; Thos. Maris, Esq., and his firstborn son John Maris; Hen. Trecarrel Esq.; John Langdon Esq., and his firstborn son Robt. Langdon; John Talcarn; Thos. Penvown and his firstborn son William Trevown; John Dynham and his firstborn son Wm. Dynham; Richard Upcote and his firstborn son Thomas Upcote; Richard Denys; Wm. Trebarfote and Wm. Whitstone.

These feoffees out of profits of the lands (above) to appoint a priest who was a Master of Arts of Oxford or Cambridge and not benefices to say daily mass at Week St. Mary church praying for souls of Sir John Percyvale, Henry Gale, Thomas Barnaby and their fathers and mothers and for Thomasine Percyvale and for the souls of John Bonventure and Joan his wife, her father and mother. Also for souls of Richard Nordon; Master John Markewike, clerk and all her kindred, for good estate of the feoffees and for their souls, for good estate of every Abbot of Hartland and for their souls, for souls of benefactors of school below.

Chantry priest, scholars and curate of Parish Church to keep Thomasine P. anniversary or obit with requiem mass on the day following.

Priest to look after scholars and see they attended matins, mass and evensong on holy days.

Priest-Schoolmaster to have six weeks leave of absence each year, and provide a deputy for that time.

Master John Andrewe appointed priest-schoolmaster for life.

Priest-Schoolmaster to be chosen by four first-named of the feoffees (above). Five feoffees to warn the master to quit the post at the end of the quarter of the year following the warning if he was unsuitable or neglecting his charge. Next priest-schoolmaster to be chosen by first-named four of the feoffees. If they cannot agree after 21 days Abbot of Hartland to chose for that time only a secular priest who is a graduate. If the Abbot deferred an election for 21 days the Prior of Bodmin to choose for that time only.

Evidences of the endowed estates to be in a box in Week St. Mary Church under two locks and keys. Wardens of Week St. Mary Church to have one key and the Abbot of Hartland the other.

Every third or fourth year Abbot of Hartland, 2 Churchwardens and four of the feoffees living near Week St. Mary to read the last deed to ascertain how many of the feofees are living. When there are only four feoffees alive they to make an estate of the properties in Devon to their heirs male apparent and to heirs of deceased feoffees in trust to performance of Thomasine Percyvale's will. One part of indenture to remain in box in Week St. Mary Church and the other at the Abbey of Hartland.

Four feoffees inspecting deed every third or fourth year to have 6s 8d to share between themselves. Four first-named feoffees to appoint an overseer of the lands to see to repairs and gathering of rents. Rent-gatherer to pay to curate or parish priest of Week St. Mary for Thomasine Percyvale's obit 12d yearly, 8d to the parish clerk, 20 pence to be shared by the two Churchwardens. Rent-gatherer to receive 6s 8d yearly. Rent-gatherer to put 5s yearly into the box in front of the Churchwardens to help cost of renewal of feoffments and payments of 6s 8d to feoffees.

Residue of rents, heriots, etc., to go to priest-schoolmaster for his salary. Rent-gatherer accountable to four first-named feoffees for this.

Copy of this deed always to remain in Church of Week St. Mary.

Sealing clause... 10th July 1506

An extract from an account of Week St. Mary by C. S. Gilbert in 1820, using a form of Old English, states:

A chantry and grammar-fchool were founded, in the reign of Henry VIII, at Week St. Mary, by Dame Thomafine Percival, a native of this parifh, "with fair lodgings for the fchoolmafters, fchollers, and officers, and twenty pound of yeerely revennue for fupporting the incident charges." Her ftory, as told by Carew, from whom the above is quoted, is, that her maiden name was Bonaventure, but whether by defcent or event he knew not; that "whiles in her girlifh age fhe kept fheepe on St. Mary-Wike moore, it chanced that a London marchant paffing by, faw her, heeded her, liked her, begged her of her poore parents, and carried her to his home. In proceffe of time, her miftres was fummond by death to appeare in the other world; and her good thewes, no leffe than her feemely perfonage, fo much contented her mafter, that he advanced her from a fervant to a wife, and left her a wealthy widow. Her fecond marriage befell with one Henry Gall; her third and laft, with Sir John Percival, lord maior of London, whom fhe alfo overlived. And to fhew that vertue as well bare a part in the defert as fortune in the meanes of her preferment, fhe employed the whole refidue of her life and laft widdowhood, to works no leffe bountifull then charitable, - namely, repayring of high-wales, building of bridges, endowing of maydens, relieving of prifoners, feeding and apparelling the poor," &c. Dame Thomafine Percival's will, which bears date 1512, throws light upon fome parts of her hiftory; it fhews that her family name was Bonaventer; for fhe leaves 2ol. to her brother, John Bonaventer: her firft hufband's name was Thomas Bumfby. She makes her coufin, John Dinham, who married her fitter's daughter, refiduary legatee, and commits to his difcretion the chantry and grammar-fchool, which fhe had founded in her life-time; to the vicar of Liskeard fhe leaves a little gilt goblet, with a blue flower in the bottom, to the intent that he fhould pray for her foul; and towards the building of the tower at St. Stephen's, Launcefton, 20 marks.

Carew obferves, that in Thomafine Bonaventer's grammar-fchool, divers of the beft gentlemen's fons of Devon and Cornwall had been "vertuoufly trained up in both kinds of divine and humane learning, under one Cholwell, an honeft and religious teacher; which caufed the neighbours fo much the rather and the more to rewe, that a petty fmacke onely of popery opened a gap to the oppreffion of the whole, by the ftatute made in Edw. the 6 raigne, touching the fuppreffion of chaunteries. Many of our celebrated foundation-fchools would have fhared the fame fate, had they not been protected by well-wifhers to their eftablifhment, who pointed out the obvious practicability of correcting the fuperftitious ufages with which they were connected; a practicability which thofe who coveted their revenues would very gladly have overlooked." [8]

Richard Carew (1555-1620)[9]

Carew was an English poet and antiquary, born on the 17th July 1555, at East Antony, Cornwall. At the young age of just eleven, he entered Christ Church, Oxford, and when only fourteen was chosen to carry on a debate with Sir Philip Sidney, in the presence of the Earls of Leicester and Warwick and others.

By virtue of his marriage to Juliana Arundel in 1577 he added yet another estate to those already inherited from his father. He entered parliament in 1584 and served under Sir Walter Raleigh, then Lord Lieutenant of Cornwall, as treasurer, before being appointed the high sheriff of Cornwall in 1586.

The work for which he is best known, locally, is the Survey of Cornwall, published in 1602, and reprinted in 1769 and 1811. Richard Carew died on the 6th November 1620. ∎

THE STORY OF THOMASINE BONAVENTURE 1450 - 1539

The cover of an early Week St. Mary magazine advertising the Flower Festival of 1991 and the epic story of Thomasine Bonaventure.

It shows her rise to fame and fortune in London, becoming Lady Percival, but not forgetting her humble origins.

She funded the original school in addition to having a bridge built at Greenamoor, on condition the tree was not harmed or displaced, among her many endowments.

Despite differing opinions as to the status of her family - some say she did not come from humble beginnings - the storyline forms the basis of a real rags-to-riches 'fairy tale'.

The Church of St. Mary the Virgin

St. Mary's ancient Church stands on the footings of its Norman predecessor in the original St. Mary's Wyke. Now, as then, all visitors are given a warm welcome.

The Parish Church is dedicated to St. Mary the Virgin. It comprises a chancel, nave, and north and south aisles. The north arcade has five four-centred arches, with monolith granite pillars; the south arcade also has five arches, three of which are obtuse pointed, and two obtuse four-centred. The pillars are of Polyphant[d5] stone and granite. The entrances are a south porch and a priest's door; the north door is not used. The tower is of granite ashlar; it has three stages and is 99 feet in height, including its pinnacles. The church, built in 1643, contains six bells, which were hung in 1731, and is finished with battlements and crocketed pinnacles, which terminate with crosses. The bells were re-hung and repaired in 1887 when the tower was also renovated at a cost of £168.

There are no remains of the Norman Church but it is reported that "a fair proportion of unworked stone from the Ventergan Quarry (a favourite stone with the Norman builders) has been worked into the later walls. The fragments of moulded stone around the exterior of the east window indicate thirteenth century workmanship, the window itself being modern. The piscina in the chancel is also of late thirteenth century workmanship. These remnants, of course, show that a church stood here at that period."

We may assume therefore that on the present site there stood first a Norman Church and afterwards one built in the thirteenth century.

Week St. Mary - Its church was built by men who may have fought at Agincourt and enriched by a great lady who married the Lord Mayor of London. It has traces of Norman work in its walls, a granite tower with bands of carving round it, fine old roofs, fragments of an ancient screen, a font carved with English roses and French lilies, and a porch with fragments of a medieval reredos[d6] built into its inner wall. Its north arcade rests on giant granite monoliths.

The outstanding features of the present Church suggest it was enlarged as follows. The first addition, late in the fourteenth century, was the south aisle with its three arches of Polyphant stone starting from the west end of the chancel. Fifty years later, about 1450, the north aisle was constructed with granite pillars and arches, and to match this the south aisle was extended two bays eastward. This accounts for the fact that the two chancel arches on the south side are of granite, while the westerly one rises from a Polyphant pillar. Probably, too, it is due to these alterations that the east window of the nave is not in the centre of the gable. The last additions were the south porch, with 'parvise', or priest's chamber, above it, and the fine granite tower rising nearly 100 feet from which a superb view can be obtained.

The three double bands of carving on the tower are exceptionally good, and high up on the west side may be seen an unusual subject, two hounds in full cry after a hare. This makes one wonder whether even in those days Week St. Mary Revel or Parish Feast began with a hunt.

Victorian Alterations

By Victorian times the church had fallen into a serious state of disrepair after generations of neglect. Unhappily, a 'restoration' was carried out between 1876 and 1881 with alleged insensitivity and excessive thoroughness - this was combined with the repairs to the church after a severe lightning strike. Major repairs of the fabric were certainly essential but the church was swept bare of most of its surviving picturesque features. Fortunately the superb medieval roofs of both aisles were conserved, together with the Tudor 'linen fold' panels of the pulpit (from which John Wesley preached on several occasions).

A tea-break under way during the annual cutting of the churchyard grass - a real community effort!

The cost of restoration was around £2,000. The architect said that, "The nave and church roofs are in a very dilapidated condition, and must be entirely removed and replaced with new wagon shaped roofs," but, fortunately, it was possible to retain and restore the fine old roofs in both aisles. The original mullions and tracery of the windows having been destroyed, these with the exception of the chancel window were all fitted with new mullions and fine through the generosity of a parishioner (Mr. C. Winbolt).

In the north aisle the stairs to the vanished rood-loft remain. Nearby, in the chapel of St. John the Baptist, one notices the beautiful Victorian stained glass window by Kempe, given as a memorial to the wife of the Rev. G. H. Hopkins, Rector. It shows St. Catherine with her wheel, St. Cecilia with her organ, and St. Agnes with her lamb, in rich quiet colours of red, blue, green, and gold. Nearby is the well preserved slate monument to Margery Gayer (1679).

Mary Week Tower

Thy praises my friend of Mary Week Tower
    Are merited all, in style and in power
And the splendid view revealed on the top
    Well repays for the tedious journey up
But nought of the past does it ever tell
    Save its age on a stone in the pinnacle.
True, the old bells speak in their long made nest
    When calling a worn pilgrim home to rest
Or ring a merry peal as they swing to and fro
    When pulled by the ropes in the belfry below
But dearer far dearer to me than them all
    Is the old grey church with its unroffed wall
And the seats tho' worn by age, and colour gone
    Have rested many a weary one
While the promise dropp'd in a sermonising sound
    Was manna to the soul heavenward bound

And often does fancy picture to me
    Dreams of the past in which I can see
Forms, oh so fair and prettily arrayed
    In the sacred aisle to the altar led
Where vows fondly made, the long ago plighted
    Are complete, when hearts are there united
Thus has the church such grand attractions
    Since here is sealed our greatest actions
Again, when time has whirled us through the maze of life
    When death ends every painful strife
We're borne there a moment by our friends so brave
    As they follow us slowly to the grave.

Jane Hutchings

Written during the Church Restoration 1879

Fragments of medieval woodwork and carved stone survive by the south door and in the porch, where the village stocks may be seen.

The Litany desk was made in 1907 from pieces of old oak, which were believed to be pieces of the old chancel screen. The oak choir seats were put in during 1891, and the organ, the work of Messrs. Bevington & Sons, in 1903. The sundial over the Church door was found at the Rectory, being used as a step to the "old schoolroom". The tower screen, the work of Mr. John Northcott, of Ashwater, was erected in 1912. The Bishop's chair was given in 1924, as a memorial to the Rev. S. H. Haslam, Rector from 1900 to 1919.

The re-seating of the Church in English oak was begun in 1926 and finished in January, 1930, at a cost of £600. Five of the seats were given as memorials of members of old and respected families in the parish, namely: Badcock, Coles, Hutchings, Martyn, and Treleven. The carving on the mouldings of the bench ends was given by Mr. and Mrs. J. Bone.

The heiress of the Marrais family married a member of the Rolle family, and on the floor of the present vestry are memorial stones to both these families.

An epitaph in the Church to one who died in 1679:

"Since man's compared to an inverted tree
To this bless'd soule that name applied be.
Sweet words, pure thoughts, good works with her endear'd,
Her leaves, her blossom, and her fruit appear'd.
Her pith was Vertue, Charity her rinde,
One verdant branch from her is left behind
Death hath not cut her downe, who rather is
To be a tree of life in Paradice.
Short was her life, yet lives she ever,
Few were her daies, yet dyes she never.
She breathed awhile, then went to rest,
God takes them soonest, whom he loveth best."

2006 A special service took place at the church of St. Mary the Virgin, Week St. Mary, on Sunday, July 30th, to celebrate and dedicate the Week St. Mary Circle of Parishes and Institution of its Rector, Revd Rob Dickenson, by Rt Revd William Ind (Lord Bishop of Truro). This service was to celebrate the union of eight parishes into the Week St. Mary Circle of Parishes; namely, Jacobstow, Poundstock, St. Gennys, Treneglos, Warbstow, Week St. Mary, Whitstone and Widemouth Bay.

Bishop Bill Ind, Rev Gavin Douglas, Rev Rob Dickenson & Archdeacon Clive Cohen

There was a large attendance with representatives from each parish. The organist was John Hopkinson and the church choir was in attendance. A presentation was made of framed commemorative pictures to the Bishop, Archdeacon and churchwardens from each parish in the new benefice. Refreshments were served in the church.

Vuyani & Phyllis Buso

On Sunday 5th November, Week St Mary church hosted a special service of Songs of Praise to celebrate the visit to the Diocese of Truro of The Venerable Vuyani Buso, Archdeacon of Umzimvubu in South Africa and his wife Mrs Phyllis Buso.

The Diocese has a twinning link with the Diocese of Umzimvubu which Bishop Roy Screech, Bishop of St Germans, recently visited to learn more about the way of life and the needs of our South African twin.

Archdeacon Buso told the congregation of his work in one of South Africa's poorest regions where each of his 18 parishes has no less than 300 AIDS orphans to care for. He spoke of his delight at seeing how willing we were to share our energy and resources in supporting his country and of his hope that once God had finished making our lives so comfortable that He would have a little left for his people in Umzimvubu.

 He said that his people were not bitter or complaining because they sincerely believe that God is good and walks with them through all of their life.

Mrs. Buso has a particular interest in the Mothers Union of Umzimvubu which has at least 2,000 members. Her work involves supporting the very many Grandmothers who have to look after all of their orphaned grandchildren in the poorest of circumstances because their parents have died from HIV/AIDS. She joined her husband in singing a lively and uplifting African prayer for us.

At the end of the service several presentations were made to the Busos to remind them of their visit to the village including a photo of Mrs Buso with the Marhamchurch hand bell ringers and a patchwork quilt made by the quilting group of Week St. Mary Churches Together.

A time of Fellowship after the service allowed us to talk with the visitors and gave Mrs Buso the opportunity to have a first lesson in ringing a church bell in Week St. Mary tower. She had a natural aptitude for this and the captain was sorry that she would be unable to pursue a career as a bell ringer in Week St Mary.

Honorary Canon

On Sunday 13th May 2007, Revd Rob was one of five new Honorary Canons installed at Truro Cathedral by the Rt Revd Bishop Bill Ind, occupying the seat of St. Winwaloe.

A large congregation witnessed this service including a coach full of 'supporters' from Week St. Mary parish and beyond.

Lightning hits the Church! Not once, twice, or even thrice!

According to the most recent Miscellaneous Register, pertaining to the church of Week St. Mary, there were several recorded instances of the tower being struck by lightning.

On 8th November 1878 the southwest pinnacle of the tower was struck by lightning, at 6.45 am, but with no record of any damage. Other occasions on which the tower was struck are recorded as follows: about 1688 the north-east pinnacle was struck and during the winter months of 1812, 1843 and 1865 the north-east, south-east and south-west pinnacles were also struck.

£2,000 Damage to Church - Lightning's Havoc at Week St. Mary as Pinnacle crashes through Roof; Beams, Lamps, And Pews Smashed

By courtesy of the Cornish & Devon Post Series of Newspapers. 1935: A close investigation made yesterday revealed that damage estimated at £2,000 was done to the ancient

Damage caused by lightning strike

Parish Church at Week St. Mary, when the tower was struck by lightning on Thursday afternoon after a short, but heavy, thunderstorm.

One of the four pinnacles crashed, portions going through the roof in several places, and inside the church oak beams splintered under the weight of the falling masonry and several of the oil lamps that illuminate the interior were smashed to pieces.

The church doors have been locked and danger notices have been posted around the churchyard. It is expected that it will take something like six months to repair the church, and in the meantime the parish services will be conducted in the rectory hall.

Storm Unexpected - Crash Drowned By Thunder Claps

The storm came on with surprising suddenness. About lunchtime on Thursday the weather was almost perfect at Week St. Mary. Then, without the slightest warning, the village was visited by a sharp thunder and hailstorm that prevailed in full force for about 20 minutes, leaving the highways covered with hail.

Above: Oswald Sandercock seen pointing at some of the damage to the church 21st February 1935

Below & Right:
Other examples of the damage caused by lightning hitting the church

Week St. Mary Tower

Thou for many years hast stood,
Overlooking field and wood;
From thy top the village green
And the distant sea are seen.

From thee also may be viewed
Widemouth beach and town of Bude,
And thro' the drear waste of night
Can be seen the Lundy light.

From thy belfry rings the call,
"Come to Church, ye people all,"
And the same bell's mournful toll
To the graves doth summon all.

Unchanged, thro many changes, thou
Art scarce the worse for age e'en now.
On thy walls so strong and grey,
The force of storms is thrown away.

Long ago was thy foundation,
Laid 'midst general exultation.
But the men who work'd that day,
Centuries since, have turned to clay.

Would that on thee were conferred
Power to tell what thou hast heard,
Things that men have said and done
In the days long past and gone.

Strange the stories thou could'st tell
Of those who in the village dwell.
Queer indeed would be the history,
Revealing much that's now a mystery.

Thro' the day dost thou look down
On the busy little town,
And at night strict watch doth keep,
While the toil-worn peasants sleep.

Since on thee the sun first shined
Mary Week has much declined,
Men have fled and trade has waned,
Markets stopped and pockets drained.

Since, on Greenmore's grass and heather,
Bonaventure strolled at leisure,
Funerals many hast thou seen
Winding o'er the churchyard green.

There, beneath thy shadow, rest
Rich and poor, whom none molest;
Deaf to all that men may say,
Sleeping till the judgement day.

Then from calm and lengthened sleep
Some shall wake no more to weep;
Some with terror and dismay
Will the trumpet's sound obey.

Scoffers then will cowards turn,
Sinful people all shall mourn
But the true and upright man
Shall be set at God's right hand.

Adieu, old Tower, tall and strong;
My stay at Week will not be long;
Like thee may I e'er be straight,
And in every act upright.

by T. C. Jacob; Week St. Mary 1879

For a while no-one noticed the damage to the church amid the noise of repeated thunderclaps. Eventually, Mr. Sandercock and his brother, who live about 200 yards away from the church, left their house to examine their bakehouse, upon which a large brick appeared to have fallen. It was then that the damage to the church was first noticed.

Of the four pinnacles at the top of the church tower only three remained, and the churchyard was strewn with masonry. The damaged tower and the gaping holes in the roof beneath told their own story, and a glance inside the church revealed the chaos that the lightning had caused.

Monster Stone

Fortunately, there was no one in or near the church at the time. The west end of the church underneath the tower was covered by the fallen masonry, and one stone weighing at least a quarter of a ton, had crashed through the roof and broken several oak beams. Many oil-lamps and pews (the latter having been placed in the church only five years ago) were smashed.

In the churchyard many of the larger stones had been forced into the earth to a depth of a foot.

The present rector of Week St. Mary is Rev. A. Hambrook. The church, which stands upon the site of a Norman church, was thoroughly restored in the years 1876-1881, at a cost of over £2,000.

The lightning strike brought down the southeast pinnacle, causing masonry to crash down and smash through the roof, resulting in such devastation that the church had to be closed. An appeal for funds was launched immediately and repairs begun. Opportunity was taken to replace the variegated floor tiles favoured by the Victorians with stone slabs and the church was duly re-opened for worship on 16th January 1936.

The church bells

	Inscription	Weight
VI fTenor J	I to the Church the living call And to the grave do summon all.	8cwt.
V.	*Abm. Ruddall of Gloucester cast us all in 1731.	6cwt.
IV.	Prosperity to the Church of England	5cwt.
III.	Prosperity to the Parish.	4½cwt.
II.	Peace and good Neighbourhood.	4cwt.
I.	Given by Cosmo Neville Peake in memory of King Edward VII.	

The bells were re-hung in 1899

*Mr. Abraham Ruddall started the Gloucester Bell Foundry in 1684. He was succeeded by his sons, Abraham and Abel, who were followed successively by Thomas Charles and John Buddall. On their retirement Mr. Thomas Mears of the Whitechapel Foundry, acquired and continued the Gloucester business under his own name, but after a few years he transferred the patterns, etc, to his London Foundry, now Messrs. Mears and Stainbank.

Church Bell-Ringers

It is probably true that there have been many bell-ringers who have been ringing church bells for 50 years but not so many of them have done so at the same church. On Monday evening, 17th August 1987, a band of 'scientific' ringers met at Week St. Mary Parish Church to pay tribute to the loyal and regular service of one of their call-change brothers who had completed this milestone.

Harold Ridgman started his ringing career in 1937 when he was taught to handle a bell by the then tower captain, Mr. Harry Rogers of Trefrouse. Harold has been a regular member of the Week St. Mary band since then.

At a meeting of the Tamar Valley Guild of Ringers at Week St. Mary earlier this summer, Harold was presented with a certificate to mark his 50 years of service by Mr. Petherick, Chairman of the Guild. Several of the ringers felt it would be a fitting way to pay a compliment to Harold by ringing a quarter peal of 1260 changes in his Honour and accepted the invitation of Mr. Sidney Heard, Tower Captain, to do this at Week St. Mary. It was a particular pleasure for the conductor, Bill Cracknell of Canworthy Water, as he had been welcomed into the Week St. Mary band of ringers by Harold and Sidney during the last year.

The band of ringers was Mr. Sidney Heard; Mr. Wilf Boucher of St. Mary's Launceston, the present Master of Truro Diocesan Guild of Ringers; Mr. and Mrs. Cummins of Lanteglos-by-Camelford and Mr. and Mrs. Brian Cracknell. The method chosen was Plain Bob Doubles and it took 42 minutes to ring the ten-and-a-half extents.

Captain of the Week St. Mary Tower

The present Captain, Lesley Booker, has kindly submitted this article about her position and responsibilities:

Tower bells exist to call the people to church and act as a visible and audible sign of the church within a community. Bell ringing is an ancient art without which the bells of all the hundreds of British churches would be silent.

The position of Captain of the Tower at Week St. Mary involves organising the ringing for services, both regular and for special occasions. The Captain is elected by the Ringers at the Annual General Meeting every year. In the past the Captain's position was more or less a lifetime's work until the captain himself decided to resign and hand over to the Vice Captain.

The Tower, when I came to the village 20 years ago, was a male dominated place, although many, many young women from the Parish have learned to ring here in the past. A group of ladies started to learn in the early 90's and we soon had enough to form a full ladies six as well as the regular men who rang.

Since then the team has gone from strength to strength led by the previous Captain Sidney Heard. I became the Vice Captain when Harold Ridgman retired from ringing in 1999 and after a suitable 'training' period have now been elected as Captain, a post which I have held for three years.

The Week St. Mary Ringers, like all ringers, are a sociable bunch and our practice night is always followed by an evening in a local hostelry. We have a Christmas Party every year and an annual Ringers Outing which travels by coach to at least five other towers anywhere in Devon and Cornwall. We take with us a number of ringing friends and non-ringing passengers who enjoy a day visiting places that they would otherwise have no opportunity to see. These arrangements all fall to the Captain to organise.

We also belong to the Truro Diocesan Guild of Ringers and the Tamar Valley Guild of Ringers. These Guilds give us the opportunity to meet and ring with other ringers from all over the county and on the other side of the Tamar. Membership gives us financial, moral and religious support and is good fun too! The Captain is also responsible for organising the various activities associated with these Guilds, the outing and other ringing activities.

One of the major responsibilities of the Captain is to arrange to teach people who want to learn to ring. Unfortunately at this time we have no young people who want to ring and learners are usually past retirement age these days. The reasons for this are many and include the very different lifestyle of people today, the mobile nature of the population and the demands placed upon everyone to take part in a huge variety of other activities. It is not a simple or short job teaching someone to ring but it is a lifetime skill which will make you very popular with tower captains all over the country. Anyone can learn to ring but young people learn more quickly. Those who do can carry on learning even when they leave home. University towns always have lots of towers and young ringers can take the opportunity to hone their skills whilst they make lots of new friends

I feel privileged to hold the position of Tower Captain and if I think about it, I realise that it is also my privilege to be the first lady Captain of the Week St. Mary Tower.   *Lesley Booker*

Church choirs

There have been several choirs over the years, one of which included myself around the 1960's. After a period of 'decline', the year 2000 saw a new ladies' church choir formed, making their debut on Easter Sunday. Mrs Higgins from Hayscott kindly donated money in memory of her late husband, Albert,

and material for robes and music books were purchased and blessed by Revd Rob. Three members of the choir made the maroon robes.

The choir has sung at various United Benefice services, Deanery festivals, weddings and carol services ably accompanied by Mr. John Hopkinson, the Church organist.

Week St. Mary Church Choir
Charles Risdon, Ivor Ridgeman, Sidney Jones
Clifford Jones, Andrew Orchard, Graham Orchard, David Martin, Bill Wadge, Michael Jones

Church clock

The late Mr. John Rogers says that his father told him there was a clock on the church tower, which went away to be repaired but was found to be beyond repair.

A postcard shows the clock to have been fixed high up on the south side of the tower (i.e. above the porch) on the louvered vents to the bell tower. The clock was wound by Mr. Brock of Fuchsia Cottage who was the churchyard caretaker. His wife cleaned the church.

In the Parish Record Book there is the following entry regarding the clock:

'1910 Aug. A clock was placed in the Church Tower early in this year. The clock was obtained by Mr. N F H Cobbald for a small sum and he and I (Rector Revd. Haslam) made the face hands and connecting parts and erected it in the tower. It has now been going steadily and keeping good time for several months.'[10]

Church organ

Mrs Dorcas Kinsman says that her father, Mr. John Treleven of Steele Farm, fetched the church organ and brought it to Week St. Mary on a wagon pulled by two horses. He also fetched the tenor bell in the same way. One was brought from Bude Station and one from Holsworthy Station. Mr. Treleven used to do various jobs for the church as his uncle, Mr. Michael Treleven, was churchwarden from 1892 -1918.

Again in the Parish Record Book, there is reference to the purchase of an organ - presumably the one referred to above. I quote: 'Nov. 1903. A new two-manual organ by Messrs Bevington & Sons, Manette Street, Charing Cross Road, London was erected in the Church on the South side aisle to replace the old organ which stood on the North side. The original estimate for this organ was £223 10s. This sum was raised by voluntary contributions, Concerts etc. The old organ was re-built and enlarged by Revd. J H Haslam and sold to Bradford Church, Brandis Corner, North Devon for £30.'

A later entry states that the organ was restored in 1958 by Mr. E Sargeant of Launceston at a cost of £178 15s. The re-dedication service was held on Friday December 19th.

It looks as though there was inflation even in those days![11]

A letter to Churchwarden, Molly Colwill, follows, dated September 4th 1994, containing some interesting information regarding the disposal and installation of the church organ:

Dear Mrs Colwill,

As promised I enclose extracts from the Holsworthy Magazine, November and December 1905 - nearly 90 years ago, and January and March 1906. As a result of a discussion at the Bradford P.C.C., with regard to a new instrument of some sort for the church, reference was made of a pipe organ at Week St. Mary, which was for sale.

The organ was inspected and purchased.

It was stated to be 'very old, but it is in thoroughly good order and very sweet in tone; by substituting a 'Gamba' stop for the present 'reed' it can be much improved' We ought to be able to do this almost immediately as subscriptions are coming in well. It was used for the first time for the Ringing Festival, November 2nd 1905. It was stated, that everyone seemed to be pleased with the organ, "and there is no doubt that we are very fortunate in getting one so cheaply; subscriptions came in so well that we were able to get the new stop at once, and to get a skilled man down from London to re-voice and tune."

In last months magazine the organ was described as "very old". The "very" must have crept in by some mistake after the notes left Bradford. It is old, but yet it is not, for at least half of it is new since it was used in Week St. Mary Church. It has been remodelled and rebuilt, and it is to all intents and purposes as good to us as would be a new organ costing by the time it should be placed in the church, £150.

I later learnt (January 1966) that a cheque for £30 was drawn in favour of the Rector and Churchwardens of Week St. Mary. Receipts were £37/7/7 plus £3 to pay all liabilities. The March magazine showed a total of £40/6/7. The Gamba stop, carriage, etc., cost £3/8/6. Messrs Taylor and B. Hutchings very kindly gave the carriage of the organ from Week St. Mary.

I wonder when the organ was replaced in Bradford Church. There is now a two manual electronic organ there. Perhaps I will discover. Your present organ must have been installed about 1906.

I should think the old Week St. Mary organ was quite small, in those days the smaller country churches had chairs and able to sing anthems - 'Thou wilt keep him in perfect peace', at the service when the old Week St. Mary organ was played at Bradford for the first time.

With best wishes,

Yours Sincerely

H. G. Jackets (?)

John Wesley

On several of his earlier missionary expeditions to Cornwall John Wesley visited Week St. Mary, one of the very few parishes where he was welcomed by the incumbent (John Turner, rector 1716-1772). Other hospitable local parishes were North Tamerton and St. Gennys. His journal recounts some of his experiences - *See Index*

Mime in Parish Church at Week St. Mary

On Sunday evening (December 22nd 1955) in the Parish Church a carol mime of the Nativity was presented by the children of the Sunday School and older children of the parish.

Those taking part were: Mary, Valerie Colwill; Joseph, Michael Hutchings; Angel Gabriel, Barbara Hutchings; Star Angel, Katherine Annett; Gift Angel, Pat Colwill; Flower Angels, Thelma Colwill, Susan Martin; other Angels, Jacqueline Colwill, Esther Colwill, Janet Ridgman, Doreen Horrell; inn keeper, Michael Jones; travellers, Brenda Martin, David Martin; shepherds, Nicholas Colton, Clifford Jones; Kings and attendant pages: gold, Sidney Jones, Sheila Annett (page); frankincense, Ivor Ridgman, Elizabeth Colton (page); myrrh, Charles Risdon, Dinah Petherick (page).

Church seating before the pews were installed

A close-up of the fine grating that was severely damaged by the
lightning on 21st February 1935 and replaced with solid slabs

The story unfolded itself in mime illustrated by carols, beginning with the entrance of angels and followed by the innkeeper, guests at the inn, Mary and Joseph, shepherds and kings with their attendant pages.

The slow and reverent movement of the children was most impressive, especially in the grouping of the angels round the crib. Particularly moving were the singing of "Sleep Holy Babe," by Katherine Annett with violin accompaniment, and "The Rocking Carol," by angels and pages.

The costumes were colourful and the angels ethereal in transparent silk and golden haloes. A large congregation first witnessed the mime on Thursday, December 22nd at 7.30 pm, in Week St. Mary Church, then at Whitstone Church one week later, on December 29th, and again in Week St. Mary Church on Sunday 1st January 1956.

The carols were sung by a ladies' choir (Mrs. Hutchings, Mrs. F. Martin, Mrs. A. Martin, Mrs. G. Colton, Mrs. A. Cobbledick and Miss W. Retallack), accompanied by the Rector (Rev. W. T. Soper), violin, and Lieut. Comdr. Annett, R.N., flute.

Collections were in aid of The Church of England Children's Society, the roof repairs of Whitstone Parish Church, and the Heating Fund of Week St. Mary Church. The mime was produced by the Rector and Mrs. W. T. Soper, who also designed and made the angels' costumes. ■

Week St. Mary church altar 1937

Week St. Mary bellringers; Sgt. James Fuller of 'Hillside' stands tall above his colleagues. 1908

TELEPHONE No.
BISHOPSGATE 8849.
~~Telephone No~~
~~8543 London Wall~~

Estab.d 3 Centuries.

WHITECHAPEL BELL FOUNDRY,
London   April 3rd.   1929.

The Rev. M. V. Hardy, The Rectory, Week St. Mary, Holsworthy, Devon.

In account with Mears & Stainbank,

32 & 34, Whitechapel Road, F.1 *(near St Mary's Station.)*

Bankers. WESTMINSTER BANK. LIMITED.   Repairs to 8 handbells, Tenor 12 F.

To recasting Nos. 12 F, 10 A, and 9 B♭ handbells.
   Refitting all springs with new felt pads,
   fitting new box wood pegs to all clapper staples,
   and leather pegs to all the clappers, also
   refitting all eight bells with new leather
   straps, including cleaning and regulating
   the set, as per Estimate;   £.   3. 10. 0.

for Mears & Stainbank
April 11th. 1929.

Received cheque
£3. 10. 0.
with thanks

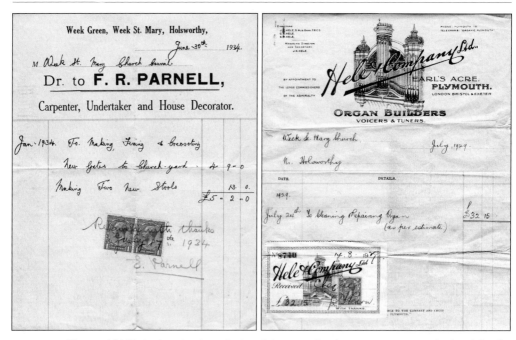

These old bills just go to show that maintenance is always necessary, whether it be for new church gates (1935) or vital organ repairs (1929).

Church expenses in 1920, ranging from the cost of oil and candles to coal, for heating and the necessary church insurance based on a building valuation of just £1,807.00; a far cry from the value of a Grade 1 listed building in todays society.

An old photograph showing the view from the top of the church tower, overlooking Box Tree Cottage, towards Sea View Farm. Notice the number of trees surrounding the houses.

The entrance to Week St. Mary church

Week St. Mary School

The first school in the village, by virtue of the generosity of Thomasine Percival, was in the building now called 'Old College' currently under the ownership of the Landmark Trust.[d7]

Between 1440 and 1530 over a hundred endowed schools were founded in England. A few formed part of collegiate churches, but most were simply schools, endowed at a cost of between about £140 and £220 and providing education, sometimes in reading, song, and grammar, sometimes only in grammar; sometimes totally free, sometimes free to specified classes of pupils, or charging low fees. Until the 1510s the office of schoolmaster was often restricted to a chantry priest, who would also pray for the founders' souls. Those who founded schools rarely explained their motives beyond the support of religion and learning, but the majority of foundations were made in small market towns rather than the bigger cathedral cities and county centres. This suggests that the fall in the size of the national population since the fourteenth century may have been a consideration. It may have become difficult for fee-earning teachers to make a living in small towns, as they had formerly done, requiring their work to be subsidized in order to continue. The founders of these schools ranged widely within the wealthy orders of society.

Old College

In the royal family Lady Margaret Beaufort was responsible for Wimborne Minster, Dorset, and among the nobility of early Tudor England Henry Algernon Percy, fifth earl of Northumberland, maintained a schoolmaster in his household and another in Alnwick Abbey, while encouraging the creation of a grammar school at Cockermouth, Cumberland. Bishops included Richard FitzJames of London (Bruton, Somerset), Richard Fox of Winchester (Grantham, Lincolnshire), Hugh Oldham of Exeter (Manchester, Lancashire), and William Smith (Banbury, Oxfordshire, and Lichfield, Staffordshire). The most ambitious episcopal founder was Thomas Wolsey, who aimed to equal Wykeham and Henry VI by founding a large college and school at Ipswich, Suffolk, in 1528 as well as a university college at Oxford, but his school foundation collapsed when he fell from power two years later.

Lesser members of the aristocracy who founded schools included such knights and lawyers as Sir Thomas Lovell (Nottingham) and Sir Humphrey Coningsby (Rock, Worcestershire), and they were followed by London merchants like the goldsmith Edmund Shaw (Stockport, Cheshire) and wealthy widows like Thomasine Percyvale, who endowed a grammar school at Week St. Mary (Cornwall), following the example of her husband, Sir John Percyvale, at Macclesfield (Cheshire).

It is not clear how the schooling progressed once the above school moved to Launceston until the County Primary School was erected on a plot at the top of the village, Week Green.

W.I. - The School

In December 1976, Week St. Mary's Women's Institute compiled a booklet entitled "Week St. Mary School - This is your life" as their entry for the Baker Cup Competition. I am extremely pleased to be allowed to reproduce the article here, for the benefit of those interested in village life; those who just wish to reminisce, whether past pupils or not; or who simply have a fascination for history.

Competition Committee: Kathleen Gubbin, Hettie Hutchings, Kathleen Watkinson, Agnes Smale & Gwen Hughes

INTRODUCTION

There you stand, grey and silent, at the top of the hill. You are built of solid Cornish stone, simple in design, with a slate roof and a modest porch. But your playground is empty, your gates are broken down, there are holes in your roof, and your bell has gone from its belfry. In the window is a sad notice:- FOR SALE.

But you were not always so desolate. For nearly a hundred years successive generations of our children passed through your doors, and masters and teachers worked together to give them an education that would fit them for life in the community, and in the world beyond.

So, Week St. Mary Village School - this is your life.

You were built one hundred years ago, in 1876, six years after Parliament had passed the Elementary Education Act, which made regular school attendance compulsory for all children, between the ages of five and fourteen.

The newly-formed School Board had appointed a Mr. Amos Grey and his wife, Elizabeth, as the first Master and Mistress, and, until your building was finished, they used a rented room in the village; there were ten children on the first register.

The numbers quickly rose, and by the end of the year fifty-four children trooped into your new schoolroom. It was a large one, which could be divided by a wooden partition. But it had very little equipment; there was no blackboard, no cupboards, no tables, and as yet, no cloakroom. The toilets were outside in the yard, but of course, with no water supply.

Week St. Mary County Primary School - Closed!

At the opening ceremony the Rector, the Reverend G. H. Hopkins, offered prayers, and then he addressed the assembled members of the Board, the two teachers, and the children. No doubt, he stressed how fortunate the pupils were to be in this new school, and would certainly have exhorted them to work hard, and to respect their teachers.

And work hard they did, as indeed did their teachers! For at that time teachers' salaries depended on a government grant, and this, in turn, depended on the standard of work achieved in the school.

This was assessed by the results of the School Inspectors' examination of the scholars' work in the "three Rs", singing, and plain needlework. In addition, parents had to pay 2d per week for the first child in the family, and 1d for all the others.

By 1879 there were eighty-seven children in the school, and Mr. Grey found the teaching so arduous that he applied for a paid Monitor to help him. This young man had to take his own lessons from Mr. Grey, in the evenings.

One great difficulty in the teaching was the haphazard attendance made by the scholars. Since the government grants depended also on the weekly attendances, the registers were very important, and numbers had to be recorded each day. But conditions of life in country areas, during the nineteenth century, were not conducive to regular school attendance. The weather was a constant hazard; snow, frost, rain and gales in winter made the country lanes almost impassable, and many children lived two or three miles outside the village.

Listen to Mr. King, the schoolmaster who came to Week St. Mary in 1882; "I found it very hard to get any continuous teaching done. Parents in those days expected their children to help at busy times on the land, at corn-tilling, potato picking, hay harvest, and even whortle-berry picking. Then there was the Village Fair, Sunday School treats, and Market Days in Launceston and in Holsworthy." I wrote in my Log Book: "It is a disgrace that children should be allowed to stay away as they do. What with Chapel Anniversaries, Bands of Hope, and seaside outings, the attendance is thoroughly disorganised."

I was continually complaining to the School Board, but it was ten years before they decided to issue summons against the parents. The children's health suffered, too, and with them all crowded into such a small space, coughs and colds, and even more serious infections, spread rapidly.

Many times I had to get the school closed for weeks on end, while scarlet fever, mumps or influenza raged in the village.

When I first came to Week St. Mary I found the standard of work rather poor. I had to correct the children's manners too,

Mr. King, Mrs. King and their daughter, with their pupils. Notice the starched white pinafores of the girls and the stiff white collars of the boys. Circa 1895

and - (I quote from my Log Book again) - "Some children are inclined to be impudent. Anything of that kind I shall put down with the utmost severity.

Giving a kind look and a little pleasant manner will never wholly do in this school." But I flatter myself that my efforts were rewarded, for the Inspectors' later reports noted that I had a remarkably well-ordered school, although the children were "shy and reticent". I taught them to have respect for their betters, and had a special ceremony on Empire Day, our dear Queen Victoria's birthday; the whole school marched into the playground, saluted the Flag, hoisted to the tallest tree, and sang the National Anthem.

The upper standards in 1908. They are standing outside the new room, added in 1906. My wife and daughter helped with the teaching. My daughter took charge of the Infant class, and I taught the two upper standards. The older girls were instructed in plain sewing by Mrs. King, and I taught all the other subjects. Writing, first on slates, and then in Copy Books, Arithmetic and Reading were, of course, the basic subjects, but History, Geography, Spelling, Singing and Drawing all came into the curriculum.

All the classes learnt poetry by heart, (known in my day as Repetition) - among their favourites were poems such as "The Wreck of the Hesperus" and "We are Seven".

With the help of picture cards I gave them object lessons in such useful subjects as Breadmaking, Salt, and Brickmaking, and occasionally I took my class into the fields to study wild flowers. I introduced skipping exercises and military drill, although at first the younger children seemed a little dense in the matter!

Being a country school, my pupils could, at first, leave at any age between eleven and fourteen if they had obtained a job on the land, but in 1902 fourteen became the legal school-leaving age.

The numbers of children increased so much that another pupil teacher, and an assistant for the Infants joined me. But gradually the work became too much for me, my health began to fail, and I had to retire in 1908.

Before Mr. King retired, however, the schoolroom had become far too small for the 115 children on the register. Here is Mrs. Smale, now a lady of over 80, who remembers those days:

"I remember our classroom being very overcrowded. It was very hot in summer, and although there was a big stove in the room it was often very cold in winter. They never seemed to have enough desks for us. In 1906 they built another room onto the school. While it was being done we could not use our playground, for it was filled with all the builder's materials, and there was sand and dust everywhere. It was finished in November, and we trod all the muck and mud into the school. The new room was very damp for a long time, and the walls were often streaming with water.

Mr. King was very strict with us, and we were rather afraid of him. If we did anything wrong he made us stand in the corner with our slates held high over our heads, and he was always quick to hit us if we made mistakes in our reading aloud."

By this time, 1906, you were no longer a Board School, for the old School Board had been abolished, and you had become known as Week St. Mary Council School. Education had become the responsibility of the County Council; schooling was free and financed from the County Rates.

WEEK S. MARY.

PROGRAMME OF ATHLETIC SPORTS

In connection with the Exhibition of Flowers, &c., to be held in the Rectory Field,

On MONDAY, SEPTEMBER 21st, 1908.

EVENTS.

No.	Event			Prizes		
1.	100 yards for Boys under 12			Prizes 1/-,	6d.,	3d.
2.	„ „ „ 16			„ 1/-,	6d.,	3d.
3.	High Jump „ „ 15			„ 1/-,	6d.,	3d.
4.	Quarter Mile „ 16			„ 1/-,	6d.,	3d.
5.	High Jump (Open)			„ 2/-,	1/-,	6d.
6.	Long Jump (Open)			„ 2/-,	1/-,	6d.
7.	100 yards for Girls under 12			„ 1/-,	6d.,	3d.
8.	„ „ „ 16			„ 1/-,	6d.,	3d.
9.	Tug of War (10 a side) ..			„ 5/-.		
10.	Quarter Mile, Handicap (Open)			„ 2/6,	1/6,	1/-.
11.	Thread Needle Race (Women only),			„ 2/-,	1/-,	6d.
12.	Hat Trimming Competition (Men)			„ 2/-,	1/-,	6d.
13.	Wheelbarrow Race (Pairs)			„ 4/-,	2/-,	1/-.
14.	Mile Race (Open)			„ 4/-,	2/-,	1/-.

COMMITTEE.

Rev. S. H. Haslam, Messrs. J. H. Thorne, R. Hooper, H. Rogers, W. Hicks, W. Colwill, W. Brock, F. Widdon, and Sergt. Jeffery.

Starter :—Sergt. Jeffery.   **Judges :**—Messrs. R. Hooper & N. Coles.

This Programme is subject to alteration if thought desirable.

The Committee reserve the right to withhold or reduce the value of any Prize for want of Competition.

The Decision of the Judges shall be final.

Admission (including Tea Ticket) 1/-, Labourers of Week S. Mary and Children, 6d.

Parry Belt, Printer, Stratton & Bude.

Mr. King had been headmaster for twenty-six years, and three generations of schoolchildren had passed through your doors.

Mr. Rablin, your next Headmaster, was a very different type of man. Mrs. Johns, one of his pupils in the early nineteen hundreds, says: "Mr. Rablin started our first school library, with books given to him by ladies and gentlemen of the village. He was very musical, being a Fellow of the Royal College of Organists, and gave recitals on our new organ in the Chapel. He formed a school choir, and we entered for some of the County Music Festivals. We came first in Choral singing and second in sight-reading. After I left, the choir won the Trefusis Banner at the Wadebridge Music Festival.

We had our first Medical Inspection in Mr. Rablin's time, and I remember my mother bathing us that morning and putting us into clean clothes. Then she came up to the school with us, while we were examined by the doctor."

The last three years of Mr. Rablin's headship saw some of the darkest days of the First World War.

Mr. Norman Gubbin was in school in 1914: "I remember a National Savings Group being started and Miss Tuke coming every week to collect our pennies. We all knew that the Germans were trying to starve us out, and as country children we knew how important the farmer's work was. Besides, round our classroom was a big poster which read Waste not, Want not, Save the Nation's Bread."

Mr. Pauling was another pupil at the school in wartime. "I lived three miles from the village school in those days. We had plenty to remind us that we were at war, for many of us had a father or an elder brother at the front. In school, we had collections for cigarettes to send to the soldiers, and we sent 12/6d to the R.S.P.C.A. in aid of wounded horses. Every week we brought eggs to be sent to the military hospitals. My friend and I walked for miles to the farms around and I was given a certificate for bringing in the most eggs.

We had many different teachers during the war. Mr. Leggo, our Head, was called up in 1918, and returned to the school after peace was signed in 1919. Then we had a collection for a War Memorial to be erected in the village Square. On the day Peace was signed we lined up below the Union Jack in the playground and sang "God Save the King". We had a football team then, but no real pitch, so we played in the field behind Reeve House.

In the twenties, Mr. Leggo had tried to interest parents in school affairs by holding an Open Day. Only six parents came, but it was the beginning of more co-operation between school and home.

The first Annual Prize Giving was held in 1922. Parents were interested in their children's school, although the first recorded instance of any combined action at this time was when folk dancing was added to the curriculum, when many parents strongly objected.

One of the children at school in the 'twenties was Miss Audrey Rogers - here she is: "I was seven years old when I started school. My sisters Phyllis and Winnie and I had to walk two miles, we left home at eight o'clock in the morning, and arrived back at five o'clock in the afternoon. We used to meet various people on the way to school, the old tramp making his way to the workhouse in Stratton, and the roadmen, cleaning the gutters and breaking stones for repairing the road. At Collaton Hill and Haydah Hill there were large stone heaps. The roadmen would stone the road, and the steamroller would roll them in. We had to carry our food for the day with us, snacks for breaks in the morning and afternoon and a pasty for lunch. Some children warmed their pasties on the stove in the schoolroom, but we were lucky as we used to drop our food into Mrs. Horrell's opposite the Chapel every morning, and she would heat it for us, and take us in and give us our lunch and a cup of tea. When we were near the village, we teamed up with other boys and girls. The big bell on the school building clanged out at nine o'clock, and it was then we lined up in the playground, the young ones in front and the older ones behind. We marched into the big classroom for a hymn and a prayer, and then each class went to its own room. I remember anything from seventy to a hundred and eight children on the register.

I enjoyed my schooldays. The teachers worked hard and so did the pupils. We took exams around Easter time to decide whether we went up into the next standard or stayed where we were. If we did anything wrong, we had to write so many lines as a punishment, and stay in after school to do it. Of course, there was a cane in the drawer, which was used occasionally. We had the Medical Officer around four times in the year, and our photos were taken once a year. Our father was a School Manager, and he and the other managers often visited the school."

Empire Day was a big Sports Day. We kept our fingers crossed that it would be nice and dry. Sports were always held in Mr. Will Smale's field, next to the school. We held some wonderful concerts - the talent was good, and the proceeds went towards the cost of the Christmas Party and a big Christmas tree.

One of the children coming over Haydah Hill to school was Dorothy Sluggett, now Mrs. Russell Orchard. She and her future husband were in the same class while Mr. Landry was the Headmaster.

'Yes, I remember those concerts. We collected money for a piano, to take the place of the old harmonium. But a great wonder was Mr. Landry's wireless. It was the only one in the village, and on Armistice Day, 1927, he brought it into the school to let us listen to the Service from the Cenotaph. Then we all marched down to the War Memorial in the Square. I was never very fond of Sports Day. I preferred playing rounders in the field. Mr. Landry was a very popular teacher, for he gave every child a halfpenny on their birthday!'

And what about the lighter side of school life? Listen to Mr. Hedric Jones, at school in the twenties: "For the greater part of my schooldays, Mr. Landry was the Headmaster, and Miss Retallack was the assistant teacher. I lived in the village, so I could come home to my dinner. I remember the Horlick's milk that we made for a drink in playtime. While it was heating on the stove we would help it on by stirring it with the red-hot poker. The resulting taste was not always palatable. The boys who brought their dinners to school had great fun in the lunch hour. I would join them for "hare and hounds" over the fields, regardless of the bell that was calling us to afternoon lessons.

Week St. Mary School Football Team 1919-20

Once a week we went up to the school garden, where we grew vegetables, and had a fine time on our own, while the girls stayed in the classroom doing sewing. I got on well in class while Mr. Landry was my teacher, and I left at fourteen to go to work on my father's farm."

These "unofficial" activities of school children are much the same in every generation. Mr. Colwill, a later pupil, says: "I don't remember much about lessons, for I did a lot of "mitching" - that is, playing truant. I would go rabbiting in the fields or spend my time playing in the woods. Our favourite game in the dinner hour was to tie a rope to a sheet of corrugated iron. Then one boy would stand on it, while the others dragged it round and round the school. The noise was really appalling! In the classroom, of course, we played all the usual tricks on the teacher. One was to collect the mud from our boots and make small pellets which we would aim at the clock when we thought the teacher wasn't looking!"

In a small, isolated community it was very natural for childhood friendships to lead to happy marriages: Mr. & Mrs. Higgins, Mr. & Mrs. H. Jones, Mr. & Mrs. Pauling, and Mr. & Mrs. Martyn all shared the same school life, and still live in and around the village.

The school-leaving age was still fourteen years, and for most of the children it was the end of formal education. Between 1911 and 1929 only five children won places for Secondary schools, but in the thirties eight children gained scholarships for Bude County Grammar School.[d8]

The number of children on the register had fallen to sixty-eight, a sign of smaller families and greater mobility of the population. Classes were therefore smaller and the quality of the teaching was good. The curriculum had widened - cookery lessons had been started in the school, and the boys had been taken to agricultural demonstrations on neighbouring farms. Eight of the girls and two boys attended classes in the Rectory Room on Practical Dairy Work, while Grafting demonstrations were given by the County horticultural staff on the Rectory lawn. The two assistant teachers appointed were still always women, and they stayed on average for about five years. The exception was Miss Retallack, still remembered by all age groups. She served the school for forty years, and retired in 1963.

The Second World War brought great changes to school and village. Let Miss Agnes Smale continue the story: "The arrival of the evacuees in Week St. Mary was a great day, and will be remembered by many of the Senior Citizens. The village was canvassed by W.V.S. Workers to arrange for their accommodation, and luckily there were enough foster homes found.

Everyone was wondering what they were taking on, - "Those town children are not the same as ours" etc! At last the day came. It was Sunday afternoon about four-thirty on June 16th 1940. About thirty children were brought to the school, each carrying a little suitcase. Then they were given a cup of tea. By this time some of the foster parents had arrived to choose the ones they thought best for them. Others had to be taken to their new homes, and the majority went in ones and twos.

I was fortunate, for I left it until there were only half-a-dozen children left. When I looked inside the door there were two pathetic little girls sitting together, aged five and seven. I said to the Warden "Those girls are for me". Their faces just lifted up and they were delighted to pick up their cases, and out we came. Nobody knows what was in their minds, having left their home and parents. Nevertheless, they settled down and were with us for five years. It was surprising how well they got used to country life.

Those two little girls were evacuated from Sydenham Infants and Junior School. Another party of boys from the same district had arrived in charge of their teacher, Mr. P. Martin. Listen to the girls' teacher, Miss Pratt, now Mrs Skilton: "We arrived in Week St. Mary at about four-thirty p.m. after travelling all day in gruelling heat, with no refreshments, save water brought to us by courtesy of the stationmaster's wife at an unscheduled stop.

We were received in the village with the utmost kindness and understanding by the headmaster and his wife - Mr. and Mrs. Sincock - and by Mrs. Sandercock of the Bakery in the Square. They, with their W.V.S. helpers, had arranged for the billeting of the children. My party joined forces with Mr. Martin and his boys. Our children's ages ran from five to fourteen. We taught them for some time in the Methodist Sunday Schoolroom, and afterwards in the village school.

Mr. Sincock lent us what he could of his small stock of equipment and books. The villagers were extremely kind to our children, and most of them settled in very happily. Just before Christmas 1940 we organised a concert with our host school. This consisted of songs, ballads, dances and two short plays, all in costume. Mr. Sincock left just after Easter 1941, and then Mr. Martin took charge of both schools. Mr. Stephens, one of the school governors, took a great interest in the children. He was an official of the Cornish Bee-Keepers' Association, and he invited groups of the children to demonstrations in his garden. Then he awarded prizes of large pots of honey."

What did the children from Croydon think of their new life in the country? Molly Tarvin was one of those evacuees: "I was thirteen when I went to Week St. Mary School. Of course, conditions were very cramped, but we managed. The age range in each class was terrific. There must have been three classes in my time. Miss Pratt took the Infants, Miss Retallack the Juniors, and Mr. Martin the Seniors. I can only remember Miss Pratt taking us for Country Dancing, which was one of her keen interests, and Miss Retallack taking me for First Aid - which I hated!

Mr. Martin was very good at reading aloud to us. I can recall him reading to us for hours at a time excerpts from classical literature - "The White Company", "The Cloister and the Hearth", the speeches from Shakespeare's Henry IV and V, and "Westward Ho!" He read with great gusto and style, mostly of battles and adventures, holding me, and most of the others, spellbound. He was also a fine artist, and possibly not many people knew of this talent. I don't know how good he was as a Maths teacher, but I wasn't a very rewarding pupil, I'm sure! We also learnt French. I had previously passed the 11-plus exam, and they tried to give us a similar educational standard, but it was hard going for them. We took some Royal Society of Arts exams, some of which I passed, and others I failed.

Looking back, it was amazing how well we were assimilated into village life, and vice-versa. For me, it was a completely new world. My "Uncle Owen" (Mr. Owen Smale) used to say to me, "When you go home, maid, I'll buy a dog", and it wasn't until years later that I realised what he meant - I literally was his dog! I followed him like a dog, and even ran around the sheep for him to round them up. I remember getting permission to be absent from school to help with the harvest and the potato picking. Anything to do with harvesting was much more in my line than games or sports.

I look back to my years spent in Week St. Mary with great happiness and affection.

Now your buildings were open not only to children, but to the whole village. Lectures and classes for adults were started in the evenings by W.E.A. and Keep Fit, Dressmaking, and Drama were all popular. The evacuees left in 1945, and with their departure the school must have seemed very quiet. But the activities started in wartime continued, and school became more involved with contemporary life. The Police sent their men to the school to instruct the children in Road Safety, and the Ministry of Information showed films. The children were taken on expeditions to local farms to see the latest modern agricultural machinery at work, and to see the dairy products of the Ambrosia Milk Factory.

The School was divided into houses, Red, Blue and Green, and competed against each other on the Annual Sports and Prize Day. It did well, too, in the Inter-School Sports, and the children were encouraged to enter in the village Flower Show, which was always held in the School building.

Conditions in your building were now very different from the early days. Cloakrooms with washbasins had been provided, although each child had to bring his own soap and towel. The toilets had been modernised, and the whole school had been redecorated in brighter colours. The water supply was never good, children were still drinking from the well outside the school and with little cooking facilities it was not possible to provide a hot midday meal.

The solution was found in 1948, when a Canteen was opened in the Temperance Hotel, with Mrs. Charlick in charge. When she moved six years later, Mrs. Edwards cooked and served dinner there each day.

Our School Meals Service gave each child a good hot dinner for 60p per week. Punctually at twelve o'clock each day they came trooping down with their teachers. They were all very well behaved, and had healthy appetites. The menus were varied, and I don't remember any child being "faddy". At the end of the Christmas term we had a special dinner of chicken and Christmas pudding. I was in charge of the canteen for eighteen years, and I missed them all very much when the school closed.

Your first woman Head was Miss Mosely, who took charge of the school in 1951. Once again, your name was changed. You were now Week St. Mary County Primary School, for, in 1952, all the "over elevens" left for the Secondary School in Stratton. Now there were only twenty-six children on the register. This is what Mrs. Pat Johns, née Martyn, tells us of her school life at this period; "All the girls wore aprons, and woe betide you if you forgot yours on Monday morning.

But on Friday afternoon we had a great spree - it was painting lesson, and it didn't matter if you covered yourself with paint. During Lent, we were invited once a week by the Reverend Townend to the Round Room in the Rectory. There we saw slides of the Cross and the Easter Story. In the summer term we practised for Sports in the Kilbroney Field, and the seniors looked after the flowerbeds and cut the grass around the main School door. Sometimes we went on Nature Walks, and I remember a wonderful outing we had to see the new Queen Elizabeth. In Coronation Year, we had an Open Day. The Juniors recited a Coronation Alphabet, and the Infants a poem to the Queen. In school, our cutout models of the Coronation coach were on display. We had planted our gardens with red, white and blue flowers, and these were much admired.

The winter term saw us all playing "shinty", a form of hockey, played in the hard playground, while the boys played football. Our milk at break-time was warmed on the stove, and served to us in blue beakers, one-third of a pint each. It might be slightly burnt, but we were told, "The flavour helps it down."

Then came the preparation for the School Concert in the Rectory Room. It was at one of these concerts that a Progress Prize was first awarded to the boy and girl who had made the most progress in the year's work. The names were a closely guarded secret until Miss Mosely announced the two winners. from the platform. Then followed the Christmas Party, with tea and games and a Father Christmas, played by Mrs. Ridgman, the caretaker. In the next term, everybody was at work, for the eleven-plus exam came in the New Year. The results came out in May or early June; these were very important, for they decided whether you went to Bude Grammar School or to the Secondary School in Stratton.

After Miss Mosley's death in 1958 Mrs Ruth Saltern was appointed as your new Head, and Miss Retallack stayed as the assistant teacher until her retirement in 1963.

Week St. Mary Revel Day came every year in September, and from 1965 the school children played an important part in it. The Infant class walked in procession before the Harvest Queen, while the Juniors joined in the Floral Dance. The procession assembled at the school, and from there proceeded down to the Square, where the Queen was crowned.

Two new teachers joined the staff - Mrs. Smeeth as Infant teacher, and Mr. J. Rees as visiting Art Master. Modern methods of teaching were very different from those of earlier years, and teachers were able to take Refresher Courses to keep them in touch with the latest teaching practice. In 1962, during North Cornwall's Education Week, the school held its own Open Day, when parents and friends could talk to the teachers, and see the children at work.

Week St. Mary School children - 1921

The health of all schoolchildren had been regularly checked for many years, but now inoculations against measles, poliomyelitis and diphtheria were given by doctor or nurse in school. The children's eyesight and hearing were tested, and any dental treatment needed was given at the School Dental Clinic in Bude. A speech therapist visited the school to help with speech defects, and a psychiatrist would give advice when needed.

Physical education was now very different from Mr. King's "military drill", and the school was using special P.E. apparatus. Mrs. Saltern started swimming lessons with the Juniors, and took them after school to swim in the pool at Stratton County Primary School.

The children of the sixties could not be described as "shy and reticent", and they certainly did not "seem scared and on the lookout for a cuff".

The project method of teaching had encouraged them to think for themselves, and through their activities to acquire knowledge that had previously been gained by repetition and memory work. Music and Drama played an important part in the school timetable.

Besides playing in their own percussion band the children listened to and took part in the B.B.C. Schools music programmes. The London Children's Theatre Company paid several visits to the school; they acted plays, and encouraged the children to take part in them. Every Christmas, the children produced their own plays for the Christmas Concert, and very often baked their own Christmas cakes for their end of term parties.

Little so far has been said about religious teaching in the school. After the denominational feuds that had hindered the passing of the 1870 Education Act, religious teaching in State Schools had been strictly non-sectarian. "Scripture Lesson" had meant the repeating of passages from the Bible only. Then came a full syllabus of Religious Education, which in a Primary School consisted of stories and activities which gave the children opportunities to learn and practise Christian behaviour. A short service of worship was held every morning, and the school held its own Harvest Festival and Christmas Carol services.

Here is Tom Watkinson's impression of school at this time: "I first came to the school when I was six. The day after we moved to Week St. Mary from Hampshire, in November 1971, Mum and I walked up the hill to the school. We met Mrs. Saltern as we came in. She then led us into the schoolroom where Mrs. Smeeth was, she was to be my new teacher. When we went in I was astonished by what I saw, there were only six or seven children in the whole room. Compared with the number of children in the class I was in at my old school, this was fantastic! It was very strange to me indeed. Mrs. Smeeth then introduced us to the class (what there was of it) and told us that there were usually more, but that five were away that day. She asked me if I wanted to stay there for the day, and I said I would, Mum said I could come home for lunch, so I stayed at the school all the morning, and came down the hill with the others at mid-day.

Week St. Mary School children

After Mum had gone I decided to sit with Michael Horrell. He was very friendly, and so were all the other children in the class. I spent half a year in Mrs. Smeeth's class. I liked her a lot.

I was moved into Mrs. Saltern's class when I was seven. This was the highest class in the school, (there were only two classes) and Mrs. Saltern was an older lady. We had Assembly in the mornings in Mrs. Smeeth's classroom, and did P.E. in our own room with some small apparatus. Apart from Maths and English, which we did from textbooks, we had a history period when Mrs. Saltern would talk to us about something, then write about it on the blackboard, and we copied it into our exercise books. We also had an Art period on Wednesdays, when we did mostly painting.

In the playground we often played a game called "Stuck in the Mud", where several people were the chasers, while the rest of us had to keep running; you had to stand still if one of the chasers touched you and shout "Stuck in the mud", in the hope that somebody would touch you to set you free again. We used to bring toy cars and lorries to play with in the playground.

We used to walk down to the Temperance Hotel for our lunch, and we brought our own soap and towel to wash with at school before going down. Stephen Colwill was one of my friends, although older than me.

We often used to walk down the hill together, when we were coming home. He always seemed to me to be quite witty. I didn't spend very long at Week St. Mary School, being there for about a year, and then it was closed, but I enjoyed my stay there very much indeed.

By the seventies, you looked decidedly old-fashioned. Although you had been modified over the years - (you now had mains water and oil-fired central heating) - you did not conform to the modern specifications for school buildings. You had no kitchen and no playing field; the Infant classroom had windows that were far above the children's eye-level, and the toilets were still outside, in a small, badly shaped playground. With only twenty-three children on the register, you were too expensive to run. A new school was to be built at Jacobstow, three miles away, which would incorporate four old schools into one. The other villages concerned being Jacobstow itself, Poundstock, and St. Gennys, six of your children joined pupils from those schools for the Foundation Stone-laying ceremony on November 10th 1971, on the site of the new school at Jacobstow; a tin containing photographs of the four old schools, pre-decimal coins, and pound and ounce weights was also buried. A few weeks later, a Statutory Notice of Closure was fixed to your main door.

On March 30th 1973 the Minister for Education, Mrs. Margaret Thatcher, officially opened the new school from Helston. One pupil from each of the four old schools was chosen to go to Jacobstow to hear her speech, which was recorded for the occasion, and David Prouse, one of the eldest children, was the representative from Week St. Mary. A few days later, Mr. Henchley from Stratton came to the school to take photographs of the children in your playground, and also, with their teachers and Mrs. Edwards, outside the Temperance Hotel.

The new school would be ready for the children in time for the Summer Term, and the last ceremony in your life took place in the Junior classroom on April 11th 1973, the final day of the Spring Term.

Parents were invited to the school, where farewell presentations were to be made to Mrs. Edwards, and Mrs. Dorothy Orchard - who had been school caretaker for some time. Mrs. Saltern and Mrs. Smeeth had organized and subscribed to a collection for this purpose, and here is Mrs. Smeeth to recall the occasion: "We thought it would be a nice idea to give Mrs. Edwards and Mrs. Orchard a parting present, in recognition of their work over the years, that had been so essential to the children's welfare. The parents subscribed very willingly to the collection, however, what we didn't know was that we ourselves were to receive presentations from the School Managers - it was a complete surprise! Mrs Saltern received a stainless steel tray and tea set, and I was given a sweet dish, and also a little silver brooch, which I treasure very much.

One of those Managers making the presentations was Mr. Norman Gubbin, himself a past pupil and an early contributor to your story. The room was filled with children, parents, and even grandparents, and to many there it was the end of a part of village life they had always known.

When the children and visitors had departed the staff closed the school gate for the last time. Mrs. Smeeth was to join the staff at Jacobstow in the new term, as head of the Infant Department, a position which she still occupies; Mrs. Saltern continued her career with the Teachers Supply Service for some time, and has now retired.

Low, as you stand empty and silent in 1976, you still remind us of all the activity that went on in your classrooms in the past. Your children have left for many different careers. They can be found in farming, commerce, banking, engineering, building, nursing, and Local Government, and many have gone abroad. But all look back on their schooldays with affection. Michael Horrell has not yet entered that wider world, for he only began his schooldays in your Infant classroom in 1970, but he is the last speaker in this record: "I live very near the old school, and when I feel "teazy" I go there and play around a bit and sing. That school had a lovely smell - sometimes I stick my head to the window that's broken and breathe in the air, it always revives me, and I sort of feel better. I hope they don't pull it down - I think it ought to be there always."

And what of your future? Speculation in the village still continues - who will buy you and to what use will you be put? A dwelling house? A youth centre? A builders yard or a furniture store? Or demolition, and old people's bungalows replacing your unwanted buildings. No one knows.

So, our village school, that was your life.

Now, in 1976, the school stands empty and silent, still reminding us of all the activity that went on in the classrooms. We are sorry those times have gone; we miss the sound of the hymns in the morning, and the school bell announcing playtime. We miss the "crocodile", going down to lunch at "the Temperance". But, as we see our children piling into the blue and white minibus in the Square, we know they are enjoying a full school life, with all the advantages that a new school can offer - modern buildings, green playing fields, a heated swimming pool. The story of our school ends where it began with the children. ∎

A typical Menu as 'enjoyed' by the pupils at the Temperance Hotel
January 15th - January 19th:
Monday: Meat pudding, potatoes, greens. Blancmange and jam.
Tuesday: Roast beef, potatoes, greens. Mince tart and custard.
Wednesday: Bacon and egg flan, potatoes, greens. Rice pudding.
Thursday: Fish, potatoes, greens. Chocolate biscuit and junket.
Friday: Mince, potatoes, greens. [blank]

March 26th - March 30th:
Monday: Roast lamb, potatoes, greens. Date squares and custard.
Tuesday: Stew, dumplings, potatoes, greens. Ice cream.
Wednesday: Cottage pie, potatoes, greens. Isle of Wight pudding.
Thursday: Fish, potatoes, greens. Chocolate pudding.
Friday: Spam, potatoes, beetroot. Fruit pudding and custard.

Week St. Mary School children

One of my first school photos

School photo - Putting my arm around my sister!

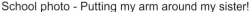

The Rectory & Rectory Room

The Rectory Schoolroom played an important part in bringing parishioners together to enjoy various small functions but provided insufficient room for large gatherings.

The lawns played host to the village for fetes, garden parties and other significant village events.

In 1921 Rev. Haslem (1900-1919) built what was called the 'Rectory Room' and was bought from him by Rev. Whitmell (1920-1921).

July 25th 1921: A Civil Engineer, Mr. A Hurse wrote to Mr. Rogers (Churchwarden), stating that he had recommended to Mr. Whitmell that the Rectory Room be put up for auction, supporting the fact that Mr. Whitmell feels that the people of the village should own the Room, thus avoiding the disturbances every time there is a vacancy at the Rectory.

It therefore appears that the intention was for each Rector, in turn, to purchase the Rectory Room from the preceding incumbent. The following letter, dated 13th August 1921, is from the Revd Hardy to the churchwarden,

Mr. Rogers:
Tooting
London S.W. 17
13th August 1921
Dear Mr. Rogers,

Thank you very much for your two letters. With regard to the Rectory Room you must do what the people consider best. I myself am quite unable to buy it. As far as I can see, I shall have very little money coming in and a great deal going out during the next six or eight months. In fact I expect to receive so little from my new Benefice between the present time and Lady Day that I shall need to raise from some other source not less than £100 to tide me over that period. Under the circumstances it is clear that I cannot think of buying the Rectory Room.

So now it rests with you. The people need have no fear that I shall object to them coming through the Rectory garden, as my object in coming to Week St. Mary is to be of what service I can to them.

As to letting the present Room go, and building another, I suppose it would mean being without a Room for some time; but no doubt if the people really felt the need of one, it would not be very long before it could be built.

Please let me know what you decide to do. As to Mr. Whitmell asking you to give him £150 for the Room, I still think that some consideration should be given to the fact that you have had the use of the Room for so long - even if the Room is not worth £150 now.

I shall certainly be in Week St. Mary for the 18th - 19th, and possibly for 11th September. Mr. Browne has suggested that I might preach on the Monday as I am a newcomer, and I told him I would: but I am quite willing for Mr. Kingdon to do so, if you have already asked him.

I shall be very glad now when the time comes.

Yours sincerely,
M. V. Hardy

The building has now been purchased from Revd Whitmell, by the Church, for £150.

As reported earlier in this book, the Rector, Revd Simpson, announced from the pulpit his decision to deny access to the Rectory Room because of a health and safety risk. This caused some aggravation amongst many parishioners. It was felt that the decision to close the Rectory Room should

The Rectory

have been delayed until the building of the new Parish Hall was complete so as to continue to offer a meeting place for the parishioners.

On 1st January 1971 the Rectory Room was sold by the Parochial Church Council, Week St. Mary, to the Rector for the sum of £60. (This was signed by the Rector, W. T. Simpson and by the Treasurer, M. Cobbledick).

The Rectory Room, for most of us older residents, became the centre of a wonderful period of entertainment, amusement, social gatherings, pantomimes, dances and whist drives. Many of us can recall the large numbers attending a wide variety of functions.

Despite the Rectory Room being of primitive construction, by modern standards, it did achieve its function of providing a community meeting-place. It was made of a wooden frame with galvanised sheets forming the walls and roof. The Room had a generous supply of forms and general seating; a well-polished dance floor and a stage upon which 'actors' and musicians took up residence. Even I can remember, with horror, at having to stand on the stage as a very young schoolboy and sing a solo about a robin!

Socials were very popular - an evening spent playing games. Assorted teams of all ages had to run around, racing each other, in an attempt to 'blow up a paper bag', 'spin the plate', 'musical chairs' and other basic tests of ability.

Many will recall the dances with a variety of visiting 'bands' providing the music.

Christmas Party in the Rectory Room for the children - circa 1955

...and then tea for the adults - circa 1955

Not the 'modern' style of dancing with great head-shaking and body twitching emulating possible signs of extreme internal pain; for us it was 'ballroom dancing', a subject still taught at Stratton Secondary Modern School up to the middle 1960s. I still remember our dancing teacher, Miss Allen, asking me not to hold her too close and telling me that I was 'light on my feet'.

Traditionally, at dances, the 'last waltz' was exactly that - the last dance of the night. When courting Jean Duke, now my long-suffering wife, my mother would suddenly appear behind me and tell me in no uncertain terms that it was the last waltz and that I should get onto the floor before the evening was over!

The Rectory Room was built on the edge of a small field adjoining a small copse of mature trees. Access to the Room was by way of a single-track through the trees from the driveway of the Rectory. Our mother always told my sisters that if they arrived home at the end of an evening with mud on their shoes it was a sure sign that they had been off the pathway!

The toilet facilities were best described as basic, with a big 'B' - simply a small room with a bucket available below a wooden seat. This facility was generally only favoured by the women - the men preferring to utilise 'alternative' arrangements outside the building. ■

May Pole dancing on the Rectory lawn - circa 1930

The Parish Hall

Before the Rectory Room had come to the end of its life in 1970, March 1968 saw a few parishioners hold a meeting with a view to rousing enough interest to build a new parish hall. The existing building was very outdated with few modern amenities - yes, we all remember the limited facilities! It was perceived that within a short while the building would become unusable by virtue of being condemned for such public use.

Squadron Leader J. Douglas first wrote to the Parish Council on Monday 23rd October 1967 asking for a public meeting regarding the ways and means of building a new Hall.

A parish meeting was convened on Thursday 7th March 1968 when a committee of 14 was formed. This eventually rose to 22 as various bodies elected representatives to join the committee. After approaching several landowners the current location was acquired from Mr. Donald Sandercock, along with a suitable parking area.

There was a small fund of some £200 in the bank, raised for such a venture before WW II but left unused due to lack of local support.

In May 1971, Mr. Arthur Cleave, of Bude, was asked to cut the first turf and a second was cut on behalf of Mr. Smale who was too unwell to perform that task but gave a contribution of £100 towards the fund.

The following July there was a large crowd at the site of the new parish hall to see the foundation stone being laid by Mr. Walter Dennis, of Launceston. Mr. Metters (architect) presented a silver trowel to Mr. Dennis with which to lay the stone. Bricks were auctioned and after being signed by the purchasers were cemented into place by two bricklayers.

Altogether the cost of the project was in the region of £15,000 including all associated costs such as professional fees, curtains, furniture and plants. Cornwall County Council and the Department of Education and Science together gave grants in excess of £9,000 towards the project, leaving the remainder to be raised by the villagers.

Fund-raising was forever evident throughout the village with a variety of activities.

Mr Dennis laying the foundation stone

74

My mother and brother, a prize-winner in 1970

These included Whist Drives and film shows in the Methodist schoolroom. Fancy-dress activities such as a pram race created much amusement and, more importantly, money!

A 10-mile sponsored walk took place with participants ranging in age from 7yrs to 73yrs. The route was from Week St. Mary to Marhamchurch and back to the village via Titson and Hannaford's Mill - first man home was Graham Orchard with Roy Cobbledick second. Over £450 was raised at this event. A successful 'Banger Race' held near Langdon by kind permission of Mr. Ellis, helped to contribute to the funds.

Gala Day at Plymswood was a major fund-raising event culminating with a real 'barn' dance, raising several hundred pounds for the appeal.

On the 3rd Gala Day (1970) a fancy-dress parade for the under-11's was held and winners were: 1st Prize 'Off to the Moon' Stephen Martin, 2nd Prize 'Cornish Pixie' Teresa Edwards and 3rd 'Mrs Mop' Rachael Horrell.

I well remember building the rocket for my brother. It was one of my last contributions before Jean and I left Week St. Mary to embark on a 3-year posting to R.A.F. Akrotiri, Cyprus. The cylindrical body of the rocket was made from a piece of 'lino', painted with aluminium paint and suitably decorated. Even Stephen's boots were painted silver for the occasion. Two loops were fastened inside so that he could 'pick it up' to move. Mother kept an eye on 5-year-old Stephen just to make sure he didn't lose his balance; after all, it was a rocket and not a torpedo!

Brother and sister at the 2nd Gala Day 1969

Grand Opening

Saturday 8th April 1972, at 2.30pm the new parish hall was opened by Alderman K. Foster, Chairman of Cornwall County Council. It was allegedly a bright sunny day with a chill wind. A good crowd was there to hear the Alderman praise the villagers for their efforts and emphasise how important it was to have a place of meeting in such an isolated village. He further added that he was sorry to hear that the school may soon be closed with the pupils having to travel to nearby Jacobstow. In excess of 400 people sat down to a tea in the new Hall that afternoon.

During the afternoon a peal of 5,040 changes in Plain Bob Major was undertaken at the Parish Church and a special thanksgiving service occurred on the following Sunday, conducted by the Rev W. T. Simpson.

Alderman Foster opens the new Parish Hall with (left to right) Alfred Sandercock, Reg Burden, John Rogers and Rev W T Simpson

By the time the hall was open only a small amount had to be found, some £850 which was soon realised by future events. During the first few months of use of the new parish hall the bookings were encouraging. The doctor used it for a surgery; there were skittles teams using it; social functions and outside interests helped to swell the coffers to cover the running costs.

In 1971 the following open invitation was published:-

Week St. Mary Parish Hall Appeal Fund

To the parishioners, ex-parishioners and all who have an interest in our village.

It is now 3 years since a Parish Meeting formed our Committee and entrusted to us the task of providing a Parish Hall worthy of Week St. Mary. The Hall is to be round in shape and of a very modern appearance, and one the Committee Members feel the Village will be proud to own.

The Village so far has raised over £3,750 since the project was first started and this, together with the Grants from the Department of Education and Science £7,238 and the County Council £1,800, on a total expenditure of £15,383.

This price includes everything, the Land, Solicitors' and Architects' Fees, building the Hall and the equipment needed for the light fittings, right down to the doormats. This leaves us with approximately £2,600 to raise.

A start has now been made on the Hall, and naturally the sooner it is built the sooner we will have somewhere to hold again, the many activities which usually take place in the Village.

We now appeal for funds, either as gifts or as interest-free loans, which can be sent to any Committee Member or direct to the National Westminster Bank Ltd., Launceston, Cornwall. Thank you for your support,

Alfred Sandercock (Chairman)

Parish Hall Committee:

Chairman:
Mr. A. Sandercock, Clifton House, Week St. Mary, Holsworthy, Devon

Secretary:
Mrs. R. M. Orchard, Plymswood, Week St. Mary, Holsworthy, Devon

Joint Treasurers:
Mrs. K. Uglow, Goscott, Week St. Mary, Holsworthy, Devon
Mr. P. Gubbin, Brendon Barton, North Petherwin, Launceston, Cornwall.

Joint Secretaries:
Mrs. C. Orchard & Miss K. Jones

Members:
Mr. & Mrs. I. Barriball, Mr. D. Colwill, Mrs. W. Congdon Mr. G. Dinnis, Mrs. J. Edwards, Mr. R. Harris, Mrs. Q. Harris, Mr. S. Heard, Mr. & Mrs. D. Orchard, Mr. L. Parnell, Mrs. H. Ridgeman, Miss. A. Rogers, Mrs. D. Treleven, Mr. T. Worden and Mr. R. Orchard.

Past Members:
Mr. J. Douglas, Past Chairman. Mr. & Mrs. O. Heard, Past Treasurers Mrs. G. Masters & Mrs. S. Parish, Past Secretaries. Mrs. T. Davey, Mrs. M. Johns, Mrs. W. Colwill the late Mrs. H. Brewer.

Trustees of the new Hall:
Mr. N. Gubbin, Mrs. A. Vedrenne, Mr. A. Sandercock and the late Mrs H. Brewer.

List of suppliers:

Main Contractor. . . . . . Mr. I. Barriball, Week St. Mary 235
Electricians . . . . Mr. F. Bright, Widemouth Bay 271
Bituminous Roofing . . . . Mr. C. Bowden, St. Merryn 413
Plumbing . . . . Mr. A. Moore, North Petherwin 224
Central Heating . . . . A.C.E. Newquay 3324
Glazing . . . . Nth. Cornwall Glazing, Camelford 2563
Roofing Panels . . . . Laminated Woods, Bideford 4091
Light fittings . . . . Merchant Adventurers 01-894-5522
Curtains . . . . Wippells, Exeter 54234
Chairs . . . . Excel, Plymouth 63334
Blinds . . . . Bayly Bartlett, Bideford 3421
China, etc. . . . . Allams Torquay 63698
Shrubs . . . . Endsleigh Gardens, Milton Abbot 235
Card Tables . . . . Colwills, Launceston 3381
Tables . . . . Moores' North Tamerton 212

Bayly Bartlett have helped to build the village hall of the future.

Architect Colin Metters, of Bude, North Cornwall, prepared and received approval for a design far removed from the traditional type of parish hall. The £15,000 project is circular in shape and built around a 1,200 sq. ft. hall.

The hall, in the village of Week St. Mary (population 400), eight miles away from Bude was built by local builder and contractor I. F. Barriball.

The villagers raised more than £7,000 towards the hall in little more than four years. The balance came from the National Council of Social Service.

Yorkshire-born Colin Metters says: "The circular interior has certainly contributed towards creating a social atmosphere. A hall which is round in shape tends to discourage people from forming their own groups. As there are no corners, people find themselves unobtrusively mixing in."

Mr. Arthur Cox, sales manager of Bayly Bartlett's Bideford branch, which supplied materials for the new hall, said his company were pleased to be associated with such a futuristic design.

Quantity surveyor for the building was Mr. W. C. C. Press, the hall, situated on a 2,200 sq. ft. site, was built in nine months.

Timetable On Opening Day

2.30 pm Opening Ceremony by Alderman Foster
3.30pm - 6.30pm High Tea in the Hall
4pm and 5pm In the Marquee - Punch & Judy shows, Sideshows and Stalls along with H. Johns and his electric organ
7pm Concert in the hall by the Whitstone Male Voice Choir and others
8pm Dance in the Hall (Admission 50p) with the Texans Dance Band
Sunday 9th April, 8pm Thanksgiving Service with St. Gennys Silver Band
Thursday 13th April Bumper Whist Drive
Friday 14th April Dance with Johnny Pett at 9pm - 1am
Saturday 15th April 2pm Beagle Meet at The Green Inn

The Parish Hall (2007)

As reported on at the Open Meeting held on Tuesday 17th April 2007.

The village hall is one of our greatest assets. It was built some 35 years ago as the result of a great deal of effort by many enthusiastic members of Week St. Mary parish. It was - at that time I suggest, a state of the art building and a credit to the team who engineered its building.

The hall has contributed to our village life but over the recent years, has been hit by a double whammy! First the continuing introduction and imposition of new regulations which we are obligated to meet in order to keep the hall open to the public, reinforced by insurance requirements and increases.

Examples are Fire regulations: An additional fire escape exit door in the hall together with the lighting signs. Curtains that needed to be of fire retardant material. Asphalt escape path at the rear of the building. Health & Safety & Welfare regulations. Disabled facilities.

Additional ventilation requirements for the heating system. At the time of inspection it was brought to our attention that the existing boiler was now obsolete and that spare parts will be difficult to obtain.

Catering regulations: An extensive upgrading of the kitchen facilities are required if we are to continue to hold functions involving the serving of food.

The second whammy is the ageing process. The building is beginning to show its age. We have endeavoured to keep abreast of this by the replacing of two or three windows and frames. Attention to the roof is ongoing as is the general repair to the internal fabric. We are aware that the overhead lighting will need attention soon. Ivor F. Barriball has carried out a comprehensive costing as to meeting our regulation obligations and carrying out necessary repairs and refurbishment. This amounts to the staggering sum of nearly £43,000.

Very few grants are available for general maintenance, only new works and these have to be generally match funded. We have discussed these issues at great length and arrived at two options. We resolve to raise sufficient funds over the next two or three years to meet our obligations for the hall, or we investigate creating a new community centre on the playing field that will totally meet today's needs, and would attract some grant funding as it would be a 'new build'. By selling the existing building and land, the money would be available for some match funding grants. We have had a feasibility study made with this possibility in mind.

As I write this, future meetings are being planned, so who knows what the outcome will be... deja vu no doubt!

Late news...

The field adjacent to the playing field has just been offered for sale by public auction and the Parish Council were successful in purchasing the ground. It is hoped that future plans will include a new Parish Hall and changing rooms for the local sports teams along with a re-positioned larger football pitch.

Any change has to be for the use of all the community so let's hope that the community has a long and useful future in its new location..., as they say, "Watch this space!" ■

Village Buildings

Including the Parish Church, there are currently eighteen buildings in the parish listed by the Department of the Environment as being of special architectural or historical interest.

The buildings are graded to show their relative architectural or historic interest:

Grade I buildings are of exceptional interest

Grade II* are particularly important buildings of more than special interest

Grade II are of special interest, warranting every effort to preserve them

Listing currently protects 500,000 or so buildings, of which the majority - over 90% - are Grade II.

GRADE I - Parish Church has a C14 south arcade, C15 aisles, late C15/early C16 porch and tower. Some masonry in the chancel may be C13. Substantially restored 1876 to 1881.

GRADE II - Brendon Farmhouse (early C19 with late C17/early C18 range) and wall adjoining, outbuilding adjoining and cart shed.

GRADE II - Brendon Farmhouse Barn, mill house and stables.

GRADE II - Goscott Farmhouse Circa 1850 with C17 range attached at rear.

GRADE II* - Leigh Farmhouse Late C16/early C17 core, C17 alterations. Incorporation of some moulded timbers from a demolished house in the village.

GRADE II - Leigh Farmhouse Cider house.

GRADE II - Lower Kitleigh Cottage Former farmhouse, circa C18.

GRADE II* - Marhays Manor, including garden area wall adjoining circa early C17 build incorporated into late C17/early C18 house. There is an elaborate plaster ceiling in high relief with putti, birds, fruit and flowers. This is a Domesday manor.

GRADE II - Sladdacott Farmhouse, with adjoining cottage and barn. Circa C17 with possibly earlier build.

GRADE II - Steele Farmhouse and adjoining outbuilding. Core C17 with C19 additions.

GRADE II - Week Orchard. The Cottage. C17 cob with thatched roof of wheat. Early roof structure intact.

GRADE II - Pigsdon/Pegsdon. Formerly a farmhouse. Late C18/early C19.

GRADE II* - Burdenwell Manor and cottage. Formerly a farmhouse. Probably C16 core. (The owner gave the date 1553). A former home of the Granville family.

GRADE II - Church Cottage. House, formerly two cottages, C17 with C20 at rear. Some original roof timbers remain. The two cottages formerly entered through common entrance door into passage with doors off.

GRADE II - Hayescott/Hayscroft House. C17 core, rebuilt circa C19. Original build may have been part of Old College complex. Shutters to ground floor windows.

GRADE II - New College. House. Late C19, perhaps earlier in part. incorporating two tympana from the 1508 Old College complex. Included for group value with Old College.

GRADE II - The Old College, outbuilding adjoining, wall adjoining front. Now a Landmark Trust holiday house, it was originally a grammar school built in 1508 for Dame Thomasine Percival who endowed it.

GRADE II - Well House. c 4m east of the Old College. Built circa 1508 for the grammar school.

One or two further details may be added from local knowledge. A former owner of Steele Farmhouse has told of large caches of drink bottles being found in the grounds and has suggested a secret ale house used during the time when early Methodism had declared war on intoxicating drinks.

Burdenwell Manor was formerly known as Burnwell Manor; the name was changed when new owners came in shortly after the end of World War II. Allegedly built around the late 15th or early 16th century, it was gradually extended and modified over the next few hundred years. The house contains a reputed priests' hole and an alleged underground passage connecting with the churchyard, although no evidence of this was found despite an in-depth survey of the Manor and Cottage by Cornwall Archaeological Unit, prior to planning approval for modernisation and extension to Burdenwell Cottage.

Several examples of buildings dating back a few hundred years can be found within the village confines although many have been extensively modernised. In Stewart's Road, one such building, Wyke House, is typical of a property, once consisting of 3 houses, now modernised and converted into one large and one small property. The original names of the buildings were; No. 1, the 'Pigs House' and the 'Stable'.

The cottages opposite Hayescott also demonstrate the combination of small cottages into larger units. These ancient buildings were named Fuschia Cottage, Lantern Cottage and Church Cottage but the two latter properties now form one house with two beautiful large open fireplaces complete with cloam ovens.

There are in the village other old houses not listed at present. Just off the Square is a small building now called "Chyvean', said to be over 350 years old and known to have been a former ale house and subsequently a Methodist chapel.

At the bottom of the hill leading from Week Green is 'Corys', a splendid old house dating from around 1400, which may well have been a farmhouse in the days when there were still farms in the heart of the village. It may also have been a typical longhouse - a thatched property with stock accommodated in an adjoining building to the living quarters. Corys has a fine example of an ancient open fireplace dating from about 1450 and constructed with monstrous slabs of granite. An archaeologist's report from several years ago suggested that stained beams in the roof area were signs of an open hearth.

It was while I was at Corys the present occupants related several instances of seeing ghost-like beings, each from a different period of history and all kind and helpful.

At the top of the same hill is 'The Cottage' which now incorporates two old cottages. Halfway down on the other side is Wentworth House, the stately former rectory, probably Georgian, with its stables, which, in 1993 housed a small honey producing business under the ownership of Mr. G. Bate.

In the Lower Square is Red Lion House, formerly a public house and later a shop, Box Tree Cottage once a farm and Sea View Farm, the last remaining working farm right in the village.

A number of houses which appear to be of 20-century builds may well be much older houses disguised under modernisation too thorough for the purist. The whole area is rich in potential gems.[11]

Delabole Head

Further south of Week Green is another example of a small cottage that is estimated to be over 250 years old even though documentation only covers the period from 1855. This early document is the conveyance of the property from John Rowe the elder to John Rowe the younger of the cottage and garden '...in consideration of the sum of thirty pounds sterling...'. It further describes the property as follows '....the Cottage or Dwelling House with the two Gardens adjoining to the same belonging commonly called or known by the name of Dinnabole...' Whilst John Rowe the Younger was able to sign his name John Rowe the Elder made his 'mark'.

The next two documents are dated 1866 and are signed and witnessed on the same date.

A Declaration by John Rowe the younger sets out his ownership of the property. He states his name and that he is 'about forty three years old' and that he had lived in the property about thirty years plus.

It confirms the purchase from his father (who had now died) in 1855 and that he had lived in the property for thirty years plus prior to purchasing the property. The document declares that John Rowe the elder had always stated that he had lived in the property for seventy years prior to selling the property to his son and that he had been 'entitled to the Property..... namely from his father before him who built it from the ground up'.

Another document refers to a loan of the princely sum of twenty pounds for a term of fifteen years that John Rowe obtained from the Provident Permanent Benefit Building Society. The payments were to be made quarterly and were eleven shillings and sixpence (57 pence approximately) of every calendar month of December, March, June and September in every year. He obviously kept up the payments as the document has been stamped and dated by the building society in 1881 confirming that the money had been repaid. This document variously refers to the property as Denebold or Dinnabole.

From the information in these documents it would certainly confirm that the property was built some time prior to 1785 and John Rowe is listed in the 1871 census at Delabole Head.

At some point the property appears to have left the ownership of the Rowe family but there are no documents in our possession relating to a sale. The 1901 census shows a John Duke resident with his wife and son.

In 1911 the property was transferred from 'The Misses Fanny Ayres and Annie Ayres to the Tilley family. The Tilley family owned the property until its sale in 1949 to Messrs 'Matera & S. Kaluzinski. It is at this time that the property is more generally referred to as Delabole Head. The property remained in the hands of the Kaluzinski family until 2000.

Lambley Park

Lambley Park was built around 1894 and had been a landmark of the village for as long as anyone alive could remember. It was with sadness that such a fine imposing building should suffer a disastrous fire on 6th April 2004. Lambley Park Country House Hotel was almost totally destroyed. Almost 20 months later very little has changed, except for demolition and site clearance in preparation for a rebuilding project.

The hotel was destroyed by fire during refurbishment, just one month prior to re-opening with upgraded accommodation. The fire started under the flat roof above one of the bays on the first floor and just 15 minutes later the roof was completely gone. After 25 minutes the fire service arrived. The water pressure in the hydrants in the village was almost zero - so the firemen took water from a nearby well. Tankers arrived and they also were emptied but only to contain the fire within the shell of the building.

Many of the residents of Week St. Mary were as devastated as the owners were at the loss of the house which had been a part of village life and history since the late 1800's.

The new owners, Andrea Peek & Alan Middleton, had moved to Lambley Park in October 2003 and started a refurbishment/renovation programme that was due to culminate in May 2004 with the re-opening of the Lambley Park Country House Hotel on 1st June 2004.

For safety reasons the remains of the hotel were demolished in July 2005.

Who could have predicted how slow the wheels would turn. Until the finances are resolved the rebuild phase cannot be started. Some 20 months on the case between the decorators and their insurance company is still on-going and currently rests with a final decision yet to be made by the Financial Ombudsman.

In anticipation of a decision being imminent, outline planning was sought and granted to rebuild the hotel.[12]

Old College

One of the most famous buildings in the village is now owned by The

Total devastation

Landmark Trust. The College is so called because it was originally a free school, one of the earliest in England to be founded by a woman. The building was originally part of an endowment by Dame Thomasine Percival - the widow of Sir John Percival, who was Lord Mayor of London in 1498. Thomasine, whose maiden name was Bonaventure, was born in the village of Week St. Mary in 1450. The story of how she first married Richard Bunsby, a wool merchant from London, and then further improved her position and fortune by two later marriages has been told by many Cornish writers, including Parson Hawker of Coombe association.

Lady Percival must have been an unusual woman of her time, because soon after the death of her third husband in 1504, she returned to the village to devote the remainder of her life to charitable work in the neighbourhood. In 1506 she founded a school, appointing her cousin John Dinham of Wortham to oversee the building work and when she died, she left the school and a chantry to John's discretion. She also settled a stipend for the schoolmaster, who was to be a graduate of Oxford or Cambridge and to pray for her soul in the Parish Church of St Mary.

The Commissioners of 1546 assigned to enquire into chantries, hospitals, colleges, free chapels, etc. reported that "that ye sayde Chauntrye is a great comfort to all ye countries, for yt they yt lyst may sett their children to borde there and have them taught freely, for ye wch purpose there is an house and offices appointed by the foundation accordingly".

Unfortunately two years later another Commission reported that the school at St Mary Week was "now yn decaye" and this was followed with a declaration by the Lord Protector Somerset that the school should be moved to Launceston.

We will never really know what happened to turn, within a few years, a flourishing school which was serving the local community well, into such an unwanted and unmanageable liability that its assets had to be transferred to the similar foundation of the adjoining town.

From 1549-1725 the buildings were owned by the Prideaux family, who sold them in the early 18th century to Thomas Pitt, first Lord Londonderry, and a first cousin to the Earl of Chatham. His sister Lucy married the first Earl of Stanhope, one of the most distinguished soldiers in the reign of Queen Anne, and the property came through her to the Stanhopes. The 7th Earl of Stanhope sold it in 1910, together with his Holsworthy estate. Mr. Colwill from whom the Landmark Trust bought it, had lived at the College all his life, and so had two generations of the Colwills before him.

The buildings of the former College were gradually pillaged to provide building materials for other village buildings - dressed granite jambs, heads and tympani can be seen built into the walls of many neighbouring cottages, although enough survives of the College to give us some idea of the imposing group which stood on the site in the reign of Edward VI.

The granite dressings of the windows, with the slightly ogee form of the head of the lights and the arch of the porch doorway, are markedly similar to those at Wortham Manor and there are other details which suggest that the same designer and craftsman were used on the two buildings, possibly under the direction of John Dinham. The granite plinth with the single course of dressed ashlar in brown sandstone immediately above it and the remainder of the walls in coursed freestone, tympanum over the entrance doorway, the stair turret with its granite quatrefoil window and the lintel of the chimney piece are all features which can be seen in the house that John Dinham was enlarging simultaneously at Wortham.

Unfortunately, nothing remains to suggest the form of the Tudor roof, floor beams and screen of the original building, but it is probable that they were similar to those at Wortham, Trecarrell and Cotehele, all buildings in the locality which were extended at the end of the 15th century or beginning of the next.

The present roof trusses are of rough carpentry which the builders always intended to conceal above the ceiling. It is probable that the first floor was inserted and the roof replaced in the late 17th or early eighteenth century when the windows on the north elevation were also changed to wood casements and a culm oven built into the medieval fireplace.

Landmark removed the more recent partitions and staircase. The first floor was replaced slightly below the 17th century level because the original turret stairs were dangerously steep and so it was necessary to lower the landing. The roof was re-laid in salvaged rag slates to continue the colour, texture and scale of other roofs on the neighbourhood.

The Courtyard: Originally the College was the central building in a large courtyard. You entered it from the North, ahead of the present front door. In the courtyard was the well, which is contemporary with the house; to your right as you came in you would have seen the castellated wall much the same as it is now, though it was then rather longer. On either side of the door there would have been gothic windows like the ones in the south wall; probably two to the right and several to the left, because the school building extended considerably further to the left than it does now and would have joined up with the west side of the courtyard, where there is now nothing but a farm gate.

The castellated wall has been repointed but not otherwise changed. The little door may perhaps have been the entrance to some very steep stairs leading to the school bell at the top of the wall; but this is by no means certain. One of the stones in the doorway has been dressed the wrong way round; perhaps it came from somewhere else.

Interior: The sitting room is the old schoolroom. Originally it was open to the roof. Mr. Pearn describes in his paper the changes that were made in about 1700, at the same time as the north wall was rebuilt. The ceiling that was then put in cut across the tops of the gothic windows, and in order to avoid this the present ceiling has been made to slope upwards in front of them. The window on the north side furthest from the door was blocked up when Landmark took over. The fireplace has been restored to its original shape. Above the fireplace is a relieving arch, very typical of early houses in the area.

The Kitchen: The floor is 2" lower than it was originally, as can be seen if you look at the mouldings at the base of the original doorway onto the stairs. The fireplace is a 19th century one in the gothic style, replacing an undistinguished modern one.

The Staircase: This was originally extremely steep; probably it led to a first floor dormitory above the present kitchen. In order to use it, it had to be rebuilt less steeply; hence the door high up in the wall on the first floor and the little landing.

Steele Farm

GRADE II - Steele Farmhouse and adjoining outbuilding. Core C17 with C19 additions.

Now usually referred to as just 'Steele Farm' it once formed part of a large Estate belonging to H. P. Leschallas. We believe that this is the same gentleman who made a number of improvements in Boscastle whilst Lord of the Manor (Henry Pigé-Leschallas).

On the instructions of the Trustees of the Will of the late H. P. Leschallas, Steele Farm was one of several properties sold at an Auction held in the White Hart, Launceston. The particulars of the sale are reproduced below, as are the specific details relating to East Steele Farm at that time.

By Order of the Trustees of the Will of the late H. P. Leschallas, Esq., deceased.

North Coast Of Cornwall

Particulars, Plans and Conditions of Sale
OF VALUABLE AGRICULTURAL PROPERTIES, ACCOMMODATION
HOLDINGS AND BUILDING LANDS, SITUATE IN THE
Parishes of Otterham, Week St. Mary, Minster, St. Juliot, Forrabury, Trevalga and Advent.

Portions of these being near to the popular Seaside Resorts of Boscastle and Tintagel and also to the Town of Camelford, and within easy reach of Stations at Camelford and Otterham, on the North Cornwall Railway, giving convenient access to the Markets at Launceston and Wadebridge, the whole extending to an area of 1,740 A. 3 R. 22 P. And producing a rental of about £806 per annum which will be offered for Sale by Auction, in convenient Lots, by MESSRS. J. KITTOW & SON, At the WHITE HART HOTEL, LAUNCESTON, on TUESDAY, the 25th day of JUNE, 1912, at 3 p.m. precisely.

THE LOTS MAY BE VIEWED ON APPLICATION TO THE RESPECTIVE TENANTS

Substantial portions of the Purchase Moneys may remain on Mortgage at 4% per annum, as set forth in the Conditions of Sale.

Further information may be obtained of the AUCTIONEERS, West Holm, Launceston; of Messrs: MERRIMANS & THIRLBY - Solicitors, No. 3, Mitre Court, Temple, London, E.C.; of Messrs: Mr. R. COUCH - The Manor Office, Boscastle; or of Messrs. J. & H. DREW - Surveyors and Land Agents, 15, Queen Street, Exeter.

And the East Steele Farm details:

PARISH OF WEEK ST. MARY - Lot 12

A Compact and Productive Farm known as "East Steele"

Situate about Four Miles from Bridgerule and Whitstone Station, on the Holsworthy and Bude Branch of the L. & G. W. Railway and about 10 Miles and 11½ Miles respectively from the Market Towns of Holsworthy and Launceston.

There is an INTERESTING OLD DWELLING HOUSE, upon which a considerable expenditure was made by the late Owner, stone built and slated, and it contains Two Sitting Rooms, Kitchen, Back Kitchen, Dairy, and Five Bedrooms.

THE FARM BUILDINGS, comprise Stables (Three Stalls), Two Bullocks' Houses, Root-house with Granary over, Calves' House and Piggery.

Included in this Lot is a Valuable Wood, known as "East Steele Wood" the Timber in which consists principally of young growing Oak of good quality, with some Beech, Ash, Scotch and Larch Fir Trees.

The whole Estate contains: 106 A. 1R. 7P. or thereabouts.[13]

The areas measured in "A, R, P" stand for Acres, Roods and Poles (or Perches) as there are 40 poles to the rood, and 4 roods to the acre.

There is a public right-of-way over the roads through this Lot. Land tax on the Farm paid by the Tenant amounts to £2 15s. Land tax on the Lands in hand amounts to 8/-. The Tithe Rent Charge on the whole of the Lot is commuted at £10, present value being £7 5s 5d.

The Timber on this Lot has been valued and is to be taken and paid for by the Purchaser at the sum of £200, in addition to the purchase money.

For those born after 1971 perhaps we should explain the earlier monetary system: 12d (12 pence) = 1s (1 shilling) and 20s (20 shillings) = £1 (therefore it follows that there were 240 pence in £1. The 'd' was used to denote the old pence whereas after decimalisation the pennies were referred to as 'new pence'.

Town Cottage

In 1875 there was a large sale of estate lands, which included the manors of Woolstone, Swannacott, Wadfast and Penlean. The following comprised of one Lot at this auction. A pasture called Twenty Penny Hay of just over ½ an acre, (this is now where a house of that name exists).

Two gardens, these were roughly where Malaga cottage and garden are now. A small pasture of ten rods, this is where Hartham Lodge now stands and the site of "Town Cottage" which is marked on the sale map in the centre of the lower green. All of this lot catalogued as Lot 10, together with another proportion of the estate for sale was held in the same tenancy.

This large tenancy also included the rights to 'tolls from fairs'. This once "Town Cottage" was likely to have previously been the market house, which once existed on the lower green. The size of this plot was 2 square rods, an area large enough for a building 24ft square or a round building with a diameter 26ft. As this is referred to as *site of* we can assume that at this date the building no longer existed, although it is possible some walls or foundations may have been visible.

By 1908 '20 Penny Hay' was in the ownership of Mr. J W Spear who also by now owned the strip field, behind the small pasture, which runs down the southern side of Hartham Lane.

In 1923 a local resident wanted to fence in an area of the lower green as it was claimed that it was on the deeds of his property New House. At the annual public meeting in July 1923 it was claimed that the site had been used as a playground for the last 60 years and the public had no wish to see it fenced in or built on. The Parish Council of the day endorsed the opinion of the parish open meeting and made it clear that this area was to remain open.

In 1967 the Lower Green and the green in the Memorial Square were registered as common land. However this failed to give the Parish Council control of the land. The parking of cattle lorries on market days on the greens continuously eroded the land. It was decided in 1972 to re-register the greens as Village Greens and the Parish Council went through a legal land ownership procedure.

On Thursday 13th of July 1972 the Parish Council became the legal owners of the village greens with substantial control over them.

During 1983 with the support of the District Council and the Manpower Services Commission the greens were curbed. This was done with higher than usual stones so that it was difficult for cars to park on them, and so protect the grass.

When the greens were registered the area didn't include the existing track-ways around them. These do not belong to the Parish Council and neither has the County Council, who are the highway authority, adopted them. Their ownership is therefore unknown, as are many unadopted roads. Although their maintenance isn't the Parish Council's responsibility, at irregular intervals as and when they have been available from 'Highways', the Parish Council has arranged the spreading of road scalpings to fill the potholes and level the tracks.[14]

The Post Office

Although the postal service 'began' by royal proclamation issued by Charles I on 31st July 1635, the Post Office as known today did not reach the village for many years.

1700s - The earliest post offices (where the public would take or collect their mail) were usually housed at inns, and were known as Letter Receiving Houses where the only duties of the Innkeeper-cum Postmaster were the acceptance and handing over of letters, the exchange of mailbags and the provision of fresh horses for the Post-Boys (few Post-Boys had a mail cart or even a horse).

1800s - New postal routes to towns and villages had been set up and to facilitate the inhabitants, post offices were established often in a room in the Postmaster's own house, with windows to the street through which mail could the be delivered or collected by callers. Few towns then had Letter Carriers (Postman as they are known today); Postmasters were willing to employ their own servants to deliver letters for a fee of 1d and 2d a letter.

1838 - Money Order Offices became official. The money order office is apart from "letter carrying, the oldest of the services. It originated in 1792 when a system of 'money letters' was established by six 'clerks of the roads' with the sanction of the Postmaster General, for the purpose of affording to the public the means of safely and economically transmitting small sums of money from one part of the United Kingdom to any other." Now an order could be purchased from a post office, sent to recipient who would the take it to a designated post office to exchange for cash.

1840 - 10th January. Uniform penny postage is introduced, establishing national minimum price of one penny. Postage rates were based on weight regardless of distance. 1840 After the arrival of Uniform Penny Postage, followed by a far greater use and range of postal services, better accommodation and separate counters for the sale of postage stamps became essential and post offices began to develop on the lines we know today.

On the 2nd July 1923 it was decided by the Parish Council that it was desirable to accept the conditions upon which the Post Master General would permit a Public Telephone Service to be installed in the village. The GPO required a guarantee of £11 for seven years. Apparently a discussion ensued as to why they would require an extra 3½ miles of cable as the wires from Bude to Whitstone passed through the village![15]

The 1881 Census records a William and Betsy Cundy living at 'The Post Office' in the village.

Although not many of us will remember the Post Office positioned in what became Tom Brommell's shippen, we can recall the days when it was opposite the Chapel, under the control of Mr. & Mrs. Donald Sandercock, with the telephone kiosk positioned beside the building.

Before the modern sorting techniques were introduced the Post Offices in rural settings had limited facilities. Letters arrived from Stratton, now Holsworthy; Whitstone was the nearest money order office and Stratton the nearest telegraph office.

Some years later the Post Office was taken under the wing of Sandercock's Shop and the kiosk was moved to the corner of the site of the old cattle market.

The telephone kiosk situated outside the Post Office and it's not red! - circa 1920

Recent changes

Up to the time we moved to Cyprus as a family, the village was, on the whole, very much the same as it had been whilst growing up. Occasionally a new house would spring up here or there but not very often.

We know that change happens! By the time we had returned from Cyprus, some three years later, that change had already begun.

The Glebe was well under way. The entrance to the Glebe was made through a recessed section of hedge upon which there was a sycamore tree with a hanging branch. All the local children played there. The northern end of the 'play area' led to the main hedge running down Week Green Hill upon which was a 'secret' passageway called 'The Parson's Walk', another great place to play, following the hedge all the way down to the original Rectory.

More buildings appeared opposite the Green Inn as they did at West Week Close and Church Mews. With the demise of the Market this area also became developed.

This year has also seen the opening of Ashbury Grove on the site of some of the historical 'strip fields', opposite the Chapel.

Social change is having a dramatic effect on the village, despite some people moving away and others arriving, the result is that the village is growing more so than ever before. Surely, this is a double-edged sword; the more houses that crop up, the more people take up residency; in another 50 years, less like a village more like a small town. The benefit though is that with more people the greater the possibility that the village clubs and meeting places will continue to thrive rather than die away through lack of interest.

As the village grows the less likely it is that the village community atmosphere will thrive. Modern technology will soon mean that one stays at home and orders everything from the Internet, even to the point of not enjoying communal activities.

Since the time I was a teenager the number of marriages that have given way to 'living together' couples; the decline of attendance at the Church and Chapel. Local employment almost totally disappeared - it is not uncommon to have to travel several miles a day to get to work, with the cost eating into the below average wage. It is impossible to foresee what these changes will mean to the village, long after most of us have left this life but you can guarantee that there will be a lot of 'locals' looking down, tut-tutting and shaking their heads! ■

Orchard's shop

Brewer's shop - early 1900's

Became Ridgman's shop - long before the garage and petrol pumps arrived (and disappeared!)

Sandercock's shop, preparing for their daily delivery service

Delivery vehicle for Coles the butchers

The Green Inn, formerly 'The Beeches', the headmaster's residence

View from bottom of Week Green hill towards the church - 1917

94

Bible Christians

William O'Bryan

Bible Christian beginnings. William O'Bryan was born in 1778 at Gunwen Farm, Luxulyan, of Anglican-Methodist parents. He met John Wesley as a boy, and felt led to become a preacher. However, he experienced conflict with chapel leaders, and after being turned down as a candidate for the Methodist ministry in 1810, he "broke away" from the home farm and local Methodist ties to "seek the wandering souls of men."

He travelled as an itinerant evangelist, linking with Methodists, at Newquay, Bodmin and Liskeard, to Stratton and the Cornwall/Devon border. Then, as an independent preacher, he conducted what proved to be the first service of a new Methodist denomination - Bible Christians - at Week St. Mary (or Mary-Week as he recorded it) on 1st October, 1815.

1831: Our Circuit. He linked with families, notably the Thorne's, of Lake Farm, Shebbear, where 22 friends formed a society on 9th October, 1815. Missions were organised as far afield as Kent, Bristol and South Wales. An Annual Conference was established, a pattern of circuits evolved and in 1831 the Week St. Mary Circuit came into existence. The official record of the Bible Christian Conference held that year at Hicks Mill, in the parish of Gwennap, shows Week St. Mary in the Shebbear District with the circuits of Brentor, Kilkhampton, Ringsash and Shebbear.

1881: Census. Looking at the census for this year shows Week St. Mary Village Chapel (Bible Christian), Week Orchard Chapel (Wesleyan Methodists) and Bakeson Chapel (Bible Christian).

1907: The name changes. The year 1907 saw the demise of the title Bible Christian Society, when it combined with the United Methodist Free Church and the Methodist New Connexion to form The United Methodist Church. This union and the later one in 1932, when United Methodists, Wesleyans and Primitive Methodists, formed The Methodist Church, produced little real change in the circuit as the Bible Christians had predominated and only two 'overlapping' situations arose.

1907: Coming Together At Canworthy Water. At Canworthy Water, the former United Methodist Free Church, Tuckingmill, linked with the former Bible Christian Chapel in 1909, when the Tuckingmill premises were substantially rebuilt.

A quarterly meeting resolution of 29th December, 1908, had spelt out the financial aspect of the "transfer" in unmistakeable terms: "That this meeting consents to pay Stratton and Bude Circuit £1/10/0 per quarter until June 1910 (or only until such funds are fused into one if that should take place at an earlier date) provided the Stratton and Bude Friends sign off the Tuckingmill Chapel to the new body of Trustees, and failing that we cease to pay the £1/10/0 per quarter and return at once to the late Bible Christian Church to worship".

The payments were duly made over the ensuing two years and there is no record of any problem arising.

Week St. Mary Merger

At Week St. Mary the two chapels (Week St. Mary Bible Christian and Week Green United Methodist Free Church) continued their respective societies following the 1907 and 1932 amalgamations until 1934 when the Week Green chapel was closed and the premises converted for use as a caretaker's bungalow. Again there were agreed payments, £4 per quarter for 4 years, from the Week St. Mary circuit to the Bude circuit with an understanding that the Flexbury Park minister would preach at Week St. Mary once a quarter. This pulpit exchange between ministers continued until 1980 and symbolised the unity of purpose underlying the amalgamation.

A great friend of the circuit, Rev. Richard Pyke, preached at the uniting service on Sunday 7th October, 1934, being then Chairman of the District and later (1939) President of the Methodist Conference. A Bible Christian pillar, he held senior appointments at Shebbear College and Edgehill where many young people from the circuit have received part of their education, scholastic and spiritual.

Changes Of District

The circuit has been involved in rearrangement of Districts from time to time. Shebbear 1831, Devonport 1843, then Devonport and Plymouth, later Plymouth and East Cornwall and eventually Plymouth, prior to becoming part of the Cornwall District in 1957.

In the Beginning.

Celebrating the centenary of the present Methodist Church at Week St. Mary has a greater significance than most events of its kind. For it was around this attractive village, the centre of a rural community on the Cornwall/Devon border, that a new Methodist denomination destined to have its own identity for nearly 100 years, first took form.

The preaching of John Wesley, on his visits to Cornwall, had helped to inspire William O'Bryan to set out as an itinerant evangelist. His parents were 'Church Methodists', attending Luxulyan Church on Sundays, and welcoming Methodist preachers on weekdays to stay with them and hold meetings in their home.

William's early travels took him to the Stratton area where a mission was gaining ground, and in October 1815 he wrote: "I entered on my circuit at Mary-Week and Hex".

He had become a Church founder, and very quickly the Bible Christian denomination was firmly established, thanks largely to early converts James and Samuel Thorne, of Lake Farm, Shebbear. Samuel Thorne later married William O'Bryan's daughter, Mary, and in 1832 they founded Shebbear College. Their son, Samuel Ley Thorne, was to become the minister in the Week St. Mary circuit at the time the new chapel was built in 1888.

The Bible Christians favoured a simpler, more puritanical tradition than Wesleyan Methodism, and their influence spread to various parts of the country and overseas, including Australia, Canada and China. In 1907, they merged with the United Methodist Free Church and the Methodist New Connexion, to form the United Methodist Church, and contributed over 32,000 members, of whom nearly 7,000 were in Cornwall.

Services were held in and around Week St. Mary from the time of William O'Bryan's arrival, and there are reports of a stone-laying ceremony in 1829 for the first purpose built chapel in the village. It is confidently believed that regular worship took place at Clifton Cottage, now named "Chyvean", at the rear of Clifton House.

Then, in 1842, land was acquired to build a new chapel, just off the main road through the village, also a Sunday School adjoining the road. The chapel bore the name "ZION", as shown on Ordnance Maps of that period, but in the 1880's was reported to have "fallen into a bad state of repair".

The Trustees, led by their minister, Rev Samuel Ley Thorne, purchased in 1887 adjacent property - a carpenter's shop and small dwelling and garden, at a cost of £32/10/0 and demonstrated their confidence by putting in hand an ambitious project to build more extensive premises on the enlarged site.

1888: The contract for the 38ft long, 26ft wide chapel, with Sunday School, furnace house and stable adjoining, was let to Messrs Bevan and Oliver of Lifton. Mr. Wise of Launceston was the architect. Foundation stones were laid on 22nd May by Rev Thorne, Mrs O'Brian Thorne, and Mr. Henry Paynter. Members of the society found all materials for the masons and plasterers, and friends undertook carriage free of cost. The Trustees had resolved that "best pitch pine be used without sap, and heart oak for beams and mortising seats".

The opening ceremonies were on Friday and Sunday 28th and 30th September. Rev H Batt, ex-President of the Bible Christian Conference was the special preacher. Arrangements for catering provided that "the water be boilt at Mr. John Ayres's, and Mr. Inch to get some faggots of wood". 160 persons sat down to lunch and 400 for tea. The net proceeds for the day amounted to £50, bringing the total to £307, just over half the outlay.

It is not easy to appreciate the financial challenge that faced our forefathers. Times were hard and it took 22 years to clear the outstanding debt of £273. Vision and determination characterised the age, and we proudly celebrate the initiative and faith of the Trustees: William Colwill, Joseph Paynter, Thomas Reed, William Rockey, Thomas Heard, Charles Honey, John Inch, William Martyn, Richard Spettigue, William Moyse, Henry Paynter, Charles Reed and Thomas Yeo.

1934: At the other ('higher') end of the village, at Week Green, the United Methodist Free Church had built a chapel on land purchased in 1855. Although both chapels became part of the United Methodist Church in 1907, they each continued a separate existence for a further 27 years, with 'Higher Chapel' remaining in the Bude Circuit.

Minutes of a Quarterly Meeting on 19th June 1933 recorded: "This meeting notes with pleasure that the Methodist Churches of Week St. Mary village are manifesting a growing desire to work together. We venture to hope that concrete proposals for union will not be long delayed".

A committee representing both chapels and circuits duly negotiated and the Quarterly Meeting of 12th March 1934 approved that "The two churches shall unite, by closing the Week Green chapel, but not to sell for the time (it was converted as a caretaker's dwelling and eventually sold in 1987), and that Week St. Mary Quarterly Meeting pay Bude Quarterly Meeting the sum of £4 per quarter for 4 years, and that the Flexbury Park minister be appointed to Week St. Mary one Sunday a quarter".

The merger went ahead smoothly on the lines agreed, and became effective at special services on Sunday 7th October 1934, when the guest preacher was Rev Richard Pyke, then Chairman of the District, and later President of the Methodist Conference.

Morning and evening services, with a joint Sunday School rally in the afternoon, were linked to Harvest Festival celebrations, and prominent in the proceedings were Revs R James and W Cann, as well as Mr. W Paynter and Mr. T C Orchard. Anthems were rendered by the newly formed choir, under Mr. H Simcock, with Miss A L Orchard at the organ.

Re-opening of the Chapel after repairs - July 1961

The fellowship at Lower Chapel was enriched by families from Week Green, including such names as Ayres, Brewer, Gilbert, Headon, Hicks, Jones, Masters, Sandercock, Smale, and many others.[16]

1961: Thursday, 13th July 1961, saw a day of celebration to mark the re-opening of the chapel after re-decoration and major repairs carried out to the floor and roof. The Superintendent Minister was Revd. J. K. Lockyer. ∎

Methodist Youth Club's enactment of '1,000 years of Bethlehem'

Methodist Cemetery

We, The People

Other than Thomasine Bonventure, there are not many people of the village who have been known outside the parish. Only one person has, for perhaps all the wrong reasons, made the national headlines. His name was....

Richard Guest

This is a tremendous story of a man who loved his children enough to try any means to have contact with them, even attempting to visit them in Canada. He was subjected to verbal and physical abuse both in Canada and throughout his incarceration in Exeter and Dartmoor prisons.

A former Olympic athlete and ME sufferer, whose wife went to Canada with their 3 children and his attempt to have contact with them. Born in 1932, Richard Guest lost his children when his wife left him, taking their three children with her.

Richard went through various legal channels in an attempt to have some contact with his children. On May 17th 1990 the judge at Truro court ordered that the kidnapped children and Mrs Guest returned to England; this order was ignored.

In September 1990 he went to Canada to persuade the courts to force Mrs Guest and the children to return. Consequently he was abused and assaulted and told to 'go home' and forget about his children.

The only way he could foresee a conclusion was to try and force the Canadian Government's hand by kidnapping a Canadian family in the hope of achieving a satisfactory means of contact or even a return of his children.

He rented a cottage in Week St. Mary and with the aid of a Canadian family pretended to kidnap the mother and her children thus alerting the emergency services to a full-scale hostage situation as a lever to try and force his wife to allow his children to communicate with him.

Just up from the Green Inn armed police and police dogs surrounded the cottage in which Richard had allegedly stored cans of petrol.

Richard Guest was finally arrested and sentenced to two years, serving it mostly in Dartmoor prison. This book is about the struggle to contact his children; the abuse in prison; and his conversion to a strong religious belief.[17]

Philip Herbert Samuel Martin

Mr. Philip Herbert Samuel Martin B.Com., A.C.I.S. was instrumental in bringing evacuees to Week St. Mary. Mr. Martin was educated at Selhurst Grammar School, Croydon, winning the Royal Society of Arts Silver Medal for Précis writing at King's College, London, where he trained for the teaching profession. He served in the First World War with the London Rifle Brigade and was badly wounded. His first professional appointment was with the Croydon Mentally Defective School, and from there he went to Sydenham Boys School, Croydon, as assistant head master. In 1935 he became an Associate of the Chartered Institute of Secretaries.

Philip and Daisy Martin - in formal dress for the Lodge Ladies night

Mr. Martin always had the boys' outside activities very much at heart being an organising secretary of the School Journeys' Association, arranging many outings, including a visit to the Royal Agricultural Show at Windsor and the Glasgow Exhibition in 1938. Twice yearly, until the war stopped it, he took a party of boys to camp for a fortnight at Caterham, Surrey. Weekly visits were also made to a farm near Croydon for the purpose of introducing town boys to country life. At the outbreak of the Second World War, Mr. Martin was evacuated with Sydenham School to Woodingdean near Brighton and while there, he fulfilled his plan for the furthering of country knowledge by forming the first Young Farmers' Club for evacuees, and for his hard work in this sphere he was mentioned in Parliament.

In April 1940 he returned to his home only to leave again the following June for Week St. Mary with a party of boys and girls. As head of the school he entered fully into all the activities of the village and figuring strongly in these were the Army Cadet Force, in which he held the rank of Captain, the Rifle Club and Observer Corps. He obtained his Bachelor of Commerce degree in 1946. Mr. Martin was a Freemason for many years and was both an ardent railway enthusiast and historian having had articles printed in the technical magazine. For several years he was a correspondent for the "Post and Weekly News" and up to 1951 was the Secretary of the Horticultural Show.

Samuel & William Dennis

The loss of the White Star Liner RMS Titanic needs no real introduction today - even if you are not old enough to remember it as a point of history at least the epic film of the same name will live on.

It was on its maiden voyage in 1912 when it suffered a glancing blow from an iceberg at around 11:40 p.m. on 14th April 1912 causing some watertight compartments to be ruptured. At around 2:20 a.m. the following day, 15th April, the ship sank.

Of the 2,228 passengers and crew on board, 1,518 lost their lives. Some four hours later, the RMS Carpathia[d9] arrived on the scene and began the grim task of recovering survivors and bodies.

A Samuel Dennis, 23, born on 17th June 1889 at Treyeo Farm in the North Cornwall parish of Launcells, was the son of William Henry Dennis (farmer) and Mary Arabella Dennis (née Sobey). He was the younger brother of Elizabeth, Olive and William. He is known to have had a younger brother also born at Treyeo. By 1894 the family had moved to Leigh Farm, Week St. Mary. It was from here that Samuel set out on his fateful journey. Samuel had been encouraged to emigrate to Saskatoon, Saskatchewan, Canada by his relatives Lewis Richard and Owen Harris Braund of nearby Bridgerule, Devon. The Braund's had a relative Leonard Lovell already in Canada and it was to him they were all ultimately travelling on Titanic.

Samuel, with the Braund's, his brother, William Dennis (born in 1886 in the village of Ashbury, Devon) and relatives John Hall Lovell (of Ashbury, Devon) and John Henry Perkin (of Holsworthy, Devon) all embarked Titanic at Southampton after a long train journey from North Cornwall. The party were also accompanied by Miss Susan Webber, a family friend of nearby North Tamerton, Cornwall.

Samuel was travelling in third class and it is likely that he shared a cabin with John Lovell. His ticket was probably obtained from the Bude White Star agent, Mr. Hawking.

Samuel and William Dennis were both lost in the sinking of RMS Titanic. In some local records the family is listed as Dinnis, a common alternative spelling.

H.R.H. Prince Charles, Duke of Cornwall

As mentioned earlier, in 1637 an order was issued for the steward and bailiff of Week St. Mary to appear "within goat skin mantles" and account before the court at Launceston Castle.

Launceston Castle is a medieval castle that was used by the powerful Earls of Cornwall to control the main route into the county. Launceston Castle is built high on a grassy mound, offering commanding views over the surrounding countryside and the town of Launceston in Cornwall.

Known as Dunheved Castle it was originally an 11th century motte & bailey wooden castle. It was built by Robert, Count of Mortain. The wooden keep was soon replaced by a stone circular shell keep. In the 12th century, stone walls and a tower were added.

The central two storey drum tower was added in the 13th century when the castle was obtained by Richard, Earl of Cornwall. He upgraded the defences with solid drum towers flanking the South Gatehouse, a new curtain wall and the re-siting of the North Gatehouse. In the large rectangular bailey, he put in the Great Hall which remained in use as the Assize Hall until the 17th century.

Launceston Castle declined in importance after Richard of Cornwall's death in 1272. His son, Edmund, moved his main residence to Lostwithiel. This building remained as both the assize and a prison.

The castle fell into disrepair after the Civil War, and large parts of the walls are missing now. By 1650 only the North Gatehouse was habitable.

At the start of the Civil War, Launceston Castle was held for the Parliament but quickly fell to the Royalists. The Castle surrendered to Cromwell's forces in 1644 but then again quickly reverted to the Royalists. The Prince of Wales, afterwards Charles II, stopped at the Castle a short while in the course of his flight westwards.

In March 1646 the Castle and its garrison again surrendered to the Parliamentary forces. However the castles walls were in such a poor state of repair that the castle defences were not considered dangerous enough to be neutralised by the Parliamentarian army when they eventually gained control over the castle from the supporters of Charles I. And in 1649 a Parliamentary Commission reported that the castle was in a state of ruin.

Demolition work was carried out in 1764 on the North Gate to provide stone for a new house being built immediately outside the North Gate.

It was used as a jail for George Fox, the Quaker preacher. In 1656, George Fox, the founder of the Society of Friends (better know as "Quakers"), and two of his friends were arrested for distributing an "earnest religious paper". They were incarcerated in the castle's dungeons for eight months before Oliver Cromwell heard of their plight and intervened.

As the venue for the county assizes and jail, the castle witnessed the trials and hangings of numerous criminals. The last execution was in 1821. A display at the castle traces 1,000 years of history, with finds from site excavations.

In 1838 the assizes and the seat of county government were moved from Launceston to Bodmin. The jail, the last remaining building in the castle grounds, was demolished. The Duke of Northumberland had the castle landscaped and turned into a public park and garden. It remained as a park until being used by the US army in 1944 for a hospital.

Launceston Castle features in the ceremony of the Dukes of Cornwall. In the 20th century, in their role as Dukes of Cornwall, both King George VI and the Duke of Windsor visited the Castle in 1909 and 1921 respectively.

The ceremony begins with the following announcement: "Oyez! Oyez! Oyez! All manner of persons appearing this day within the Great Gate of this Castle and all persons that do offer Suit and Service to His Royal Highness, Lord of the Castle and Honour of Launceston according to the Ancient Custom thereof draw near and give your attendance."

Week St. Mary's Bethuel Hutchings, of Swannacott, was presented to the Duke of Windsor whilst wearing the goatskin mantle on his visit as Duke of Cornwall to Launceston on 25th May 1921. He repeated this honour by being presented to King George VI on 1st December 1937.

The King was already crowned when in 1937 he made a state entry into the Castle, being welcomed with age-old ceremonial affairs and presented with feudal dues - a pound of pepper and one hundred shillings, to name just two, which were set down in a charter of 1230 by Richard, King of the Romans, then Earl of Cornwall.

Launceston Castle is run by English Heritage and owned by the Duchy of Cornwall.

William the Conqueror allocated Cornwall to one of his relatives, and by 1337 Edward III created the Duchy as an estate for the eldest sons of the monarch. This has remained the case down the ages, through 24 Dukes of Cornwall, to Prince Charles today.

Edward the Black Prince rode into Launceston Castle in 1337 to be proclaimed the first Duke of Cornwall. This was the first Duchy to be created in England. Apart from owning large estates the Dukes of Cornwall claimed taxes from tin and other mineral rights. The taxes on tin continued until 1828, although after this date they still received income from mineral rights.

In 1760 the Crown gave up its estates to the nation in exchange for an income, but the Duchy of Cornwall estates were not included in this deal.

It was customary for certain people to meet with the Duke of Cornwall and present him with gifts appropriate for his visit to his County, although not all of the gifts would be of much use today.

Prince Charles became Duke of Cornwall at the age of 4 when his mother ascended the throne. However it was not for another 20 years, in 1973 that he was actually proclaimed Duke of Cornwall in Launceston Castle.

On the 19th November 1973, the Manors of Swannacott and Week St. Mary in the Hundred of Stratton held by Knight Service, and their representatives appeared within goatskin mantles before the Duchy Court at Launceston. Bethuel's grandson, Keith Hutchings, represented these Manors.

The Manor of Cabillia was held by the service of paying to the Duke one grey cloak as often as he should pass through Cornwall and the Manor of Pengelly was held by Serjeanty of receiving the grey riding cloak when the Duke should be coming towards Cornwall and of carrying that cloak with the Duke throughout all Cornwall.

Then the Bailiff recites each Tenant, his holding and the rent offered, in token, in recollection of days long past.

Each Tenant in turn presents his rent in the following order:

1. The Mayor and Commonalty of the Borough of Launceston held the Borough in Fee Farm rendering therefore one hundred shillings and one pound of pepper. The Mayor of Launceston makes the presentation.

2. The City of Truro will render one Bow de Arburne. The Mayor of Truro makes the presentation.

3. The Manor of Elerky in Veryan in the West Division of the Hundred of Powder held, prior to dismemberment, by the render of a brace of greyhounds. Lt. Col. J. A. Molesworth-St. Aubyn makes the presentation.

4. The Manor or Barton of Penvose in the parish of St. Tudy in the Hundred of Trigg held under knight services by the render of a pair of gilt spurs. Mr. M. W. B. Scurrah makes the presentation.

5. Battons otherwise Battens in the parish of Northhill in the North Division of the Hundred of East held under Knight Service by the render of one pound of cummin. Mr. E. B. Latham makes the presentation.

6. The Manor of Clymeslond otherwise Stoke Climsland in the North Division of the Hundred of East rendered a salmon spear and one carriage of wood daily when Our Lord the Duke should come to Cornwall. Mr. K. J. Uglow makes the presentation.

7. The Manors of Swannacott and Week St. Mary in the Hundred of Stratton held by Knight Service, and their representatives had to appear within goatskin mantles before the Duchy Court at Launceston. Mr. L. K. Hutchings represents these Manors.

8. The Manor of Trevalga held by the render of one pair of white gloves. Mr. C. G. Peter, Steward of the Manor, held by Marlborough College, makes the presentation.

Having given each a white rod, His Royal Highness then says:

"I hereby confirm you, and those you represent, Tenants and give you and them peaceable and quiet seizin and possession of the Manors, Lands and Tenements which you hold or represent according to ancient custom."

Then the Bailiff says: "Let every man depart and keep his day here upon a new warning and so God Save The Queen and the Lord of this Honour."

Most of the inanimate objects can be seen encased in a display unit within Launceston Museum.

Bethuel Hutchings

A grand social took place in the Rectory Schoolroom on Thursday 27th December 1906. A goodly number attended, and thoroughly enjoyed the comforts provided.

The gathering was made for the occasion of presenting Mr. Bethuel Hutchings (churchwarden) with a marble timepiece, as a token of sincere regard for his many years service as a chorister in the Parish Church.

For 59 years he had taken part in the musical services, and listened to five successive rectors.

'In the old gallery, in front of the grand old tower, has he attuned his voice to the accompanying violins; in the old choir-stalls, very crude and primitive, has he taken his stand; and now in the finely carved stalls, enrobed in a surplice, we see him still. His hair has whitened, but his face has lost none of that pleasant smile, which is a reflection of the heart's trueness. May he be spared many years to sing God's praises, and to listen to the tick-tick of the testimonial which we know was so heartily given.'

Bethuel Hutchings had the distinction of being presented to the Duke of Cornwall in 1921 and 1937 wearing the 'goatskin mantle' on behalf of the manors of Week St. Mary and Swannacott.

This was my village: 1921

Bethuel Hutchings recorded the following list of occupations in the village:

1 Blacksmith	2 Carpenters (2 shops)
4 Tailors (2 shops)	4 Dressmakers
1 Milliner	2 Masons
2 Stone Masons	1 Meal & Coal Merchant
1 Ironmongers Shop	1 Little Woolworths
4 Grocer Shops	4 Butchers (2 shops)
1 Doctor & 2 Nurses	1 School Master
2 Lady Teachers	1 Sergeant Policeman
2 Sets Ringers	1 Football Team
1 Young Men's Club	

Gordon Bate - Beekeeper

Many of us remember the building, formerly the Rectory stables, becoming a builder's workshop before being known as 'Honey Stores'.

The following booklet from the days of honey production is re-produced by kind permission of his children.

How it began

As a keen naturalist during his early boyhood days, Mr. Gordon Bate spent many hours listening to the hum of the large bumble and native honey bees foraging for pollen and nectar in the huge sycamore trees which surrounded his birthplace in Cornwall.

This aroused his curiosity immensely and, whilst still at school, his father purchased a hive of bees, and later in the early 1930's he became established as a beekeeper. As those early years developed so the bees increased in numbers and the story of Bate's Honey began.

Where it is produced

The delicious honey is gathered by British bees from numerous apiaries situated in valleys, orchards and woodlands lying within approximately a 25-mile radius of the little village, which dates back as far as the early Saxon times, known as Week St. Mary, in the Southwest of England and on the borders of Devon and Cornwall, separated by the glorious Tamar Valley with its waters flowing into Plymouth Sound.

Clover and flower honey - all about it

Far from any industrial towns, this area provides a perfect environment for the bees to produce a delicious soft, light coloured, creamy honey, which is ideally palatable for everyone, and for which England is famous.

Because our climate is so unpredictable, quantities of this honey is often limited, and only the largest beekeepers are able to maintain a steady supply. The unique flavour of our West Country honey gathered by our hard-working honey bees is due to the English climate varying so considerably from day to day. The bees are often forced to find new sources of flora which yields nectar at lower temperatures, and having derived from such a variety of flowers, our honey has a distinct appreciable flavour.

Often the bees fly many miles a day before finding a rich source of nectar and even though strong breezes from the Atlantic may prevail, they are tough and do not retire to their hives until many loads of nectar have been safely gathered. The honey is then removed from the hives and extracted from its pearly white combs using the latest modern equipment. It is then carefully stored in bulk, until we are ready to bottle it for your table use.

The heather season

In either direction, on yonder hills, the moorland landscapes can be seen. To the East, lies the Devonshire highlands of Dartmoor, and to the South-East, the Cornish Bodmin Moors. It is in these areas that the rich Ling Heather thrives, providing a magnificent purple carpet covering many thousands of acres of hills and deep Valleys, flowing with crystal clear waters. In early August our hives are transported to these moors, packed with vigorous bees, and between the morning and evening mist some very delicious nectar is gathered.

This honey has such a high density that it is not possible to extract it from the comb direct, as other honeys, but the quality and richness of flavour of the heather nectar gathered from these South Western Hills, more than compensates the bees for the extra work involved. On some days the bees are only able to forage for a few hours.

To conclude - Bate's English Honey has a freshness, purity and flavour often unmatched by any other. It soon stabilises after bottling and can be made clear by gently warming whether you buy it Set or Clear, according to your taste, it is still the same honey.

Its value and uses

Once honey is eaten it releases an immediate supply of energy. It is an invaluable food for those doing tiring work. It will aid and soothe digestive troubles. Athletes eat it before their races. Children love it, and it gives much pleasure and satisfaction to older people as well. It is said that babies grow better when fed with honey instead of sugar. There are many recipes in which honey can be used where sweetening is required, and we feel sure that Bate's honey will satisfy and fulfil all your future requirements.

You deserve the best why not get it

Produced and Packed by:- G. Bate, Week St. Mary, Holsworthy, Devon.

Moses Roper - Slave

Moses Roper was an American slave, bought and sold by several 'masters' before finally escaping on board the 'Napoleon', bound for Liverpool, departing 11th November 1835, arriving some 18 days later.[18]

His story is told in his book, "NARRATIVE OF THE ADVENTURES AND ESCAPE OF MOSES ROPER, FROM AMERICAN SLAVERY", published in 1848.

He says; "What I shall now relate, is what was told me by my mother and grandmother. A few months before I was born, my father married my mother's young mistress. As soon as my father's wife heard of my birth, she sent one of my mother's sisters to see whether I was white or black, and when my aunt had seen me, she returned back as soon as she could, and told her mistress that I was white, and resembled Mr. Roper very much. Mr. Roper's wife not being pleased with this report, she got a large club-stick and knife, and hastened to the place in which my mother was confined. She went into my mother's room with a full intention to murder me with her knife and club, but as she was going to stick the knife into me, my grandmother happening to come in, caught the knife and saved my life. But as well as I can recollect from what my mother told me, my father sold her and myself, soon after her confinement. I cannot recollect anything that is worth notice till I was six or seven years of age. My mother being half white, and my father a white man, I was at that time very white. Soon after I was six or seven years of age, my mother's old master died, that is, my father's wife's father. All his slaves had to be divided among the children."

Slaves are usually a part of the marriage portion, but lent rather than given, to be returned to the estate at the decease of the father, in order that they may be divided equally among his children.

"Soon after my arrival in England, I went to a boarding-school at Hackney, near London, and afterwards to another boarding-school at Wallingford, and after learning to read and write and some other branches, I entered as student at University College, London, which place, I very much regret, however, I was obliged to leave, in consequence of bad health; and during the time I was at school I lectured in different towns and sold my Narrative or book to pay for my education. On the 29th of December, 1839, I was married to a lady of Bristol, and, after travelling tens of thousands of miles, and lecturing in nearly every town and hundreds of villages in England, at the commencement of 1844, I left England with my family for British North America, and have taken up my future residence in Canada West, it being as near as I can get to my relations (who are still in bondage) without being again taken..."

As he says above, he travelled extensively throughout the United Kingdom, visiting Week St. Mary to preach to the Bible Christians. He preached to those of the following beliefs: Baptist, Independent, Bible Christian, Friend or Quaker, Wesleyan Methodist, New Connexion, Primitive Methodist and Reformed Methodist; in Churches and Meeting Houses in over 920 villages and towns, plus many public halls.

Thomas Orchard

We know that many people leave their homelands for a variety of reasons and Thomas Orchard is no exception. This article came about quite by accident when a lady in Canada contacted her cousin in the U.K. to ask about the possibility of obtaining some information about Bude, in Cornwall, as she had information about a 'Thomas Orchard' and his family who had left their home village of Week St. Mary, just outside Bude, to find 'lands anew'. He contacted a local Orchard family and this information was passed onto me allowing me to make direct contact with the lady in Canada. She was so surprised to receive my initial email; she replied almost instantly, the forerunner of many more emails, each containing more information about the origins of the Orchards! This is Marguerite Caldwell's story...

From the Old World to the New

So many pioneer families made a great contribution to the Canadian landscape. One such family named Orchard, came to the area of Grey County, Ontario, in late 1841. Their story is not without many hardships.

Thomas & Betsy (Wilton) Orchard decided to leave Week St. Mary seeking a new life in the new land. They had ten children ranging in ages from 6-26 years. Possibly they thought of finding better opportunities for their family. Thomas Orchard was 53 years of age, while his wife was 43. It took between two and three months for them to cross the Atlantic Ocean, and it is thought they landed at New York. Father was not well when they landed, however, travelling from New York to Cleveland by stagecoach. Thomas Orchard passed away at Cleveland and was buried there just two weeks after their arrival.

This must have been a shock to the family, but, determined to gain a foothold in the new land, they pressed on to Toronto.

John Orchard, the eldest son who had been a war veteran, made arrangements here to receive a land grant. With this grant of 100 acres there was a stipulation that he should build an inn or hotel about half way between Mount Forest and Durham, then known as the Maitland Hills and Bentick settlement. Elizabeth Orchard (Betsy) the widowed mother also claimed her lots, divison l of Lot 14 Concession 1 Egremont.

A settler was required to build a cabin or log house and make certain noticeable improvements such as clearing the land for a period of five years before receiving the patent or Crown Deed.

Thus sprang up the community of Orchardville. It was situated on the old Garafraxa trail, being the boundary line between the Townships of Egremont and Normanby.

Charles Rankin was instructed to survey a line from the Fergus settlement to Owen Sound then known as Sydenham Settlement. The survey was temporarily stopped with the outbreak of the Mackenzie Rebellion in 1837. Then the Government thought that Rankin's survey was too crooked and too long, so sent John McDonald to re-survey it in 1841. About the only difference made in this area was that instead of going West of the 40 mile long swamp as Rankin had done, McDonald came through the centre of it. McDonald also surveyed farm lots on both sides of the Garafraxa trail.

Each Lot was comprised of three divisions of 50 acres. Settlers who came into this area immediately after the survey had the choice of one 50 acre division. The one beside the 50 acre was held in reserve for a few years. These first lots were soon claimed. It was noted that John was the only one to receive two fifty-acre lots side by side. He acquired the crown deeds to the same in 1846 and 1847.

After receiving the lots, they then travelled back to Hamilton and north to Guelph by stagecoach. They were known to have friends in Eramosa Township. As autumn was fast approaching, it is assumed that once Elizabeth and her two older sons had laid claim to their land, that they would have travelled back to the Guelph area for the winter. The whole family then moved to the area in the Spring of 1842.

John Orchard claimed another 50 acres between his original and his mother's in 1842. He lived in Eramosa Township from 1843 to 1856 and married Sarah Parkinson. John had a village site surveyed off the front of Div. 2, lot 13, con.1 Egremont in 1858, consisting of 12 quarter-acre lots and two streets that he named after his sons, John and Thomas. A two-acre lot was also set aside then, for a fair ground on the north-west corner of div. 3 lot12. Eight more lots were surveyed off the front of Div. 3 in 1876.

A Post office was established in 1847. At first the name was Normanby but later changed to Orchardville but that name was too long for the stamping hammer so was changed to Orchard, July 1st, 1862. This name still exists in 2007. John passed away in 1872, age 65 years.

School was the next priority. A school property was taken off the mother's farm. It was called U.S.S. #2, Egremont and Normanby, otherwise known as the Orchard school. In 1849, Simon, as one of the trustees, beseeched the government for funds to pay a Teacher. The brick school one sees on Highway #6 was built in 1902.

Another daughter, Mary-Ann, married Samuel Rowe, from a neighbouring farm. He had come out from Truro, Devon.

Later, in 1851, these two families, Simon Orchard and Samuel Rowe became the first settlers to establish Paisley. When the two families left the area of Orchard, Simon sold his farm of Div. 3, lot 14, con.1 Egremont. Samuel rented out his land, across the road in Normanby.

Simon had been born July 26, 1823, at Kitsham, Week St. Mary. He was about 18 when he had left England. He had married Lily-Ann born July 20th, 1823 in Scotland. It is stated that he was a 'Yeoman'.

Simon & Lily's first child was born in 1847, named Eliza Jane. A second child was also born in Egremont, initials M.A., in1850. We wonder why Simon and Samuel made the decision to come down the Saugeen River back in 1851, to seek new lands. However, the land in Bruce County was just being opened up. Perhaps it was the sense of a new adventure. Maybe it was the stories of the fertile land in this area of the Bruce. However, the men took their belongings over in the winter of 1851, to Walkerton. They brought their families in the early Spring and then prepared to set sail on rafts down the river once the ice was gone.

Before the Surveyors Ever Ran Their Line

Standing upon the Main Street Bridge in Paisley, Ontario, Canada, it is very fascinating to watch the fast flowing swollen waters of the Saugeen River in springtime. That must have been some trip coming down the river on a raft from Walkerton back on April 18th, 1851! What a brave family to attempt this journey into the wilderness of the Queen's Bush. The Orchard family had left their home in Orchardville, just nine miles or so, south of Durham, in Egremont, Grey County. Their belongings had been taken by sleigh that winter to Walkerton. They had come over later in the Spring preparing to navigate this large River in hope of finding better land. A large 30ft x 15ft. cedar log raft was built by some French Canadian loggers in the area.

A plaque to honour Simon Orchard positioned outside the Paisley Museum

With their possessions stored in trunks, a meagre amount of furniture, a Family Bible, and provisions of food purchased at Walkerton were all stacked on the raft. As well, there were the few necessary tools given to early settlers by the Canadian government in order to make a start on the land and to build a home.

As night was descending, they watched anxiously for a place to rest for the night. No wonderful motels in this land! Eventually, they saw a large elm tree at a bend in the river, which just seemed to beckon them. They drifted to the north bank, tied up their raft, and climbed ashore. The big tree later became known as the Tidings Tree only dying in recent times (1968). The location was also near by the present day Baptist church. They had brought a few planks from Walkerton and thus set about to make a lean-to for the night. This may have been an adventure for the family but after having left the few comforts of a log cabin, this must have seemed very primitive! Simon and Lily Ann, his wife, and small child made the best of the situation. Upon rising the next morning and seeing the beautiful trees and flat valley he decided that the area was a desirable place, at the confluence of the two rivers. Simon decided to make this their destination, to begin life anew. As you now know, this was the beginning of Paisley.

This is a view of the Saugeen river and the location where Simon Orchard, wife Lily and little daughter, tied up his raft for the night. He had left Walkerton on a big raft loaded with many supplies. He did not know where he might stop, but after a night's rest and then surveying the landscape the next morning he decided this was the place! It later became known as Paisley.

A few days later, along came some surveyors, led by Alex Videl, who were blazing a new road from the Durham Road, north to Southampton. This later became known as the Elora Road, and today as Bruce County Road #3.

"Sure we will give you a hand to build you a cabin. We see you have been busy chopping logs in readiness," Vidal told Simon.

Yes, Simon was so thankful to find this location, a place of which he had dreamed! "For sure, my brother John is happy with his grant of 100 acres, but look what I have, fresh water, an abundance of fish, good soil, large trees, and NO stones! I even beat the surveyors as well!"

Paisley's Second Settler

"Well, my dear Mary-Ann, it is already May 9th 1851. Time to leave Walkerton. I know it is sad to leave behind the precious memories of our beloved wee son. We did all we could to help him here. Cousin Jasper's two-story log home has been set up. He has in turn helped us to build our large rafts for this journey. The cattle are being loaded on one.

Your brother Simon will be wondering when we are coming. It has been three weeks since we saw him leave. Word has been received that it will take most of the day to make the trip to where Simon and family have chosen to settle. I am counting on his good judgement that he has found the best land. However, I have only rented my farm back in Normanby, so if we choose, we could go back." Those were the words spoken by Samuel Rowe as he and his young family prepared for this perilous journey down the Saugeen River.

They had two experienced hardy river drivers from the Ottawa Valley to help with the rafting. The river was high. It almost proved too much for these drivers. However, the important cargo of travellers, with provisions, including flour and salt pork, along with their cattle, survived the hazardous journey. The day was overcast, cold and dreary. How grateful they were to see Simon and family waving to them as they rounded another and final bend. A warm cheery fire awaited them in Simon's cabin. They agreed that Samuel would set up house-keeping on the south shore.

Yes, Simon had made a good choice. This did indeed seem a worthy site. With the help of oxen, a log shanty was built where the Paisley Inn now stands. Although the families were separated by the Mud River (later called the Teeswater River) and the Saugeen River, the men undertook to build a foot-bridge. When it washed out the following Spring, a dog called Danger was trained to swim across, to carry small items from one shanty to another.

Samuel and Simon knew they had to get official permission to own the land where they had settled. They saw the possibilities of setting up a town here. In desiring to secure a patent from the Crown they paid early into the hands of the Crown Land Agent the required amount. It seems that others in the political field thought the same thing.

Were they speculating? The Crown patent remained un-issued year after year. Mr. Rowe made repeated visits to the Crown Land Department at Quebec and Toronto. Finally in 1856, Francis Kerr, P.L.S. decided to have a town plot laid out and made the necessary survey. Rowe's and Orchard's rights were respected. Thus, patent after patent in their names were issued September 17th, 1856, creating village and parking lots which were entered in the books of the Registry Office.

Let's Build Us a Village

Exciting times lay ahead for Simon Orchard and Samuel Rowe. First Samuel Rowe erected a log building, called Rowe's Tavern, near to the present day site of the Paisley Inn.

During the Land Sale at Southampton in 1854, Mrs. Rowe was said to have cooked a whole ox along with potatoes. In two days it was all gone, as so many people had passed through on their way to Southampton.

In 1853, Thomas Orchard (born:1830; married: Christina Brown in 1850), Simon's younger brother, moved from Orchard in Grey County to Paisley and established the first store, supplying hardware, dry goods and groceries etc.

Thomas Orchard also opened the first Post Office, becoming the first Postmaster. Many names were suggested for naming of this new village, but the Government selected "Paisley" after a town in Scotland. During this time in Paisley he was the 1st Postmaster, Justice of the Peace, and also served on the Council. He lived 16 years in Paisley before moving to Carrollton, Missouri USA in 1869.

The first municipal council of Elderslie township, of which Paisley was a part, met on January 22,1856 in Rowe's Tavern, Paisley. Samuel T. Rowe was elected as first Reeve. Streets were named after the battles of the Crimean War, being the war was just over. Balaclava, Inkerman and Alma being some of the names used.

Later Paisley was organized as an urban Municipality on January 19th, 1874. The Town Hall, built to hold the Municipal offices, was opened in 1876.

Samuel Rowe donated land for the erection of the Anglican church which opened in 1864. You can see a plaque inside the church on the wall remembering the Rowe Family. He also donated land for the Agricultural Park where the Fair is held each year.

There are a few homes in Paisley that Samuel Rowe built, that still stands today. One is a Bridal home on Albert St. that he built as a wedding gift for daughter Julia.

Simon Orchard was known as a builder of bridges and of laying out roads in all directions from Paisley. Simon also established a trail to Port Elgin in the very early times. He was paid to help chop the trees on roads leading to Paisley.

These men worked hard to make this settlement in the wilderness become what it is today. Simon passed away in 1873 at the age of 50. He had lived to see the first train come to Paisley in 1872. This would have truly been a big event in his life.

Samuel, who was born in Truro lived to be a ripe old age of 85, passing away in 1904. Both men were considered to be very kindly and helpful to the early settlers.

Today in 2007, there are plaques to honour these first settlers in front of the Paisley Library. You can also see their tombstones in the Paisley Cemetery, where details of their life are found inscribed upon the granite or limestone. They are not to be forgotten, no matter how far from home they roamed! ∎

Hundreds

The reign of King Alfred saw the offices of headborough, boroughead, bortholder, tithingman and chief pledge being recorded, even though they are generally considered to be one and the same in status. It was Alfred that divided England into shires; these shires were sub-divided into laths, the laths into hundreds and the hundreds into tithings.

For the purpose of administrative convenience Cornwall (Kernow) was originally divided into shires. Hence the names Pydershire, East and West Wivelshire and Powdershire first appeared between 1184-1187. Although Cornwall and England relied on separate, wholly different, mechanisms of civil administration, shires in Cornwall mirrored the administrative apparatus of shires in England. Where English shires were split into hundreds each having their own constable, Cornish cantrevs had constables at parish level. The Cornish cantrev replicated England's shire system on a smaller scale. Although by the 15th century the shires of Cornwall had reverted to being called hundreds, the administrative differences remained in place long after.

Constables existed as constables of hundreds and franchises and constables of towns and parishes within those hundreds or franchises. The first were called high constables whereas the latter were called petty constables. Petty constables were originally formed about the beginning of the reign of King Edward III, to help the high constables of the said hundred.[19]

Cornwall (Kernow) comprised of 10 Hundreds in 1841: Penwith, Kerrier , Pydarshire, Powdershire, Triggshire, Lesnewth, Stratton, West Wivelshire, East Wivelshire and Scilly

The parishes in the Stratton hundreds are as follows: Boyton, Bridgerule, Jacobstow, Kilkhampton, Launcells, Marhamchurch, Morwenstow, Poughill, Stratton, North Tamerton, Week St. Mary and Whitstone.

The Parish

In the 13th and 14th centuries a parochial organization, created primarily to meet the temporal needs of the Church, had gradually become more and more concerned with the business of civil administration. As a rule the Church had adopted the old Anglo-Saxon township as the district of the parson or parish priest. The cost of maintaining the fabric and furniture of the church would be laid upon the landowners in the parish and it became the general practice of the parson to summon from time to time a parish meeting for dealing with expenses. All members of the church came to these meetings - the Vestry, so called from the place where it met. The officers to look after church matters were also elected at it - the sexton, clerk and churchwardens. With the Reformation the State had to aid the poor and the parochial organization was adapted to the purposes of the Poor Law.

The Vestry was a very democratic type of local government. In larger parishes inevitably sub-committees were formed. The Select Vestry was a standing committee recruited by co-option. Hence there was a move away from a democratic form.

So, after the early 18th century there were Open Vestries mostly in the smaller parishes and Select Vestries.

In the 19th century there was reform and reorganization of the internal administration of the country which entirely neglected the parish. The establishment in 1834 of the Boards of Guardians reduced the Vestry to little more than a shadow of its former importance. Church rates were abolished in 1868 and so completed the downfall of the Vestry. The Parish Councils Bill passed by Gladstone in 1894 gave universal suffrage to the ratepayers. The former urban and rural sanitary authorities became the urban and rural district councils, The Boards of Guardians were reconstituted and provisions were made to establish administrative relations between the county, district and parish councils. The responsibility for roads went to the district councils. Boundaries were to be rectified so as to bring all districts entirely within the relevant administrative area.[20]

Hundreds are no longer used for administration; instead Cornwall is now divided into district councils. There are 6 district council areas: - Caradon; Carrick; Kerrier; North Cornwall; Penwith and Restormel. The District Councils are divided into civil parishes; these originally were based on the old ecclesiastical parishes, but now the boundaries of each are quite different.

There was a Reeve (law officer) for every Hundred, presided over by the Shire (County) Reeve of Cornwall. The office of Shire Reeve (Sheriff) is the oldest law office in the world, dating from Saxon times.

Before the Constabulary was formed in Cornwall, around 1857, parish constables were elected once a year by the vestry meeting in each parish. The office of parish constable was frequently an unpopular one; they received no wages and some tried to buy their way out of the service. Once the Constabularies had been formed the locally-appointed parish constables soon became just another element of local history. It was not until 1st June 1967 that Devon and Cornwall combined their resources to form the Devon & Cornwall Constabulary.

Churchwardens and Overseers of The Poor [21]

The position of Churchwarden is a very ancient office, with specific tasks and responsibilities, although many of these have disappeared over the years, namely:

'They are not to permit any to stand idle, walk or talk in the church or church-yard; to take care that no persons sit in the church with their hats on, or in any other indecent manner, but that they behave themselves orderly, soberly and reverently, kneeling at the prayers, and standing at the beliefs, etc., that none contend about places and they may chastise disorderly boys, etc.'

'All quarrelling is prohibited either in the church or churchyard; and if any offend in such case the ordinary man may suspend him from entering the church, etc. Where one is assaulted and beaten in the church, it is not lawful to return blows in his own defence; for striking or laying hands on another there, the offender shall be excommunicated.'

116

The responsibility of Overseer of The Poor came about as a result of the first statute made for the relief of the poor.

'Overseers are to take care that the poor be set at work, or relieved if not able, and to settle them in their habitations. But none are to be relieved, whose names are not registered in a parish book, kept for that purpose; unless by authority under the hand and seal of a justice, or in case of pestilential diseases, viz. the plague, or the small pox, in respect of their families only'

'Persons relieved must have, on the uppermost garment, and upon the shoulder of the right sleeve, a large letter P and the first letter of the parish, or otherwise one justice, upon complaint, may cause their allowance to be abridged or suspended, or may commit the offenders to the house of correction, not exceeding one and twenty days.'

'There are reckoned three sorts of poor people; such as are poor by impotency, (which takes in the aged, decrepit, lame, blind, distracted persons, infants, etc.) such as become poor by casualty, (which includes persons maimed, undone by fire, overcharged with children,) and such as have made themselves poor by rioting, idleness, drunkedness, etc. As to the first sort, the poor by impotency, the overseers are to provide for them a necessary relief and allowance. As for the second sort of poor, those by casualty, if they are of ability and strength, they are to be set on work by the overseers, and to be farther relieved to their necessities. But for the third sort, they are not to be relieved, except it be in cases of great extremity; but are to be sent to the house of correction, and there set at work to maintain themselves by hard labour.

Overseers of the poor have power to rate and tax every inhabitant and occupier of houses, lands, tithes, underwoods, mines, etc. to raise money towards the relief of the poor, providing s competent stock of flax, hemp, etc. to set the poor on work, and also for the putting out poor children apprentices; which rate being allowed by two justices, the churchwardens and overseers may levy the same by distress and sale, and for want of distress, the party may be committed to gaol till payment'

The above controls on the poor explain why, in ancient church records, there are considerable entries where parishes contest most strongly the place of residency of such poor persons because it had to support them accordingly. If they could only persuade them to move to another parish - although there were often 'deals' with neighbouring parishes to take under their care such other families that may have differing demands on the parish by way of support.

Surveyors of the Highways [22]

The position of Surveyor of the Highways gave the officer the right to impose charges against those failing to repair, or contribute to such a repair, a road or such 'highway' that suffered wear and tear beyond an acceptable level.

Not only did they have these responsibilities, it is recorded in this reference material that they be also responsible for ensuring that cleanliness of the streets be maintained:

'Inhabitants to cause the streets to be swept twice a week, under penalty of 5/-; no rubbish or other annoyance to be thrown in streets under penalty of 10/-. Soil, and other filth, to be kept till the scavengers take it away. Scavengers to come twice a week for the dirt and to give notice of their coming, and carry away the sweepings of the streets, under penalty of 20/-. Rubbish occasioned by building to be carried away by the owners.'

One significant responsibility laid upon these officers was to ensure that carts did not linger unnecessarily when loading or unloading - so Traffic Wardens have been around for quite a while!

Parish Council

By the Year 1601, Church Vestry Meetings were so organised and workable that it was quite natural for legislators to give them the responsibility of levying the poor rate. These were the first effective local taxes. Everyone in the parish was entitled to attend Church Vestry Meetings but in practice the work fell to a few individuals, rather like Parish Councils today.

Although the 1834 Poor Law Amendment Act removed from Parish Vestries the responsibility for poor relief and handed it to Poor Law Unions (the origins of our present District Councils) parishes had naturally accumulated responsibility for administering local charities, managing commons under distribution of land as a consequence of the 18th Century Enclosure Acts.

In 1894 although the Squire, the Parson and sometimes the Schoolmaster were still the leaders in the village, popular education was spreading and more people wanted a say in managing local affairs.

The great Victorian Prime Minister, W.E. Gladstone, piloted the 1894 Local Government Act through the House of Commons. It met a lot of opposition, for example there were over eight hundred amendments moved during its passage through the House. Nevertheless, the Act became law and Parish Councils were formed.

Parish Council Snippets

The first Parish Council Meeting was held on December 31st 1894. The proceeds of Poor Man's Piece, some £2.10.0 was paid out to 38 local residents under the terms of the charity by order of the meeting dated April 15th 1895.

At the May 13th meeting 1895 a discussion was had concerning the proposed new road from Haydah to Wax Hill, the current way being up and down the old road leading up through lower square. This scheme was recommended to start on Monday September 30th 1895, after reaching agreement with the then landowners over rights of way issues. The Stratton District Council were in favour of this new deviation to the road and decided to grant half the cost provided it was made according to the Act of Parliament.

February 11th 1896 saw discussed at the Council meeting, that iron railings would be preferable as a fence in the field at Haydah.

April 15th 1896: the recipients of the proceeds from the Parochial Charity known as Poor Man's Piece, included one Charlotte Kinsman. Ancestors of my wife, the Kinsman family were, in the main, millers, notably at Trefrouse Mill (of which nothing remains).

September 26th 1898: The Council wrote to the London & South West Railway with reference to the new station being opened soon, called the Whitstone and Bridgerule station, suggesting that the mail could be offloaded there instead of going on into Bude, then sent to Stratton for onward delivery to Week St. Mary. A reply was duly received from the Postmaster turning down the suggestion.

The Parish Council wrote several letters to owners of wells requesting that they be made of good order, both in the Square and at Week Green. All the Parish meetings had been in the County School but the Educational Authority had recently notified the council that a permit would be required to allow future meetings. It is noted that the following meetings were held in the Church Rooms.

On August 24th 1941 a committee was formed to oversee Civil Defence. May 16th 1944: A meeting was held in the School to make arrangements for "Salute the Soldier" week. Mr. P. Martin (*my grandfather*) was elected Chairman of the Committee. The target for "Salute the Soldier" week was set at £2,000.

July 18th 1945 saw another meeting in the School Room to make the necessary arrangements for the "Welcome Home Fund".

A meeting on 29th April 1946 took place in the School Rooms to make arrangements for the "Victory Day" celebrations.

9th May 1946 saw the Parish Council writing to the County authorities protesting against any possible closure of village schools.

September 1970 saw the suggestion that future Parish meetings be held either in the Chapel Sunday School Room or in the County Primary School.

Thursday 20th June 1974 finally saw agreement for full lighting through the village. Despite repeated suggestions that a public telephone kiosk be erected at Week Green this still failed to come to fruition.

July 1975 finally saw the Parish Council receive permission allowing the installation of village lighting. ■

World War I (1914-18)

As the German U-boat menace of the First World War gained strength and many merchant ships, bringing much needed supplies from Canada and America across the Atlantic, were sunk, a new way of protecting our convoys was envisaged: U-boat surveillance by airship.

Although early days as regards aircraft taking an active part in the war, Airship patrols tackled the German U-Boats and flew many miles out into the Atlantic Ocean, Irish Sea and the Bristol Channel looking for the German threat to our shipping.

Bude-Stratton museum, has recently acquired a rare photograph of an anti-U-Boat airship, CIO, flying near Marhamchurch, to add to its collection of photographs of airships already on display.

The Royal Naval Air Service operated these airships on anti-submarine patrols, convoy patrols and mine-spotting sorties off the coast of Cornwall from 1916-1918. They flew from Bonython Manor near Mullion but had a satellite station at Langford Barton, two miles south of Marhamchurch, called R.N.A.S. Bude.

At Langford, woods were cut down at both sites to provide mooring protection. It was a real "combined services operation". The Army provided tents and manpower - very necessary when hauling down or releasing airships, with the Royal Flying Corps providing some of the aircrew.

For example, the museum has a photograph of Stephen Henry Broomhead who joined the RFC in 1915, and after an air communications course at Cranwell, joined RNAS.

Looking every inch an aviator - dressed in leather coat, goggles and boots - he was photographed at Langford Woods, where the station complement was around 100 men.

Soldiers and seamen pulling on the ropes to guide an airship down to its mooring position at Langford

Between 1916-18 Airships operated from a 'satellite' RNAS station at Langford with primitive living conditions for the enlisted men whilst the officers had a solid roof over their heads!

Week St. Mary
church tower

A modern-day photograph of the approximate site of RNAS Bude, with a clear view of the surrounding area, particularly Week St. Mary's 99ft church tower on the horizon

On a calm day it needed 25 men to grab the three guy ropes but more if the weather was bad. Once hauled down they were attached to very large concrete balls, two of which have been retrieved from a hedge at Langford Wood and now reside peacefully in a secret garden in Bude.

The SS Z airships were made by Vickers and had one 240bhp Rolls Royce engine, with petrol carried in tanks on either side of the gondola in fabric slings. The armaments were two 100-pound bombs and one Lewis Gun.

The pilot used a short-wave radio for Morse code transmission to shore and ship-based radio stations, but for ships without radio a Morse lamp was used at night and semaphore by day.

As a teenager Den Colwill remembers seeing airships flying over the village during the latter part of the first World War.[23]

A 'Peace' Letter sent home from Frank Rogers:

Cornwall Barracks,
Delhi, India

November 11th 1918

Dear Harry & Kate,

Just a few lines to let you know that I am still in the land of the living and in the best of health, hoping you are all in good health. Well, since I wrote to you last there has been a great lot of alterations in the war. It is looking splendid now. Don't think it will go on much longer. Turkey and Austria soon followed Bulgaria, and Germany won't be long, so roll on the time when it's over. I see on today's paper that the Kaiser has abdicated the throne, he ought to be slung up, and that would be too pleasant, don't you think so, so I should think we shall soon have a chance to go back again, within the next twelve months any way. Well by the time you get letter Xmas will be pretty close if not over, so I wish you all a merry Xmas and a happy new year under the circumstances.

November 12th 1918

Well, old boy, the news came through that the war had ended while I was writing your letter, so I had to drop it then you bet. It came through 20 minutes to nine, some of them didn't sleep much that night there's two Regiments of natives here pretty close, we had greatest part of them up here and their bands, but I could hardly realise that it had finished, after being raging for over four years. I should like to have been in England when it came through, I'll bet there was some rejoicings, but it will renew it again to the parents that has lost sons in the war when the rest of them come back, but I expect it will take a decent time for them to demobilize the army, and I expect married men will have the preference then so roll on another year, I was offered a decent job the other day to go as Sergt Instructor to a Native Regt, but I don't want it, I think they have to sign for so long after the war, of course it's pretty good pay and I'm jolly glad now. I wouldn't stop here another four years for five hundred rupees a month, because it cost anyone so much to live and keep up to it. Well old boy get the bells well oiled up. It won't be many months anyway now before we get back if all goes well. The fever has broken out very bad here in our Batt, but much better again now we have lost a lot of fellows with it. I won't state the number, and the natives are dying wholesale with influenza and pneumonia, I have been fortunate up to now not to have it, Emmanuel tells me it's just the same where he's too, but glad to say he is quite well, all being well he intends to come up here for Xmas for a months holiday.

Well I hope that you are all in good health remember me to the children, hoping Phyllis is alright I will close now.

With best love to all

From your loving brother, Frank

Peace Celebrations

On Sunday 6th July 1919 there was Service of Peace in the Church & Chapels. On Saturday 19th July, in accordance with the King's Proclamation there was a General Holiday. A house-to-house collection had been made and a free tea was given to all parishioners; the tables being laid out on the drive at Stewarts, through the kindness of Mr. Willett. All kinds of sports were held in an adjoining field. A bonfire was lit at 11p.m. in a field at Week Green.

On the next day, Sunday, at 3p.m. an outdoor service was held in the Square at which Rev. J.M. Milner (Rector of Poundstock), Rev. M. Hoare and Mr. J. Wickett spoke. Prayers were offered and hymns sung. A collection was made for the War Memorial.

War Memorial

The first meeting of Week St. Mary's War Memorial Committee took place on the 28th of April 1919. By June the 25th 1919 a sum of £109 had been raised by public subscription and the granite cross had been ordered. On October 27th the decision to prepare the site was taken and materials were ordered for the foundations. Further monies were raised by a public tea; Price 1/- (one shilling), followed by a magic lantern show on Palestine; Admission 6d (sixpence).

The war memorial was unveiled by Sir George Croydon Marks MP for the Launceston Division on Saturday 6th of December 1919 (Parliamentary divisions have been reorganised and renamed several times since). Prayers were lead by the rector, Rev. Charles Thomas Witmell; a lesson was read by Rev. T. Rud and followed by a hymn. A tea followed in the Council School to which all service men had free invitations. After the tea Sir George gave a lecture on the League of Nations to a crowded audience.

At that time the fund contained a total of £134/11/6. The memorial cross was supplied by The Bodmin Granite Company Ltd, and invoiced on the 9th of December 1919 for £123/10/4d.

Those who gave their lives are remembered annually on Remembrance Sunday when the brief but poignant service concludes with the laying of a wreath and the sounding of the Last Post.

WORLD WAR I

•Private Ernest James HIGGINS (Duke of Cornwall's Light Infantry) Died: 18/09/1917 - Aged: 19 Son of William and Susanna Higgins, of Week St. Mary.

•Private W. J. COLES (Duke of Cornwall's Light Infantry) Died: 23/05/1919 - Age unknown

•Private John KINSMAN (Duke of Cornwall's Light Infantry) Died: 2/10/1916 Aged: 19 Son of Richard and Mary Kinsman, of Kitleigh, Week St. Mary.

•Private Sidney LAWRENCE (Duke of Cornwall's Light Infantry) Died: 10/09/1914 - Age unknown

•Lance Corporal Hartley Owen ORCHARD (Military Police) Died: 21/11/1918 Aged: 21 Son of Thomas and Mary Ann Orchard, of Carey House, Week St. Mary.

•Sapper George Frederick Wright REED (Royal Engineers) Died: 1/12/1915 Aged: 36 Husband of Alice Moyse Reed, of Week Green, Week St. Mary.

•Private James ROGERS (Devonshire Regiment) Died: 4/11/1917 - Aged: 21 Son of John and Mary Mason Rogers, of Week St. Mary.

•Private William John COLES (Duke of Cornwall's Light Infantry) Died: 18/09/1918 - Aged: 23 Son of John and Emily Coles of Parsonage Green, Week St. Mary. ■

World War II (1939-45)

War Memorial

In October 1946 the balance of the "Victory Day Celebrations" £15/6/3 was passed on to the 1939-45 War Memorial Fund. In April 1947, £7 was spent on cleaning and painting the memorial and in May 1948, £8/5/0 was spent having the names of the fallen added to the memorial.

WORLD WAR II

•Private Wilfred Richard Pengelly ROWLAND (Duke of Cornwall's Light Infantry) Died: 30/11/1943 - Aged: 21 Son of Albert and Hilda Rowland, of Week St. Mary.

•Sergeant Eustace Henry ORCHARD (Royal Air Force Volunteer Reserve) Died: 15/03/1944 - Aged: 23 Husband of Doris Mary Orchard, of Week St. Mary.

Week St. Mary War Memorial is unique in that not only does it record those who lost their lives during the two World Wars but also honours those 'who served'.

At some time after the initial erection of the war memorial the maintenance and upkeep was taken on by the Week St. Mary Branch of the Royal British Legion and this they did until the nineteen-sixties. By this time the railings had deteriorated and in November 1964 the Week St. Mary Branch of the Royal British Legion wrote to the Parish Council to say that they were no longer able to be responsible for the memorial.

In November 1967 responsibility of the War Memorial had been taken on by the Parish Council. Week St. Mary Royal British Legion passed the money in the war memorial fund onto the parish council. In February 1968 the old railings were removed at a cost of £5 less £1/15/0 for the scrap value of the old railings. In March 1970, £50 had been raised towards the new posts and chains which cost £55/9/0 to install.

Royal Observer Corp 'Lookout Post'

The Royal Observer Corp lookout post has been neglected for some time and if not maintained will undoubtedly lead to demolition on the grounds of safety.

To the Northwest of Week St. Mary, on private land, stands this disused Post. This has been there so long that we accept it as part of our landscape. This landmark is set high on a hill and is clearly visible as we approach the village from Week Orchard or Treskinnick Cross. It is usually referred to as the Lookout Tower or the Observation Post. Officially, it was designated as N2 of No. 20 Group, Truro. When the Observer Corps first established a Post at Week St. Mary in 1941, a flimsy wooden structure was erected. The present brick tower was not built until three years later in 1944.

The first Cornish post was established at Veryan in January 1940 and was soon followed by others. By 1942 there were 36 aircraft recognition and reporting posts in Cornwall. Across Britain there were over 1,600 reporting posts and these were connected by telephone to one of thirty-five operations rooms. These in turn, passed on all aircraft movements to their appropriate RAF Sector Operations Room. A limited number of Observation Posts, three of which were in Cornwall, were equipped with High Frequency radio equipment. This communication could be used to contact air-crew, who were lost or in distress, and helped to save lives and planes.

Although the Week St. Mary tower has deteriorated with age, its layout is still complete. The area was once fenced off from the public with barbed wire. Some of the concrete posts are still in situ. Its structure is brick built and of two floors. Sleeping accommodation was on the ground floor with a stove for warmth. The hearth and flue pipe exit are still clearly visible. The original external wooden steps have been missing for many years. These led to the upper floor, which contains a shelter and the observation platform. Originally linked by telephone, a rusty hook-up bracket is still visible at the top of its South West corner. A more specific feature to have survived is the chart post. This reinforced concrete pillar supported the large brass plotting chart on the upper floor of the tower. This was used to plot the direction of aircraft movement. Observers were experts at identifying aircraft and this information used by the RAF to intercept enemy planes.

At the end of Word War II, Week St. Mary along with other posts was stood down. However, only a couple of years later in 1947, it was reactivated. At first its previous aircraft recognition work was its primary role, but as weapons became more sophisticated the Observer Corps' role gradually changed and along with this a new type of structure was needed. This later structure is not so clearly visible. Despite neglect and some vandalism, Week St. Mary's WW II Observation Post has managed to keep its aircraft plotting chart post. Even more unique is that it is a World War II reporting post that still stands alongside its later Cold War monitoring station.

Children have recently done some considerable damage kicking out the upper parapet wall. Not only are they putting themselves at risk, but have damaged an important part of our local heritage. There is a high probability that the structure is unsafe and children should be discouraged from climbing it.

The Royal Observer Corps Association has recorded details of both posts in their work which is now lodged in the Defence of Britain Project and held by the Imperial War Museum at Duxford.

After the Royal Observer Corps was reactivated in 1947 their role was to gradually change and in 1953 the Week St. Mary post was re-designated as 132 of the re-numbered No. 10 Group Truro. From 1955 the Corps was given the new role of detecting and reporting nuclear attacks on Britain. They were to become part of the United Kingdom's Warning and Monitoring Organisation (UKWMO).

The threat from the Soviet Union had now become Nuclear and from 1960, observation posts and operations rooms were placed underground. By 1963 aircraft-reporting had virtually disappeared and from 1964 the role of the ROC was entirely Nuclear detection.

In June 1960 Week St. Mary's observation tower was discontinued. A new belowground post or nuclear bunker was constructed only a few yards to one side of the original observation post. Nuclear monitoring and training was carried out at Week St. Mary and continued until October 1968 when a restructuring programme reduced the number of ROC posts to 875 and operational rooms to 25.

It was at this time that the Week St. Mary's branch of the Observer Corps was stood down. The site was closed down and the bunker abandoned. The bunker was constructed to give almost total protection against a nuclear attack.

By the late eighties communism became less of a threat and the Soviet block started to collapse. The last of the Observation Corps posts finally stood down in September 1991.

A good view of the tower can be seen from the road and is more clearly visible from the lane. This is, however, on private land and it is hoped that those reading this article will respect this.[24]

Local Defence Volunteers / The Home Guard

Wonderful Spirit of Patriotism: On that momentous 3rd of September in 1939 when Mr. Neville Chamberlain, in his broadcast talk, told the British people that they were at war and that it would be evil things they were fighting, how many of his listeners foresaw the very narrow margin by which the perpetrators of that evil were to be held in check?

Thousands of citizens, many of whom had seen service in the war of 1914-18, had no idea that within a very few months they would be carrying on with their normal civilian jobs and at the same time straining all their spare-time energies to fit themselves to fight as part of the armies of Britain to counter an invasion that seemed inevitable.

In the early days of the war, even the Government had deemed it necessary only to provide services to counter the effects of enemy action by bombing from the air and these known in the first instance as A.R.P. services, were purely of a passive nature, and were not equipped or intended in any way to hit back at the enemy; no-one visualised a situation that might need a vast number of the civilian population to stand and fight to repel invasion.

The position changed so quickly, however that when the Hun was over-running the Low Countries and Northern France, Mr. Anthony Eden broadcast an appeal for volunteers to form Local Defence Companies throughout the length and breadth of the land, to ensure that no part of it was left unguarded and so available as an easy target for enemy Airborne Troops.

It is doubtful if anyone, least of all Mr. Eden himself visualised at the time what the response and its effects on the future would be. Before he had ceased broadcasting, Police stations all over the country were being besieged by men all anxious to join the new force, and such a vast number were enrolled, that the question of equipping them became a matter of the first urgency.

Week St. Mary Home Guard

The men of North Cornwall were no less eager than those in other parts of the country, and within a very few days of the call, a live organisation was in being. Parties were formed in each parish and night after night every vantage point was manned from dusk till dawn, eager eyes scanned the night sky, and whilst the weapons to hand were, in many cases primitive, there is not the slightest doubt that they would have been used with great determination had it been necessary.

Many were the alarms and excursions of those days, and by those men who shared those early watches, many will be the incidents which will be re-told in years to come. Leadership was vested in those with some knowledge of military matters, and their authority was never questioned, irrespective of the civilian status of the individual members when off duty.

And so the days and weeks went by. It is ancient history now that the invasion did not come but it is fitting to recall the splendid spirit of service which the early volunteers of the Local Defence Volunteers displayed, because it was very largely their example which encouraged an ever-increasing stream of recruits to join, and so in due course caused the whole organisation to be remoulded on more military lines, and become embodied in what has since been known as "The Home Guard."

This change of status was not effected without a certain amount of criticism, both from within and without. One contention was that it was not necessary or desirable to give to the officer and Non-commissioned ranks, titles equivalent to those of the regular services, but the significant feature of this was that the highest military authorities had been quick to appreciate the potential value of the spirit of service exemplified by all members of the force and had decided to take advantage of it.

Quite apart from the value of such a vast force, as it had by now become, from a tactical point of view, there was also the fact that many members were in due course called to service in the regular army, and without exception they found the preliminary training they had received invaluable.

A point that cannot be stressed too frequently in connection with the Home Guard, and also with its sister services of a part-time nature, is the very remarkable fact that, no member officer or man has been paid for his services, and when the amount of time put in by all ranks is taken into full account a wonderful picture of self-sacrifice is presented. The more so in the case of the officers entrusted with the higher ranks, and therefore with added responsibility.

It is true in the later stages they have had the assistance of full time regular officers and instructors all of whom have been of tremendous help, but it should never be forgotten by the public, that, the raising and maintenance of this magnificent second line army has been possible only because of the readiness of men in every town and every remote country parish to accept the burden of leadership, often at great inconvenience and in many cases to the detriment of their own personal affairs.

Where so many have done so well it would be invidious to select a few for special mention, and really there is no need because they are already well-known in their own areas from the work they have done, and in many cases well beyond these areas.

Now that the time has come for the "standing down" many of its members are wondering and discussing how best the fine tradition that has been established can be carried on. Many hold the view that, the spirit of mutual service which has been inculcated within communities, both large and small, is bound to be an influence for the greatest good when the problems of peace confront us. May this prove to be the case.[25]

The Home Guard, originally the Local Defence Volunteers, was set up in May 1940 to defend the Home Front and to assist in the repelling of any invasion. The Home Guard was never tested by an invasion and it operated under inevitable constraints. However, it made an important contribution to the defence of the British Isles. The Home Guard was instructed to "stand down" at the end of 1944.

War time air raids brought death, destruction and disruption. 60,595 civilians died as a result of enemy action in the United Kingdom. Streets were subject to lighting restrictions - the blackout.

Volunteers needed to be trained in civil defence duties. These included fire-fighting, first aid and ambulance driving.

Civilians were instructed in how to protect themselves against poison gas attack and issued with gas masks, which they were encouraged to carry on all journeys.

Aircraft Crashes

During the course of researching for this book, it came to light that an aircraft had crashed near Week Orchard, however, talking to Reg Risdon, of Bowdah, there were actually two aircraft that met their end in our local area of the Cornish countryside.

The details of these 2 aircraft were revealed by some detective work conducted by Michael Croft of Maidenhead. He was staying at Bowdah and became excited by the story and the collection of 'bits' as souvenirs.

Michael wrote to Reg in 1985 with these details:-

The first aircraft was a P47 Thunderbolt, from the U.S.A.A.F., 353rd Fighter Group, based at Metfield, Suffolk, but operating from Thorney Island, on 15th September 1943, piloted by Captain Durlin. The aircraft apparently ran out of fuel forcing Captain Durlin to bail out. He landed safely before the aircraft crashed.

The second aircraft to crash, at Bowdah, was a Typhoon JB431 from 183 Sqdn. On a training flight the aircraft suffered engine failure and after circling for a while (including clipping the tops of some trees), failed to land in big field and was forced to land in a short field occupied with sheep.

Despite the loss of some of the flock, the aircraft slid across the ground, coming to rest against the far hedge. The pilot, Flight Sergeant W. F. Tollworthy R.A.F.V.R. was only slightly injured and by the time help arrived from the farm, had managed to climb from the wreckage.

Regrettably, Flight Sergeant, later to become Warrant Officer, Walter Frederick Tollworthy, Service No. 1334758, of 183 Sqdn., was killed in action over France on 9th August 1944, flying another Typhoon, MN638. ■

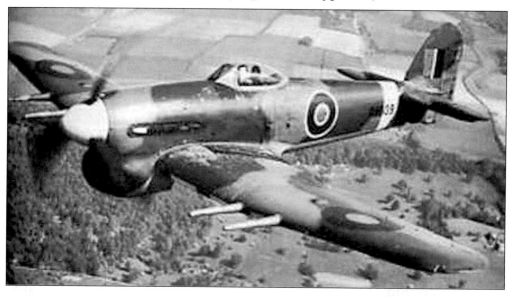

A typical Typhoon aircraft

Evacuees

E vacuation plans had been in preparation well before the outbreak of war. Small scale evacuations of women and children were carried out at the height of the Munich Crisis in September 1938 but the real evacuation began in September 1939. The government had planned to evacuate about 3,500,000 people but in fact only 1,500,000 made use of the official scheme. Almost all had been evacuated from the danger areas to the reception areas by the evening of 3 September, a few hours after the official declaration of war.

War Time In Week St. Mary

by Philip Herbert Samuel Martin

(Week St. Mary Correspondent)

The following was written some time after the last war: "I remember well, Sunday, June 16th 1940, for I left my home in Surrey at 7 a.m. to take charge of a party of Croydon children going on evacuation under Plan 4. The authorities had been alarmed by the drift back of children under the previous arrangements and determined to send them further afield, but all I knew was that we should detrain at Bude. The long journey ended about 7 p.m., when several hundred tired children and teachers detrained at the station and were shepherded into Cann Medland's Garage[d10] where a real Cornish meal was provided and the children were medically examined. I remember walking down the line of buses parked at the side and reading the names of the destinations. North Cornwall was unknown to me then, but it struck me that Week St. Mary was an attractive sounding name, and I gave instructions for my kit and party to be loaded as far as possible for this place. I never regretted this decision.

Somewhere about 8.30 Mr. Len Maddock drove the bus up to the school where the late Mrs. Sandercock, and her willing band of W.V.S. helpers assisted by many others set about distributing the children around the parish.

A view of Cann Medland's garage, situated opposite the Railway Station, just visible in the bottom of the picture

131

Every child had a stamped post card on which to write its new address, and those in charge of parties sent telegrams to Croydon giving the location of each school party. The information was posted up outside the Town Hall and must have relieved many anxious parents. By 1945 Croydon children were to be found in 40 different counties.

Back in Week St. Mary the children were rapidly absorbed into the homes which had given them shelter and most remained until they were due to leave school or the end of evacuation in 1945. A few still visit the village or keep in touch with their foster parents but the numbers are now sadly dwindling.

When the attack started in August, 1940, the wisdom of evacuating the children was more evident and there were additions to the evacuees. These continued and in 1941 parties arrived from Bristol and Plymouth, so that the School and Methodist Schoolroom were crowded with 156 children and 6 teachers.

The "fly bomb" period in 1944 brought the last party of evacuated children and mothers to the village this time from West London, but with the end of the German War most of these returned after a short stay.

Evacuation brought many problems and difficulties, but this was well worth while. It may be a sign of toughness to stick it through the raids, but no child should be forced to experience the sight and sound - and possible injuries which go with a modern air-raid. Those who returned from North Cornwall had had a period of loving care in a peaceful countryside, with the continuous education which every child needs.

My grandfather, Philip H.S. Martin, with his young pupils fresh from Croydon, outside the Chapel

Naturally, they compared favourably in health and development with those who grew up among sleepless nights - and worse and interrupted schooling. The success of the movement was due in great measure to the whole-hearted help of the Cornish people who received the children and treated them as their own.[26]

My Life As An Evacuee In Week St. Mary *by Audrey Tarrant*

Our school party left Croydon in the very early hours on 16th June 1940, we boarded a train not knowing where we were going. The journey took all day, and in hindsight the teachers who were with us must have had a very daunting job in keeping us all amused, fed and toileted throughout the day. We finally arrived at Bude station at about 7pm and were walked, crocodile fashion, across the road to a big garage which was full of large tables with ladies waiting to serve food to us. After this we were all assembled and escorted onto the fleet of buses there.

In all this time I must say I had no fear of where I was going, I remember being sad at leaving Mum and Dad, but knew that it had been arranged for Mum to come as a helper when the school was settled in. On arrival at Week St. Mary I realised I had lost my two brothers since leaving the train - then I began to worry!!!

We must have looked a very 'bedraggled bunch' when we arrived after being on the move all day, but we were all gradually taken in ones and twos by our foster parents and I went with Les & Mary Colwill to a large house, (well I thought it large after our little one in Croydon).

When I woke up the following morning I couldn't believe the amount of 'country' all around.

After a few days my brothers were found, Colin had been kept at Bude for a medical exam and was eventually sent to Nath & Winnie Coles in Week St. Mary, and Peter was discovered in Whitstone - he obviously joined the wrong bus. As he was happy there with Mr. & Mrs Will Stanbury it was agreed he should not be moved.

These were my first foster parents in Week St. Mary, Les and Mary Colwill and they lived in New House, Lower Square. The house was on the corner of the square with the road leading to Steele Farm in front of it, and the lane to Swannacott at the side.

I remember waking up on the first morning there and looking out of the bedroom window, to see a beautiful country lane filled with wild flowers just waiting to be picked, and that is what I did!

Not realising it was only about 6 o'clock, Les and Mary were in a panic as you can imagine. When they looked into an empty bedroom, they must have thought they had lost me on the first night.

After a few months it was decided Mary's health was not too good (I don't think this was anything to do with my earlier escapade!) and I was then transferred to the Temperance Hotel.

Audrey Tarrant

We started school in the room beside the Methodist Chapel under the direction of Mr. Martin and Miss Pratt, two classes with two teachers in one room could not have been easy. I think there was a small room at the back where we went for reading etc.

Eventually several children returned home and the rest of us were filtered into the main village school at the top of the hill, where 'Pop' Martin later took over as headmaster. During our early days in Week, I remember most of us caught Impetigo which of course, being infectious, we were all treated with a medication which turned all our spotty faces, arms and legs mauve. I'm sure this did nothing for the local residents trying to endear themselves to this 'bedraggled lot'.

However everything turned out well in the end, because my memories of life in the village and being accepted by the villagers will stay with me for the rest of my life, and in spite of the war I look back at my time spent in Week St. Mary as some of the happiest days of my life. We had some very good times especially trying to do a bit of drama in Audrey & Sheila Jones' father's barn, (was it called Cawsey?) This was behind Orchards shop on Week Hill.

20th June 1940: Ned Masters (village blacksmith) is on the left of the picture. The chap with the box was from Sandercock's shop in the square, and was carrying the box from their store room down the road. Another of his jobs was to fetch water from the pump, across The Square, in a large barrel on wheels, something remembered by others.

Our meeting place always seemed to be by the pump in the square, we would sit on the trough and talk for ages and plan what we could do or talk about tomorrow.

Some of us would go after school to the Blacksmith's Forge and help Ned Masters with the bellows. It was fascinating watching him shape the iron into a shoe and then burn it onto the horse - we learnt a lot there! The forge at this time was between the market place and Ivy Cottage, where George and Edna Masters lived, down a rough little lane. Photos on the website seem to indicate it as being in the square now.

Another meeting place was at 4pm every day when the incoming post arrived at the Post Office, which was then opposite the Chapel in Mr. & Mrs. Sandercock's bungalow. After a quick sort, Mrs. Sandercock would come out and call out the names for us 'regulars' there and we would take it away. There was always a lot of chat as it was a mixed crowd of eager youngster as well as some of the older folk expecting the letters etc. If anyone was lucky enough to get a parcel - well there was no holding them!

As I was later billeted at The Temperance Hotel with Mr. & Mrs. Ned Masters and their daughter Christine (later Mrs Den Treleven) I probably had more contact than most with the schoolteacher Miss Retallack who also lived there. I regarded her as much of a 'demon' as the rest in school, but indoors she did seem to relax and she was always more friendly. I remember her helping me if my knitting went wrong (as it often did) and she always used very long needles and tucked them under her arms when knitting - which seemed very strange to me with my short 'learners' needles.

The Temperance was quite the hub of the village with people, farmers and market personnel being constant visitors, and with a view from the window onto the square, we were aware of all the 'goings on.' On Market Days the hotel almost exploded with the comings and goings of the farmers and others visiting the Auctioneer who used the small sitting room as their office for the day. Most of the farmers and auctioneers had the lunch cooked by Mrs Masters This was always a roast meal and because of all this catering, extra rations were available. Compared with a lot of others during the war, I consider we fared very well there, and I think most villagers did by helping one another with foodstuffs that were in short supply. I seem to remember we had jam and cream at most meals, and meat nearly every day!!!!

As I have said, my childhood in Week St. Mary was a very happy time, and when my mother gave birth to my sister in 1941 I thought life was wonderful. We all integrated so well with the local children (as any villagers who are 70/80years 'young' and were in the village during the war will readily agree.) It was very strange, on looking back, how we all settled so well, but this must be credited to the villagers who made us all so welcome, and treated us as extended families, not just 'VACS'.

My heartfelt thanks go to one and all in Week St. Mary for making my wartime experiences so easy and pleasurable to remember. They will remain my GOOD & HAPPY YEARS. I look forward to visiting again soon.

20th June 1940: This was probably our first encounter with 'real' horses, being on a walk around the village when we met them with Eddie Coles. I am on the front of the large horse who was called Cricket and the pony was called Stella. Both horses were characters in the village for as long as I can remember.

The Village pump in the left of the picture was a 'meeting place' for most, especially children and this was an obvious point for us strangers. A lot of the houses around The Square did not have their own water supply and had to fetch it by buckets etc. from this pump.

The house on the right was owned by Sandercocks and was also used for their storage. Beyond this was the police station. It was an ordinary house with a notice on it, I cannot remember any action taking place there! In the distance; the white cottage was owned by the Pooleys. Mrs ran a shop and Mr (a tailor) also operated a Taxi service for trips to and from Whitstone station, like when our parents came to visit us. Petrol was only available for tractors and farm vehicles (and a Taxi !!)

The other building was part of a farm, and I recall going there from where I was first billeted in the house opposite to fetch milk.

August 1940: Outside The Temperance Hotel
Back row, left to right:

My father, Mr Ned Masters, my mother, Mrs Gillam, Mrs Lilian Masters, Miss Christine Masters (later Mrs Den Treleven)

Children in front row:

Eileen Hawk, Audrey Tarrant, Sheila Gillam, Colin Tarrant, Pauline Gillam

Evacuees see hunt for first time!

Although shorn somewhat of some of its usual features, Week St. Mary revel was faithfully observed by the local parishioners over the week-end, and numerous Week St. Mary natives paid their customary visits to their homes and friends.

The dedication services, on Sunday, were conducted by the Rector, and drew large congregations.

The meet of the South Tetoott Hounds, under Harry, on Monday morning, attracted about twenty riders and a large crowd of followers on foot. Craddacott Moors provided two 'kills' in full view of the majority of walkers, much to the delight of the locals, and to the wonderment of the evacuees, most of whom were having their first introduction to such a sport. Cawker's Moors gave the riders a short, but brisk gallop until the fox 'went to holt' and the hounds were called off about 1 p.m.

February 1941: These giant snowballs were made one Sunday after a very heavy snowstorm during the night. We started off throwing small balls, as one does, then decided to roll them around The Square to see what happened. The size of them can be judged by the children behind. I can remember boring the holes through them to try to make them look like igloos.

My Life As An Evacuee In Week St. Mary *by Peter Tarrant (Audrey's brother)*

Peter wrote and said that as we had contacted his sister regarding the evacuation from Croydon to Week St. Mary, he wanted to add 'his six-penny-worth' to the story.

It was June 16th 1940, just 2 days after my 7th birthday, when Audrey, Colin and I were bundled on a train in Croydon and sent to what appeared to be the end of the earth.

I remember being quite terrified when I became detached from my brother and sister. I had been given a boxed set of Dinky aeroplanes as a birthday present and I clutched these close to me as they were my sole worldly goods. It was a very long arduous journey interrupted by stops along the track where kind people were waiting to pass us drinks.

Eventually we arrived at Bude and were then herded into the bus station where we were put on coaches and transported to the local schools. Here we were lined up and our future guardians paraded past to select their quota of scruffy urchins. I am sure we must have looked like very thin and pale creatures from another world. I was chosen together with another boy by a very kindly looking couple. We were logged out and told to report to school the following morning.

Our new parents were a couple about 40 years old. We were bundled into the dickey seat of an ancient bull nosed Morris car and driven to a large farmhouse. I remember being frightened by lots of animal noises, by the trees, fields and another boy also called Peter (renamed for convenience as John, his other name) who was 5 months older than me. I do not know if Philip Martin ever knew of my disappearance or in fact if I was his responsibility, but I do recall it was two weeks before the whereabouts of my brother and sister was made known to me to be in Week St. Mary. It was a long time before I saw them again. I was at Whitstone some 4+ miles away, and there was no way of getting there.

Mr. and Mrs Stanbury with whom we were billeted had no children of their own and insisted we did not forget our Mums and Dads, we always referred to them as Master and Mrs.

He was a farmer but was also what I could best describe as a part time Ministry appointed fat stock assessor at the Week St. Mary's monthly sale of animals for slaughter. A position of some importance which gave strength to the farmer's side whilst a man called Coles (I believe) was a Week St. Mary butcher and added that element.

The village community was split between the Chapel and the Church goers. For 6 days a week they conversed with each other but on the Sabbath they avoided contact if possible. My mind is a bit vague at this point but the chapel people would not let a drop of alcohol pass their lips and people that did were very much regarded as the other side of the street people. Anyone who wanted a tipple really earned their drink as they had to go to the nearest pub in Bridgerule several miles away. The method of transport was probably by horse. These were trained by their rider to get home unguided once he had been helped onto it.

I feel very guilty when I think that the war years were some of the happiest of my life due to the Cornish people who were so kind to a couple of ragged urchins in desperate need of love and affection.

I know this sentiment is shared by Audrey and Colin. In 1941 another important event occurred in your village! My Mum had come away from the Croydon bombing and was accommodated in the Temperance Hotel. There my sister Betty was born on the 21st June.

I am not really part of the Week St. Mary history but as an evacuee I have my own memories and experience of your village and those Cornish people who graciously took on the challenge of what must have appeared to have been people from another planet or race. Thank you Week St. Mary, Whitstone and all the many other villages who saved some of the children of England. You have earned your place in history.

The Temperance Hotel, before its replacement by the modern houses on the Market site. Upstairs there were 4 large bedrooms and one very small bedroom. There was also a chemical toilet, in a small cubicle, which had to be emptied daily - Chris would carry this down the flight of stairs, through the main living area and way down the back yard ! (No Health and Safety in those days!). There was also a 'bucket house' in the back yard, I remember this would only be used by the men in the house, (and also me if I came back with muddy wellies.) Downstairs there was a Front Room, used mainly on Sunday evenings, in there was a piano, and we usually had a sing-song with Chris playing and Ned Masters singing with Miss Retallack, both had beautiful voices - or so I thought at the time. The main living room had a very large table with a reversible top, plain wood for everyday and turned over for the polished side for Sunday teatime. There was on open range fireplace which always had kettles and a large urn (they called it a fountain) with constant hot water, and an oven where all the baking was done. Off this room was a small sitting room used during the week. My memories of this are the many games of cards, mainly Solo I think, played in there. Bill Smale from Week Green was a regular visitor as were 2 or 3 soldiers who were based at the camp in the Goscott road.

The kitchen seemed enormous to me at the time. All the preparations were carried out there, also the washing-up with water in a bowl and dishes drained on a tray. The bowl was then emptied out into the yard from the top of the steps. The Temperance Hotel was far from today's idea of an hotel, but it did excel at least once a month on 'market days' when farmers from all around, together with the auctioneer's men would gather around the large table for a meal. I was usually required to help serve at the table, but mainly my job was in the kitchen helping with the washing-up. I remember this as quite a 'fun time'.

My Life As An Evacuee In Week St. Mary *by Monica (Molly) Perry*

My friend Audrey Tarrant passed a letter on to me that you had sent her Mid-November about the web site you are promoting for Week St. Mary, and you were asking her for her memories of being an evacuee in the last war. I was also an evacuee during this time and I have presumed that you might be interested in my experiences. I was a great friend of Audrey's, indeed after the war we worked for the same business and have remained in touch ever since.

I should perhaps explain that I was just 11 when the war started in 1939. I had been a pupil at Sydenham school (for girls) and had passed a scholarship for Lady Edridge school. I have a sister Beryl, four years younger than myself, and at first we were evacuated to Brighton, which seems an odd choice of refuge, since it was much nearer the French Coast than Croydon! However it was the "phoney war" and nothing much was happening and most people drifted back home. I started school at a Grammar school, and in the meantime my sister Beryl was evacuated to Week St. Mary with Sydenham School. My Father worked for British Airways and was sent to Wales for safety together with my Mother and younger sister, leaving me living with an Aunt so that I could continue attending Lady Edridge School. Soon after this we began to experience bad air raids, and I remember my Father coming to Croydon, on the weekend of the "Battle of Britain" in Sept. and taking me back with him to Wales. Sorry this is so complicated. So at Christmas 1940 we all went down to Week St. Mary to visit my sister, Beryl who was living at Week Green Farm, with Will Smale, and daughters Agnes and Doris, and quite unbeknown to me, organised that I should stay there with a relation of theirs, Owen and Olive Smale, who lived at Waxhill. I can remember going to visit Waxhill and I suppose I must have made a good impression, anyway that was it, and I stayed with them until early 1945. I can't remember ever being homesick, or questioning their decision. My Mother was a very matter-of-fact person, and one of her favourite phrases in wartime was "we must make the best of things" and I suppose we did.

I hadn't known your grandfather (Philip H. S. Martin) until then because he had taught at the boys' school in Croydon which was next door to mine and fraternising was not encouraged, but of course I did know Miss Pratt and of course there was Miss Retallack whom we all avoided like the plague, if we could. Your comments on her are interesting; obviously we weren't the only ones to suffer. I remember on one occasion I overheard her remark about me "Why do they call the child Molly, it's a cows name." And I've never forgotten it. My family always called me Molly because my sister Beryl called me "Molica" and since then I have always hated it.

Since living in Cornwall I have never been able to settle down to life in the suburbs. I think I must have gone a bit wild at first. I loved the country life, all the hay and corn harvesting, planting and harvesting potatoes.

I was especially good at running around the sheep and cattle to round them up. In fact I can remember "Uncle" Owen saying "When you go home maid, I'll have to buy a dog" and it only came to me years later what he meant! Aunt Olive used to say "The trouble with you maid is you think you'm a boy". The Smale's and the Horrell's were keen Methodists, so I was encouraged to attend too. Great fun at "Anniversary" time, games, and enormous teas, as I recall.

School was presided over by Mr. P.H.S. Martin, we secretly called him "Pop" Martin. I don't know if he ever knew, but it was a compliment because he was a father figure for all of us. The thing I remember most about his teaching style was that he was a wonderfully dramatic reader, and instilled in me a love of literature for which I am eternally grateful. He read Pickwick Papers, all the funny bits in character, Henry V, the Gadshill Robbery, with Falstaff and Poins and made the characters live, with the appropriate accents! I wonder how many other fellow pupils were as influenced as I was. White Company, Treasure Island and any other exciting adventure stories came alive for me.

Miss Pratt was the teacher who was an expert for Country Dancing, which she was very keen on, and she also produced the many little plays that you probably have photographs of. I met her again years after the war. After she had retired from teaching she married, and was living in Shirley, near Croydon. I don't know if you know, but the W.I. in Week St. Mary published some information about the wartime evacuees. I recall I was approached for comment and I did reply, but I have never seen the results. It was quite a few years ago.

Miss Pratt with some of the evacuees

I returned to see Olive and Owen many times since the war ended, and we always corresponded until they died. I have very happy memories of those times. I married in 1950, and had two children, and now 4 grand children. When my husband retired we moved down to Dorset, and have lived here for 22 years. We commenced walking the South West Coastal Path, on and off, when the weather was fine, and completed it some time ago, even though it took us 8 years. We saw the best of the West Country, and Cornwall will always be home to me. Incidentally I found out years later that my Grandmother was of Cornish stock, from Hayle. Her family names were Hamlyn and Pascoe, of which there are many in the Cornish phone book! Perhaps that explains something.

My sister Beryl emigrated to New Zealand in the 60's, and has been back to England a couple of times. In fact she came with her husband last Summer and stayed with us whilst he, with 10 other mad Kiwi's, cycled from Lands End to John O' Groats.

My Life As An Evacuee In Week St. Mary *by Beryl Denton - New Zealand*

I've received the 'nudge' from big sister Molly (Monica)! I remember the occasion when the very dominant Miss Retallack stated in class that she couldn't be called 'Molly'. It was a cow's name!

Your letter to Molly brought back a lot of memories of my stay in Week St. Mary, in fact I was the last evacuee to leave the village just before VE-Day which I celebrated back in Lady Edridge School, in Croydon.

I scarcely know where to start but maybe my first experience of being an evacuee. Initially Molly and I (11 and 7 years old) were both evacuated with the school, a short train ride to Patcham, Brighton. I can remember standing on the doorstep of a house and meeting Mrs Weland who was informed by the adult with us that her allocation was two. I remember sleeping on a 'camp bed' in the small bedroom upstairs with Molly on the 'proper' bed. I'm sure our stay here was quite short not quite the ideal spot for evacuees with the German troops now occupying France and looking for the opportunity to extend their territory just across the Channel into England. I understand that the bodies of German soldiers were being washed up on the beach at Brighton at the time. One morning on the way to school with Molly I saw Mum with 3 year old sister Sheila, standing on the roundabout in the middle of the road. Molly said "Don't be silly, it can't be Mum!", my reply was "Yes it is, she is waving to us!" Mum too had been evacuated - (I didn't realise it at the time but she was pregnant with yet another daughter, who was born back in Croydon and died just a few days old).

I don't know exactly how long the stay was in Patcham, but certainly it wasn't more than 3 or 4 weeks. Sadly I didn't ever talk to my Mother to learn more about it. It was after this that Molly passed the scholarship and went to Lady Edridge School and I remained at Junior School, Sydenham Road. When evacuation time came again Molly was evacuated to Windsor with her school (she has probably told you more of that!) and I went on the long train journey to Devon, this time on my own, aged 8 years.

I was 8 on June 6th 1940 and recall having to go to the dentist on my birthday! And my mother gave me permission to grow my hair and have a ribbon! I can remember feeling quite grown up! I was fitted with a gas mask and my little sister had to have a 'Mickey Mouse' one designed for infants. I also remember that 'Pop' Martin drove me to Bude to the dentist. When I came out of the dentist (minus tooth with abscess) he asked if I would like an ice cream. I said, "Yes please" very quickly and they laughed. My first ice cream in years!

Almost everyone made a special fabric case or cover for their gas mask box. The originals were just manilla cardboard with 'TOP' embossed on the lid in large letters and a string 'handle' that you could put around your neck. We were supposed to carry them everywhere including to school and down into the Anderson (corrugated iron shelters that were issued to every dwelling) shelter when the siren sounded during night or day!

It must have been a terrible time for parents, sending their children off with teachers, not knowing where they were going. Mum had made a drawstring bag out of curtaining fabric and inside was a postcard that was addressed to her and stamp affixed, that I was to send as soon as I arrived, giving her my new address and the name of the people I was staying with. A packed lunch including an apple, a bottle of drink, a pack of cards, drawing paper and pencils, and a comic were the other contents of the bag.

141

The train journey took us to Bude and we were taken to a large marquee where we were fed on currant buns and lemonade in a glass. We all had a luggage label in our coat lapel with our name written on it (probably our identity card number too. I imagine mine was CLLK563!).

From Bude we were put into groups to travel to various villages in the area. The bus (we called them charabancs at the time) I was put on was full of kids of various ages and 2 teachers: your grandfather 'Pop' Martin and Miss Pratt. As it happened I 'knew' Doris Pratt because she was in the same class as my mother, Gladys Maynard at Cross Road Junior School in Croydon. According to Mum she had to sit next to Doris Pratt to learn how to behave!

It's amazing to reflect on the selection system that occurred when we arrived in Week St. Mary. We all sat on chairs around the large room and residents came in and 'chose' who they would take as they walked around the room and 'inspected' us!

I know that the room was getting pretty empty by the time my turn came! Maureen Davidson and I had decided that we wanted to go together. She was quite a few years older than I, maybe a big sister replacement! So, Agnes and Doris Smale led us off down the lane to the farmhouse where they lived with their father, Will. Doris was 21 at the time.

We arrived to a meal quite late in the evening and I know they had made jelly especially for us, 'cos children all like jelly, don't they? Naturally I insisted on posting my postcard off to Mum without delay and we walked with torches in the blackout up to the post-box in the stone wall on the far side of the school playground. (I wonder if it is still there?)

Initially our Schoolroom was the Methodist Chapel down in the village, the background to quite a few of those early photographs. Incidentally, I'm the one that was sitting in front of 'Pop' Martin, with his hands on my shoulders. This photo was also the same grouping and occasion as the one with Miss Pratt in - they just changed places. I think it was Miss Pratt's camera.

Uncle Tom Cobley re-enactment outside the Chapel

My chief memory of those early days in the chapel schoolroom were of children crying. They seemed to have problems, being separated from their Mothers. I knew that crying wouldn't help and I certainly wasn't going to join them. In any case I knew that when the war was all over we were going to be back with our families. I remained convinced that that would happen. No doubts!

Molly and I talked about our evacuation when I went back to England last year, at 78 and 74 years old. We agreed, "Weren't we well prepared!"

Drama featured quite a lot in my activities at school. Miss Pratt must have been keen! We had to work at our Devon accents for 'Widdecombe Fair'. Each individual had to say their name.... "Wi' Bill Brewer, Jan Stewer, Peter Gurney, Peter Davy, Dan'l Whiddon, Harry Hawk, old uncle Tom Cobbley and all, old uncle Tom Cobbley and all." The last bit in unison. I was Peter Gurney the one in the bowler hat and smock coat at the right hand side. I can't recall who, or rather which 2, played the horse!

Molly had a photograph of an excursion into the countryside to pick daffodils and primroses and Miss Pratt was keen for us to learn the names of the flowers and weeds. We pressed flowers and labelled our collections and mounted them on cardboard. I was very proud of mine.

On another occasion we went to see a Mr. Stephens (or was it Stephenson?) who kept bees down in a lane off the village. We had to write up a story about our visit and information and drawings about bees. I won! The prize for the best entry was a jar of honey.

After a while the number of evacuees that remained in Week St. Mary had reduced considerably and we then combined with the local school. Your grandfather's account will have recorded the move. Possibly he was appointed Headmaster at this time too, that's a don't know, but certainly at this time I became acquainted with the dreaded dragon, Miss Retallack! She had quite a bark - and was quite handy with the ruler and stick.

At some stage quite early on Mum came down to visit me and assure herself that I was being well looked after. She had removed Molly from her place in Windsor. I got the impression that her hosts weren't 'clean' enough by Mum's standard. So, Molly came down to Week St. Mary with Mum, in search of a safe billet away from the bombing in Croydon.

As Molly will have told you in her letter/account, she found a home with Owen Smale, brother and uncle to the family I was with. Uncle Owen and Auntie Ivy had no children of their own and they doted on Molly and treated her like one of their own out at Wax Hill. Molly stayed there until she was 15 or so when she went to Whitchurch, outside Cardiff, S. Wales, where Mum, Dad and Sheila were lodging with the 'Browns' 'cos Dad was working at Croydon Airport (Directed Labour) and was transferred to an aircraft works in S. Wales.

Before the war Dad had a greengrocery business in Croydon, but the war put an end to that. As a young man he had trained as a mechanic and his skills were of use to the war effort.

What an upheaval it all must have been for families all over the world. I am full of admiration for families like the 'Browns' with their 4 children, sharing their house with another family for 4 years or so. The miracle is that they remained life-long friends.

Let's see what other memories I have of Week St. Mary - it was quite a new experience for me, a 'townie' being billeted on a farm and living in a farmhouse with no electricity, a kitchen sink with a hole to a gutter outside. A huge 'dairy' cool storage room, with an 'Alfa Laval' separator. Oil lamps and candles.

The fireplace was an open one with a chimney corner where I used to sit on a stool and poke little sticks into the fire until I was told to 'stop playing with the fire, maid!' The kettle was hanging on a hook over the fire and a large boiler where small potatoes were boiled to squash up with the pigs' mash. There was a clome oven in the chimney corner that was heated by burning a faggot of wood inside. The sisters baked bread and made huge pasties which were a mainstay of the diet, eaten hot or cold. There was a little Primus stove in the kitchen for use when the fire was out and an oil heater type oven that sat on top of two chimney-like burners. It smelt and made the food taste a bit funny too.

Doris and Agnes did the milking, in the morning and evening - there were about 9 red Devon cows. Feeding the calves was a new experience for me too putting my fingers into their mouths and holding them down into the bucket of milk. Haven't even seen that system in New Zealand. There was the occasional lamb being bottle-fed, wrapped in a blanket near the fire. And a pit toilet near the end of the garden with newspaper for toilet paper!

We were encouraged to help at harvest time, even allowed time off school to work in the fields. Molly and I had a good reputation for planting spuds pacing along a furrow spacing seed potatoes into the ground, from the bucket we carried. Another potato job was 'tatie picking', collecting up the potatoes scattered on the ground, a pretty back-aching job. All the farm work was done by horse-drawn machines. The only other machine was when the huge threshing machine came and made quick work of the stored sheaves of corn stacked under the roof of the open shed down in the farmyard, leaving us with sacks of corn and a new straw stack.

All the washing was done by hand with 2 huge galvanised baths standing up on a wooden bench. All the water heated on the fire and every drop of water used came up from the well just up the garden path. Hauled up by hand with the bucket on a length of rope. No taps, inside or out! The final job for the washing water was to clean the Wellington boots. Some of the washing was dried on the line in the garden with a wooden prop but a lot of it was just draped over the thorn hedge around the garden.

Sometimes the Wellington boot job was left for me, and putting together a small pile of chopped sticks for fire lighting. Mr. Smale provided the bundles (faggots) of wood for the fire from a plantation on the farm. All these were tied bundles fastened with a wrap of wooden stick, twisted somehow to hold it together, no string!

You used a little hook tool to chop with. I seem to think they called it a matchett or something like that.

Now back to my education. 'Pop' Martin took the senior class and I was in the same class as Molly (4 yrs older). I know I enjoyed Maths, and was good at it. I didn't cheat even though the answers were in the back of the book! It must have been difficult organising the teaching for such a wide range of age groups. I have fond memories of English with 'Pop' Martin, he was such a marvellous story teller. I am sorry you won't have experienced your grandfather reading you a story. We all listened in awe as he read aloud to us. I am sure Molly has mentioned this too.

White Company, various bits from Dickens or excerpts from them. Bits from Pickwick Papers and Christmas Carol, enactments or performances really. Poetry too. I remember 'Down by the great, grey, green, greasy Limpopo river all set about with fever trees!' We didn't do any flower picking with Mr. Martin but had a great cultural introduction to Literature. We did various exam papers too, RSA Exam papers in English, and Molly and Audrey Tarrant were learning the basics of book keeping and helping to run the 'pig club'. Did Molly mention that?

Watching killing a pig was also part of my farm experience and hearing the squeals as well as being part of the butchery and cleaning process. I can recall clearly now, standing over the bath of intestines, holding one end of a length, with Doris at the other, swishing back and forth until the end was considered 'clean'. Clean enough to stuff with minced oddments of meat and offal, tied into sausages, ready to be sliced later and fried - 'Hog's Puddings', I wasn't sure if I dared eat them but eventually I was brave enough.

My Art education was not a major part of my schooling but occasionally 'Pop' Martin would do a demonstration painting on a large sheet of paper pinned to the blackboard. We were expected to copy what he did, in stages. Watercolour washes and imaginative landscape. I don't think that happened often but I did quite a lot of drawing 'at home'. Maureen Davidson went back to Croydon after about 6 months. I met her in the street in Croydon years later. She was pushing a pushchair with her first baby inside. I was 14 and she would have been about 18 or so. Married to a sailor! Haven't seen or heard of her since.

I took the 11+ exam sitting in the back of the classroom and passed. It would have been possible to go and live in Bude and attend a secondary school there, but it was decided I would stay in Week St. Mary, the war would soon be over, or so everyone said. That was 1943. On my 12th birthday, 6th June 1944 it was D-Day, and I had a watch for my present!

Throughout the years I had received regular letters from my Mother (none from Dad) and had written back, receiving parcels for birthday and Christmas and probably just one visit a year from my parents, them coming down to visit in Week St. Mary by train. On occasions I was taken back for the summer holiday or part of it, visiting relatives in Croydon or staying with the Brown family in Whitchurch.

I haven't really mentioned the Chapel and the great times we all had at Anniversary times. We learnt a whole lot of new 'songs', occasionally with solo verses and Miss Orchard playing the organ. (Incidentally, I had piano lessons with her at some time too. Didn't come to anything. I never really did catch on, but enjoyed singing!)

There were organised 'Faith Teas' too and Sunday School and organised sports on the field opposite the Chapel.

My experience of the war itself and the bombing was very limited. As a child I sang the wartime songs heard on the radio. Vera Lynn and the 'Workers Playtime' programmes and of course the 'News' and Winston Churchill's speeches. I felt very patriotic.

We did concerts in the barn. We saw German and Italian soldiers who came as prisoners to work in groups on the farms.

There was an American soldiers camp on the outskirts of the village. The source of supplies of chewing gum, cigarettes and even nylon stockings and other things that I was too young to understand!

We had air-raid practices at school. When the whistle sounded we went quickly (and orderly) across to 'Parson's Walk' where we crouched in the bushes until we were given the 'All Clear'.

The scariest bit was hearing the heavy drone of German bombers overhead on their way to bigger cities to drop their load. On one occasion we could see a red glow in the distance, Plymouth on fire! We'd hear the planes go back later having dropped their bombs, a different sound.

It was August 1945 before my family regrouped after the war. This meant buying new furniture, etc with special issue coupons; even curtain fabric needed coupons to purchase. We rented a house in South Norwood. Dad went to work at Heathrow Airport working on aircraft maintenance and pressurised cabins. I was very fortunate that Croydon Education Committee organised a special class for returned evacuees at Lady Edridge School for Girls. There were just 24 of us in that class. We started in Form 2 when most of us were 13 years old. We tended to work hard and appreciated the opportunity we had been given to have a Grammar School Education and I went to Bretton Hall in Yorkshire where I specialised in Art. It was a brilliant environment. Now home to the Yorkshire Sculpture Park in some of the grounds, specialising in Art, Drama and Music. We lived in the 16th Century mansion for the 2 years we trained.

I met my husband, Jim Denton, whilst I was there. We married in '53 (53 years ago!) and emigrated to New Zealand with our 2 young children in 1966. We continued to teach in New Zealand, in Auckland and retired to the 'Bay of Plenty' in Katikati, (east coast north of Tauranga and 2 hours drive from Auckland Airport). Our property there is 26 acres on estuary land. Jim designed and built our house. We've been there for 25 years odd now. ■

Parish Magazine

The Reverend Townend M.A., R.A.F. Chaplain was inducted in the parish Church on July 4th 1947, at 7.00 pm, by the Bishop of Truro and the Service was followed by a social evening in the Rectory Room.

In the autumn a Sunday School and a Choir were formed. The Reverend Townend also decided that a Parish Magazine, to be called "The Beacon" should be introduced to the parish. This begun at Advent and was priced at just 2d.

I am indebted to Audrey Tarrant, David & Shelia Coles and Pat Barriball for the inclusion of the following extracts from "The Beacon", starting with the first edition in 1947 and some others leading up to 1963.

The Beacon

Week St. Mary Church Notes   Advent 1947 Price 2d.

Rector's Letter

Parish magazines are sometimes called "The Vicar's monthly nightmare" and I expect they often are. I hope this isn't going to be mine. I don't think it will. It may be a little rash to start a magazine. Many would be only too willing to give up the ones they have got if they could, but I have been wanting to start one ever since I came here. The Parochial Church Council has now given me the chance and here it is.

As usual it is a question of Finance. It will be extremely difficult to make this magazine pay its way. We can hardly charge more than two pence for such an infant, the circulation can never be very large in a small parish and so there will always be an adverse balance to be made up. The Church Council has agreed to back my efforts out of Church Funds for a year's run. Please be kind to the infant. Every two pence will be a little less for the Church to find.

This is my first attempt at such a publication. Like the notice hung over the piano at the Wild Western concert, "Don't shoot the pianist he's doing his best", don't expect it to rival The Times or even the Whitstone Parish Letter all at once. I hope to publish it every two months to begin with and see how it goes, whether it is too much of a nightmare either for me or for you.

What's in a name?

Why The Beacon? I wanted a name which would both express what the magazine was intended to do and which would also be expressive of Week St. Mary. A name which would make you say "That's just like the Parish." You know what a beacon does. It gives warning of danger (beacons were lit on all the hills at the coming of the Armada). It calls people together (beacons were prepared in 1940 for the invasion). It announces news (beacons were I believe lit at the Coronation. It guides people to safety (the shining light in Pilgrim's Progress, the lighthouse we see from Plymouth Hoe.)

Isn't our Church tower just like a beacon? From whichever direction you approach Week St. Mary there is our Church tower standing up in the distance. It must always have been a great guide to travellers, especially in earlier days when roads were few and the country chiefly moorland. Its bells have been rung on many occasions to announce tidings; (Waterloo, Trafalgar, Blenheim). They were ready to warn in the event of invasion and week-by-week they are rung to call us together for worship. "The Beacon" is a good name for our Church.

And what about this magazine. I believe a magazine should fulfil the same purposes. It should be used to announce parish news and call people to coming events (be a diary and an engagement book). It should give teaching on Christian beliefs so as to guide people through the wilderness of this life and it should also, when necessary, warn the heedless of the dangers that come from the neglect of spiritual things. May the Holy Spirit cause this magazine to fulfil these requirements. ***NOEL TOWNEND, Rector***

Parish Diary - The Bible Class

This class is held in Church at the same time as the Sunday School although quite distinct. There is no age limit above eleven. It is recruited from the Sunday School and I would welcome all older people who would like to come. In this connection I would like to say that there is no necessity for those coming to Morning Service to wait in the porch. The porch is cold and draughty. Its warmer in Church and neither they nor the bells will interrupt my lesson.

Sunday School

This was restarted on September 14th, thanks to the interest of Molly Rogers and May Cobbledick who offered themselves as teachers. Almost every possible child is a regular member, some coming from quite an appreciable distance and very few ever being late. Quite an achievement on the part of the parents. Sunday School begins at the Rectory at 10.30 a.m. the children going on to Church at 11 a.m. This gives parents who live at some distance an opportunity of worshipping with their children, otherwise difficult for them to arrange. I wish all the parents would take this opportunity of coming to Church as a family. One of the strongest ties in family life.

Confirmation Classes

These are proceeding steadily in preparation for the Bishop's visit on Sunday February 29th. This will be the first occasion that a Confirmation has been held in our Church since 1936. At the moment there are eight candidates, both adult and junior. There is still time for others to come forward for preparation. Believing as I do that Confirmation is essential to our Christian life and welfare I would urge this on all adults who have not yet been confirmed.

Guides

Mrs. Townend has started a Girl Guide company which at present meets in the Rectory on Tuesday afternoons from 5 to 6.30 p.m. It is an open company which means that it is not affiliated to any particular religious body. Any girl who is over 10 and under 16 years can join. I can recommend this to all parents as a good thing.

Remembrance Service

We had a full Church, on the afternoon of Sunday November 8th and we were fortunate in the weather, which remained fine until we had just finished the Service at the Memorial. The only point I would like to make is that the Service is not over until we have left the memorial. The walk from the Church to the Cross then is of the nature of a procession of all the congregation headed by the choir. We will have to practise so that next time we can all sing the hymn as we go along.

The Choir

The keenness of its members makes up for the smallness of the choir. It is once more in being and numbers are only limited by the supply of cassocks and surplices. We would be grateful for one or two volunteers from the ladies who would be willing to undertake the care and maintenance of the robes.

Electric Boiler

The long hoped for boiler has now been installed in the Rectory Room. It will be a great boon to the ladies and a valuable asset to the Hall. It will be under the charge of Mrs Ridgman. We have still to raise most of the cost. This will doubtlessly be forthcoming in due course.

Arrivals and Departures

We were sorry to have to say goodbye to Mrs. Cadman although glad to know that she and her husband have at last found a temporary home together. Michael and Sophie will be missed in the Sunday School. We are pleased to welcome Mrs. Jenkinson once more to the Church. We were sorry to hear that Mrs. Martin had gone to Plymouth Hospital but glad to know she is doing well. We wish her a complete and speedy return to health.

THE CHURCH CALENDAR

Advent

The four Sundays before Christmas when we prepare ourselves both for Our Lord's immediate coming on Christmas Day and also for his final coming at the Day of Judgement. Let us keep in mind that Advent is, like Lent, a period of fast rather than festival.

Christmas

As in the past we hope to begin this Festival with the Midnight Eucharist on Christmas Eve. We hope to hold a special Carol Service in the evening of the Sunday after Christmas.

Sunday School Party

This will be held in the Rectory Room on Monday December 29th. It will be open to all children who are regular members of the Sunday School and those not yet old enough.

Church Party

It will, as in the past, take place in the Rectory Room on New Year's Eve.

The Beacon

Week St. Mary Parish Notes   May 1951 Price 2d.

Rector's Letter

I would like to thank you all for the welcome you have given to the Beacon in its new form. What expressions of opinion I have heard have all been appreciative of the fact that it is going to come out once a month. That does show, I am glad to say, that you find the notes interesting; I will try to keep up the interest. I was only sorry that, through being laid up for a few days just at the beginning of the month, I was unable to distribute all the first copies personally. I am very grateful to the Guides who took round the copies for me and so got them out in time.

Garden Fete

We have fixed Thursday, June 21st as the date for this year's Garden Fete. With the rise in cost of everything, it is increasingly important that we should reach our target of £40 for the Cornish Church Thanksgiving Fund. There are so many things for which the Church is responsible and of which the cost is steadily rising. Schools and orphanages, evangelisation, building and repairs. They cost more and yet more money every year, and in spite of the generally accepted idea, that the Church has a lot of money up its sleeve, the money ultimately comes out of our pockets in the parishes, since the Church is us and, we are the Church. So please, in the words of the Sunday evening Good Cause appeal on the wireless, do all you can to help us find our £40.

Bell Fund

By the time you read this, Messrs. Gillett and Johnston's bill for the repairing of the bells will have been paid in full. This would not have been possible without the help of Mr. J. Cobbledick, who has most generously lent us the balance required free of interest. We are very grateful to him for this and we must, in consequence, try all the harder to repay him as soon as we can.

Mr. T. Rogers. As we have had a change of People's Warden this year, I want to take this opportunity of publicly thanking in the name of the Parish, Mr. T. Rogers, the retiring Warden. He has been a Churchwarden since 1936 and the treasurer of the Church for the past four years. In these positions he has loyally done his best in the interests of the Church. For his years of service we are indeed grateful. *NOEL TOWNEND, Rector*

Parish Diary

Mothering Sunday. This year Fr. Wyatt preached at our Family Service in the afternoon. There was a good attendance of parents and children although we would like to have seen more fathers present. For their play the children produced an acting lesson on prayer, in the rectory before tea. This they performed very effectively.

Church Fellowship

Our March meeting was most successful and produced some interesting papers, read chiefly by our younger members on subjects drawn for the month before. Some good discussions arose in the course of the evening.

British & Foreign Bible Society

The annual meeting was held in the Rectory Room on Friday, March 16th and was addressed by Mr. Foster the area representative. We are greatly indebted to Mrs. R. Orchard, the secretary, for her work in keeping the interest of the parish alive in this Society.

The Bishop's Tree

We planted the camellia in the churchyard on the afternoon of Palm Sunday. The ceremony was performed by Mr. J. H. Rogers during a short and well attended service in the open air. We have placed the tree on the south side of the Church close to the path between the porch and the vestry door. We hope it will do well there although the weather hasn't been too kind to it since. The collections on this Sunday were given to the late Bishop's memorial fund.

Passion Play

On Monday in Holy Week Mrs. Oke of Holsworthy gave us, with the aid of a filmstrip, scenes from the last Oberammergau Passion Play which she attended. A good number gathered in the Rectory Room to witness it. It took the place of Mr. Petvin's usual visit on Good Friday, which he was unable to pay this year.

Good Friday

We had our usual services but with smaller congregations than last year. It is unfortunate that we cannot get a full Church on this day, because it is the day of all the year that should be given completely to God in worship and reflection. I feel that Christians are largely to blame that while their regard for Sunday has restricted what anyone can do on that day, their neglect of Good Friday has allowed it to be turned into a public holiday on which almost anything is allowed.

Easter Day

The Church looked beautiful in its clothing of Spring flowers. We again built our Easter garden at the children's altar that we might take in the Easter message with our eyes as well as with our ears. Our Communicants were as many as usual although we missed a few of our number.

Personal

We welcome Mr. S. Ridgman as people's warden and Church treasurer for the year and wish him success in his responsible position. We also welcome three new arrivals to the Parish in the persons of an infant daughter to Mr. and Mrs. J. Colwill of Marhays, and of sons to Mr. and Mrs. L. Parnell and Mr. and Mrs. Gilbert. Unfortunately at the same time we have to say goodbye to Mr. and Mrs. Gilbert who have left the village. Mrs. Jenkinson is unfortunately confined to her bed at the moment and Mr. Kinsman is in hospital after an accident. Miss Audrey Jones has been sick but is now better. We wish them all speedy recoveries.

The Beacon

Week St. Mary Parish Notes   June 1951 Price 2d.

Rector's Letter

The letters which boys at boarding school send home to their parents, are supposed to deal chiefly with finance, that is, appeals for more pocket money. This letter may seem rather like that, but it won't all be begging. Mr. Stacey and I attended the annual meeting of the Tamar Valley Ringing Guild in Holsworthy on April 4th. There the Guild very generously voted us the sum of £10 towards the cost of our bells. As the Guild hasn't a large bank balance, this is a generous offer for which we are very grateful.

I made an appeal a few Sundays ago for an increase in our Church collections. My points were: we must pay our way and with our own money and we must also find some money to help others and that this, with the increase in the price of everything, was becoming impossible on our old income from collections. I am grateful to say that you have risen nobly to my appeal, I knew that it was just a question of the realisation of our need. Our collections since have shown a definite increase. For this we are very thankful.

As our Sunday School grows so does its expenses. As it has no funds of its own, we have decided to give the 11.00 a.m. collection on the first Sunday in each month to this purpose. This alone won't be sufficient, but I would commend it to your notice. We chose the first Sunday in the month as the parents make a special effort to worship with their children on that Sunday morning.

May 10th will be a big day for the Methodists of Week St. Mary. The Chapel is looking very spick-and-span in its new coat of paint. By the time this Beacon is in your homes the re-opening will be over, but we all hope that May 10th will be a fine and most successful occasion, and they have our prayers and best wishes for the great event. *NOEL TOWNEND, Rector*

Parish Diary

The Church Fellowship

The last meeting of the Winter was held on April 5th. As the evenings are getting longer the attendance wasn't as good as usual. For the final occasion we relaxed a little in an atmosphere of general religious knowledge and other competitions.

Ruridecanal Conference

This annual event was held in Stratton on the afternoon of April 16th. All our representatives were present. We heard a most instructive talk by the Sub Warden of the Community of the Epiphany on the subject of, "The Church as the living Body of Christ." This was followed by the business meeting and the reading of the reports of the various deanery secretaries.

U.M.C.A.

We welcomed Mr. Phillips, the area secretary of the Mission, once again to the Parish on Sunday, April 15th, when he preached at the Morning Service. He told us how, in little bush churches in the centre of Africa, congregations of black African Christians would be gathered that Sunday morning. They would be having the same service and saying the same prayers as we were here. All sharing in the same worship. He said how you could always tell a Christian village or Christian person from a heathen by their happy appearance.

Personal

We were very happy on Rogation Sunday to welcome into the fold of Christ's Church, Thelma Grace, the daughter of Mr. and Mrs. J. Colwill, who was baptized after the Morning Service. We have had to say goodbye to Mr. and Mrs. Lyle and Mrs. Jewell, who have all lived for many years in the parish, but who have now gone to live with their children. We are glad to see our District Nurse home again after her illness.

The Week St. Mary district is a large one which makes heavy demands on those who staff it. We cannot be too grateful to the District Nursing Service. We hope Nurse Jones will soon be quite well again.

The Beacon

Week St. Mary Church Notes   July 1951 Price 2d.

Rector's Letter

In May the chief event in our village life was certainly the re-opening of the chapel after extensive renovations. The weather was perfect for the occasion and the Methodists are to be congratulated on their efficient organisation of the various events. To feed such a number was alone no small undertaking, but it was very well done. And to raise the greater part of the money required on that one day and so much of it by straight out giving, is a result of which they may well be proud.

I would like to say again as I said then, that we are blessed with a friendly relationship in Week St. Mary between Church and Chapel and this we must do our best to foster by co-operating where we can and by being sympathetic and understanding about things in which we are unable to agree.

By the time this is published our new Bishop will have been enthroned. I am sure he will have the prayers and good wishes of us all as had his predecessor. I hope it won't be long before we come to know him and appreciate him as much as we did Bishop Hunkin.

The Rectory Room

We are again in trouble here. An inspection of the floor in the ladies cloakroom brought to light the fact that part of the main floor beams in that area had perished. This will mean some fairly extensive repair work to make the room safe. For this we will have to dip into our very slender reserves. I reckon that over a year's working, if there are no special extras or repairs, the Rectory Room should produce a profit of £8 to £10 which is paid into the reserve fund for future painting and repairs. Unfortunately there always seems to be something needed, a new stove or more crockery. Consequently, in the last four years, while we have drawn heavily on the fund for the repainting of the building, we have not been able to put anything by and so the reserve is at a low ebb. This isn't a plea for funds, but just that you should know how things stand. **NOEL TOWNEND, Rector**

Parish Diary

Ascension Day

Thanks to the co-operation of the day-school teachers we had a good children's service this year as in the past. There was also a slight increase in the number of communicants for which we are thankful.

Ringers' Festival

This was held at Launcells on May 5th. In spite of it being a showery afternoon the Church was crowded. The sermon was preached by Archdeacon Boreham. A busload went from Week St. Mary and stops were made at several towers.

Sunday School Van

On Monday, May 7th, the parish was honoured with a visit from Miss Bartlett the secretary for religious education of the Church Assembly. She brought with her samples of the latest help and methods in the religious teaching of children. Invited to meet her were the Sunday School and Day School teachers and the parents of the Sunday School children. Miss Bartlett gave a most interesting and instructive demonstration and answered many questions.

Chapel Reopening

On May 10th this event brought many visitors to the village. After the official opening in the morning, lunch was served in a marquee. In the afternoon the Whitstone choir gave a concert and the day was concluded with an evening rally.

Whitsun Day

This weekend did its best to make up for Easter by turning out fine and warm. The Services in the morning were well attended, but numbers dropped in the evening. We did our best with the decorations but flowers were scarce due to the lateness of the season and the earliness of the Festival.

Personal

We are grateful to Mrs. J. Cobbledick for taking the place of Mrs. Lyle in the cleaning of the Church brass in conjunction with Mrs. Cotes. Mrs. F. Martin has been in hospital and Mr. Smith is there now. Mrs Martin is home again and we hope Mr. Smith soon will be. Most of the children have had colds and some whooping cough. This has affected our Sunday School attendance. Miss Audrey Jones was married on Whit Monday. The first wedding in the chapel since its renovation. She is now living near Marhamchurch.

The Beacon

Week St. Mary Church Notes   January 1953 Price 2d.

Rector's Letter

Here we are at the beginning of another year. It is my earnest wish that it may be both a holy, a happy and also a prosperous one for us all.

We live in such eventful times, that we can never hope to prophesy what this year will bring forth. The older ones among us may be able to look back to times when life seemed peaceful and secure and when such a future as we have known since 1914 seemed quite impossible. If we can, we should not necessarily regret that these times have gone. I believe that far more spiritual progress has been made as a result of the trials and tribulations of the past forty years than would have been possible under conditions of security and comfort. This is always true and it is the reason why riches, which bring comfort and security, can be such a hindrance to entrance to God's Kingdom. We only stir ourselves when we feel the prick of trial and uncertainty.

Fr. Kingdon's Memorial: You will remember, that when we took the Church collection on the Revel Monday evening following Fr. Claude Kingdon's death, we decided to devote the money to the placing of some small memorial in the Church to commemorate the long succession of sermons which he preached here.

After much thought, we have come to the conclusion that the most fitting memorial and one which would please Fr. Kingdon more than anything, would be the hanging of a Crucifix on the pillar directly behind and above the pulpit and the placing of a small tablet, suitably inscribed, in some convenient spot adjacent to it to indicate the memorial and explain its purpose. Now some may think; "but why a Crucifix and why just there?" The reason is this: It has always been the custom but one that has been discontinued unfortunately in many churches owing to an ignorance of its purpose, to hang a Crucifix behind and above a pulpit. The purpose of all sermons is to set before our minds "Christ crucified" as our hope of Salvation. It is, as St. Paul says, "But we preach Christ crucified."

Now we not only learn by hearing, but also by seeing. (That is why we use pictures so much in school and why seeing someone's example is so much more powerful than hearing what they say). The pulpit Crucifix is a sermon in wood and is in fact the greatest of all sermons, the words of the preacher in the pulpit being a commentary on and an explanation of that sermon. It is eminently suitable then, that above that pulpit, in which Fr. Kingdon preached so often and so eloquently of the benefits of Christ's Passion, we should restore to its rightful place this sign of our Salvation.

By the time you read this the memorial may be in place. It is now in hand, following the unanimous decision of the Parochial Church Council, and when ready, we hope it may be dedicated and unveiled by members of Fr. Kingdon's family. The details of this ceremony will be announced when arranged.

The Revd. M. Y. Hardy: At my request, Mrs. Cotes has kindly written for The Beacon an obituary of Mr. Hardy. In consequence of this, what I was writing on the subject of "the Parish and the Diocese," will have to be carried over to a future edition.

NOEL TOWNEND, Rector

THE REVD. M. V. HARDY by Mrs. Cotes

News of the death of the Revd. M. V. Hardy came with tragic suddenness on Nov. 10th. We had welcomed him and his family with open arms only three months before, when after an interval of 21 years, they had returned to the Rectory while our Rector and his family were on holiday. The warmth of their reception quite surprised him, for he was a man of deep humility. On Nov. 5th, Mr. Hardy had taken the services as usual, returning to the Vicarage after Evensong. Shortly afterwards he collapsed and soon became unconscious and he died twelve hours later of cerebral haemorrhage. The funeral service was held on Nov. 13th in his own church at Flintham, which was beautifully decorated with flowers by some of the parishioners, and his body was cremated at Wilford Hill, Nottingham. It is hoped that a faculty will be obtained for the burial of his ashes in the church at Flintham.

Maurice Victor Hardy was born on Aug. 23rd, 1887. He was the youngest of five brothers and had one sister. He was educated at Dulwich College, then studied Classics at Sidney Sussex Cambridge and took his M.A. degree. He was a keen oarsman. He obtained his theological training at Westcott House and was ordained in Exeter Cathedral; deacon in 1910 and priest a year later.

Mr. Hardy's first curacy was at St. Michael's, Stoke, Devonport. (This church was destroyed by bombing in World War II), There he met Miss Stella M. Cole, daughter of a churchwarden and became engaged to her.

Believing a period of first-hand experience in the Mission Field to be an essential part of the training of all Clergy, he went to Canada in 1913 with the Archbishop's Western Canada Mission. With a number of other Clergy, he worked from a base Mission house at Cardston, a small town with a largely Mormon community in the foothills of the Rocky Mountains in Southern Alberta, only a few miles from the U.S. border. He lived in a small village called Foremost for some time, under very primitive conditions, even baking his own bread. The villagers built a small log church for him, but his parish was 60 miles square and he covered it on horseback, holding services in farmhouse kitchens, with congregations from 15 or 16 miles distant.

Parish Diary

Remembrance Sunday. As usual the two-minute silence was observed in the Church at 11.00 a.m. The memorial service was this year begun in the Chapel and afterwards at the War Memorial in the Square. The British Legion was present in force, but on the whole the congregation was not as large as usual.

The Revd. M. Hardy: A requiem was said in the Church on the Friday after his death and a muffled peal was rung on the following Sunday morning.

The Women's Institute

The W.I. is to be congratulated on an excellent evening's entertainment put on by its members in the Rectory Room on November 15th. A variety concert by members of the village is for us an unaccustomed thing. This attempt drew a large and appreciative audience.

Church Fellowship

There was a good gathering on Dec. 4th to listen to Mrs. Vedrenne, who spoke with enthusiasm and feeling to a deeply interested audience, on her experiences as a hospital nurse and sister. It was obvious to all that she was deeply interested in this work and her talk would have inspired anyone thinking of taking up nursing as a profession.

Personal

We were very sorry to say goodbye to Nurse Jones who had been our district nurse for several years and who had endeared herself to us all by her care for the children and the sick. We wish her success and happiness in her new work and welcome her two successors to our village. We would congratulate David Coles and Sheila Jones on their engagement and wish them every happiness for the future.

The Beacon

Week St. Mary Church Notes   February 1956 Price 2d.

Christmas 1955: Whist Drive

This, the first of our Christmas festivities, was very well attended: a most successful evening, in the spirit of sociability, the number of good prizes won and the gratifying result of £16 12s 8d towards the Church Heating Fund.

Village Celebrations

The origins of the popular annual Week St. Mary Revel are lost in the mists of time although we recall again John Wesley's comment in his journal for 15th September 1746; "A guide, meeting us at Camelford, conducted us to St. Mary Week.... It was the time of the yearly revel, which obliged me to speak very plain".

The first Harvest Queen was Joyce Cobbledick - around 1961

The Harvest Queen is a fairly new innovation. When Week St. Mary Carnival ceased to be held there was a lapse of some years before the Harvest Queen was crowned in Revel Week to take the place of the former Carnival Queen.

High up on the west face of the church which was built in 1643 are three bands of carvings depicting two hounds in full cry after a hare. This could well indicate a connection with the Revel celebrations which have always featured a hunt which met in the square early in the morning of Revel Monday.

This was followed by sports, dancing to a band and fun for the old and younger, including a public tea and a service with a visiting preacher in the evening.

At one time there was a Revel King who was drawn in a farm cart sitting on a pumpkin. This old custom was revived for one year in 1937 when Jack Colwill, sitting on a pumpkin, was crowned 'King' by Rev Hambrook. The King's identity was kept strictly secret until the last moment, adding spice to the occasion.

In former days, celebrations were confined to the Sunday and Monday following the feast day of the patron saint, St. Mary the Virgin. Revel is remembered with great affection by the older inhabitants of the village, not least because Revel Monday meant a day off school. It was a day when any absent member of a family would make a special effort to come home.

The Harvest Queen was crowned as part of the celebrations and her crown, made of corn, was constructed for each Harvest Queen by Mr. Norman Wilton and treasured as a keepsake by the wearer. Many of the old traditions remain though now festivities last a full week, providing entertainment to suit everyone.

The following song was written by Wilfred Rablen, Int.Mus.Bac., F.R.C.O. He was Headmaster of Week St. Mary Council School from about 1903 until the middle of the World War I. He was very musical forming a school choir and entering pupils for some of the County Music Festivals. The song certainly gives a cheery start to Revel time and we are indebted to the late Mrs Vedrenne for producing it.

WEEK ST. MARY HARVEST HUNT AND REVEL

Rise and sing this happy morning:
Hail with joy the festal day.
Week St. Mary holds her revel,
Mount your steeds and ride away.
Join the huntsmen on the moorland,
Parsons, Doctors, Farmers all.
Greet with smiles each jovial sportsman,
Short and fat, and thin and tall.

Refrain:
Shout hurrah! for Week St. Mary:
Shout hurrah! for Revel day.
Jolly boys and buxom maidens
Mount your steeds and ride away!

Ladies fair, with shining tresses
Gaily decked, shall grace our band.
Come my lads, and bring your sweethearts,
Fairest beauties in the land.
Farmer Bunt shall blow the bugle:
Doctor Dick will sing a song.
Hark! the merry bells are pealing.
Get your horses: come along.

Then when all the sport is over
And o'er earth the shadows steal,
To the dear old church we'll wander
Where the Village ringers peal:
Join in harvest hymn and anthem
While the mellow organ rolls:
Render thanks for village comforts,
Pleasant homes and happy souls.

Summer Fete

Somewhere around 1955-57 a Summer Fete, in aid of the Church Heating Fund, was held on the Rectory lawn, Week St. Mary.

The report goes on to say, '...and was opened by Mrs. W. Congdon (Kitsham), made a profit of over £35. Mrs. Congdon was presented with a bouquet of flowers by Avril Coles. During the afternoon, sideshows were kept busy, those in charge being Messrs. Terry Martin, F. A. Swindells, E. Brown and many helpers. The ringing the bottle competition was won by Mrs. Alan Martin [*my mother*] and Mr. Slee from Bradworthy [*my grandfather*], the prize being a bottle of Port.

Mrs. Vedrenne was in charge of the hidden treasure, fully equipped with a "smuggler's map" and these prizes were won by Doreen Horrell and Peter Annett. Also on the lawn, was a cake and sweets stall (in the charge of Mrs. Maddock); and a jumble stall (Mrs. Pearce and Mrs. Masters). Madame Helena did a good trade with her card readings.

A public tea was held in the Rectory Room, convened by Mesdames F. Martin and G. Cobbledick helped by Mesdames L. Hutchings, H. Ridgman, W. Ridgman, V. Coles, J. Colwill and Miss V. Colwill.

Susan, Linda & David Martin

The fancy dress parade followed tea, and was led by the Rector (W. T. Soper) playing, "Country Gardens" on his violin. Prize-winners were: children under 5 - Daffodils and Roses (Linda and Susan Martin- my sisters!); 2, Gnome (Trevor Squire); 3, Charlie Chaplin (Trevor Horrell). Girls under 8 - Polish Girl (Johanna Kaluzinski); Gypsy (Barbara Harris); Buttons and Bows (Avril Coles). Boys - Scarecrow (David Dawe); Zebra Crossing (David Martin - yes, me!); Tommy Tucker (Mervyn Colwill). Girls over 8 - Queen of Hearts (Pat Colwill); Naughty schoolgirl (Doreen Horrell); Dartboard (Jacqueline Colwill). Adults - Charlie's aunt (Mrs. W. Ridgman); Mrs. Mop (Mr. Anderson); Love me, love my dog (Mrs. Pearce). Adult couples - Before and after the Church Heating Fund (Mesdames. J. Colwill and F. Martin).

The judges for the fancy dress were Mrs. Congdon (who presented the prizes), Rev. A. L. Parish (Vicar of St. Gennys), Rev. R. E. Underwood (Rector of Whitstone) and Mrs. Underwood. The day concluded with a dance to music by the Blisland Accordion Band. The M.C. was Mrs. Brown. The competition for the tablecloth was won by Mrs. P. Pearce, who gave it back and it was sold in aid of funds.

Door-stewards for the day's events were Messrs L. W. Vedrenne and F. A. Swindells (for entrance to lawn), P. Smith (tea) and Mr. F. Martin (dance).'

Carnivals

For quite a few years leading up to the 1960's the village played host to an annual Carnival. Typical of the days before television large crowds were drawn to such functions. I can distinctly remember one entry in which I was a cowboy. In another I remember my mother, dressed as a

Me (*the author*) as a cowboy - dated by the cars!

My mother's entry as a Nurse

nurse (nanny) pushing a pram in which was one of the workmen from Creddacott Farm.

Mother had written to Heinz for some decorations for the pram and they sent strip after strip of Heinz baby food labels which were duly used to decorate the pram.

His Majesty King Edward VII - Coronation

Coronation Day was celebrated here on August 9th 1902. The day began early with a merry peal of bells. Holy Communion, with special prayers and intercessions taken from the Authorized Form, was celebrated at 8.30am there was a fair attendance. At 2 p.m. the portion of the Coronation Service not already used, including the Litany, Sermon and Proclamation, was said and the Service, which was attended by about 100 people, concluded with "God Save the King." In the afternoon the festivities took the form of a "High Tea" and "Sports." Bells began to peal again shortly after six and by shortly after 7 the people had gathered together in considerable numbers to the Church (the Nonconformists having their own services in their own Chapels at the same time), and an Evensong of Thanksgiving with a Sermon brought the services of the day to a suitable close. Nothing remained now to be done but to ring the bells once more and to light the huge bonfire.

The whole tone of the day was one of Loyalty and Thankfulness. Much hard work had to be done and we owe a debt of thanks to many willing helpers; the committees for tea, sports, bonfire, and decorations, all deserve the thanks of the whole community; besides these our special thanks are due to the ladies who kindly undertook to preside and help at the tea tables; and if there is one individual to whom we are more indebted than another for his indefatigable zeal I would single out our honorary secretary, Mr. King.

Her Majesty Queen Elizabeth II - Coronation

To celebrate Her Majesty's Coronation on 2nd June 1953, three trees were planted. One, the W.I. tree, was planted by Lady Warren of Marhamchurch on the piece of land by Efford

Stores, owned by Mr. Brewer. The other two were planted on a different day by the Parish Councillors who then stood around the trees and sang "God Save the Queen". These trees are on the grass outside Mr. Brewer's bungalow, Trekelland, and on the Green, Lower Square.

The children were presented with Coronation Mugs. Sports for the children were held and, later, a bonfire for all the Village. There was a Church Service at which the Rector, the Reverend Noel Townend, officiated.

Her Majesty the Queen's Golden Jubilee Celebration

Week St. Mary was a riot of red, white and blue for the Golden Jubilee Celebrations, writes Lesley Booker. A Best Decorated House Competition spurred the residents on to make their houses as pretty as possible for the big day and the result was one of the finest displays in North Cornwall.

In the week before the Bank Holidays there were several events to get people

in the mood for celebration. The first was an Elizabethan Evening held at the Green Inn which was attended by 'Lord and Lady' Booker and their brilliantly costumed guests. The company ate in the Long Room of the Inn and as was the custom of the day had to use their fingers for the banquet.

The Best Costume was judged to be that of 'Lady' Margaret Johns. The guests were grateful to the Landlord, Mr. Vic Thurston and the Serving Wenches, Barbara Thurston and Liam Tye for a very good evening.

On Friday, Saturday, Sunday and Tuesday there were 21 gardens open in the village. The event was organised by Margaret Taylor and was well supported by visitors from all over the parish and beyond.

On the Saturday, the entertainment continued with a Barn Dance in the Green Inn car park, which was very well attended. Mike Caesar-Gordon was cook for the evening and provided a steady supply of hot pasties and burgers to go with cider from the bar. Les Burden was the caller and had no trouble persuading the revellers to dance the night away.

For the Sunday, the children of Jacobstow School re-enacted the Coronation in Week St. Mary Church as part of the Family Service. The children were beautifully dressed and took their roles very seriously. The result was a magical experience, which everyone will remember.

When finally the big day dawned, dull and damp, there was a little concern, but preparations continued and by lunchtime the sun came out and helped to make the square bright and cheerful. There were seven teams of five for 'It's a Knockout' on the village green which was watched by a large crowd, who cheered and drank tea all afternoon. The Street Party continued with a public tea where a vast amount of food appeared as if by magic. The bouncy castle and ball pool were forgotten for some time as this mountain of goodies was consumed.

Competition winners were: children's Jubilee cake, Jasmine Parkin; adult Jubilee cake, Margaret Taylor; plate of vegetables, Hilda Axford; children's posy, Jessica Dolton; small flower arrangement, Norah Jewell; vase of mixed flowers, Ann Gubbin; vase of one type of flowers, Joyce Orchard; odd shaped vegetable, Daniel Parkin. Chris and Allan Chesney of Oaklands won the best-decorated house and the winners of the Knockout Contest were 'The Mad Marys'. Team members were: Jaci Mathews, Annette Dolton, Joy Dolton, Jessica Dolton and Sue Booker. All the prize certificates were presented by Bob Johns of the Robert Johns Leukaemia Fund and the cakes auctioned by Sidney Heard in aid of the Fund. The auction raised over £60.

During the day the final signatures were added to a special card in folder form of village photographs signed by everyone in the Parish, to be sent to the Queen to congratulate her on her Golden Jubilee.

In the evening James Bromell provided a disco in the Square which was enjoyed by young, not so young and old alike.

At 10pm the whole village gathered in the churchyard to see the Jubilee Beacon being lit. The beacon was specially made for the occasion by Tim Ward and shone out into the night to join those at Marhamchurch, Jacobstow, Whitstone, Launcells, High Cliff and Trevose Head which could all be seen from the village. When the crowds left the churchyard their path was lit by dozens of candles which had been set up whilst they watched the spectacle. Dancing continued on the village green until past midnight when it was all hands on deck again to clear away.

The events of the week have all been recorded in photographs, a total of 250 of which are available to choose from, as prints or as a complete collection on CD-ROM. They have been included in a folder, souvenirs of the village celebrations' and added to the Parish Archives.[27]

Week St. Mary Harvest Queen 2005

...and 50 years earlier!

Assembly of the hunt in The Square - Revel 1951

A fine collection of Queens to celebrate some bygone years, with only two missing!

An unhappy Linda Martin despite being under the watchful eye of Miss Retallack (right)

David Coles (right) wearing my grandfather's Army uniform - Carnival circa 1950

Owen Smale provided transport for the Queens for many years

Week St. Mary Carnival 1932

Week St. Mary hunt meet on the village green - circa 1920

170

Week St. Mary Revel hunt meet in The Square 1988

Nothing has changed - 2007 is reportedly our wettest summer since records began!
Week St. Mary Carnival - circa 1953

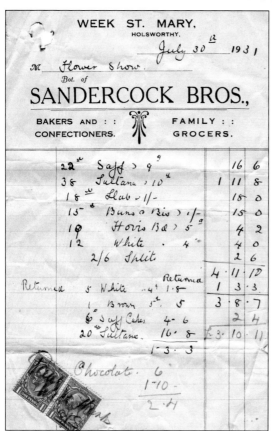

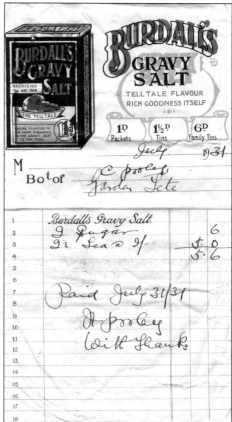

Scarecrow Festival

In 2002 the village grew in population overnight when the first scarecrow festival was held, lasting one week around the August holiday weekend, coinciding with the Craft Fair held in the Parish Church.

This was one of the most successful ideas since the cessation of Week St. Mary Carnival, drawing many visitors to the village, following a prepared map showing their locations in order to assess the skill used by the participating households and apply a donation to suit.

The first year saw a unique event when Rev. Rob Dickenson permitted the scarecrows to be gathered together in the Parish Church for a further week. This equally put many a smile on the faces of visitors to the church.

To complement the Scarecrow Festival and the Craft Fair, cream teas are traditionally served on the village green over the Bank Holiday period. This combination has been run successfully each year and participants are to be congratulated for their ingenuity and creativeness. ∎

The Weather

The South West is no stranger to stormy weather but 1990 was called by many 'The year of the great storms' making the recent period one to go down in the annals for not only the ferocity but the duration. I believe there was only one period of 24 hours during the three weeks that was free of strong winds with rain, thunder, lightning, fog and power cuts thrown in to create variety!

Thursday 25th January 1990 saw the gale force winds hit with tremendous ferocity doing any amount of damage removing tiles, sections of roofs, demolishing sheds, greenhouses, stables, farm buildings and tossing large sheets of lead off the roof of Lambley Park Hotel. The gusts were so strong that it was impossible to walk to the village without periodically clutching the walls; cars stayed firmly in the garage - if it was still standing!

Electricity was lost but we in the village were lucky only losing it for a few hours although our outlying parishioners were without for much longer. Week Ford was without for three days. In one instance cows had to be taken to a neighbouring farm to be milked.

The following Thursday 1st February the gale force winds were reinforced by torrential rain. Roads turned into streams as water streamed off hedges and gushed out of gateways. Gallant work was done throughout the region in repairing the damage and restoring electricity and telephone supplies. One felt very sorry for all these people working in such adverse conditions and often seeing their work destroyed the next day.

However, for Week St. Mary Sunday 11th February proved the sting in the tail, when during the strong winds in the evening one of the two trees in the churchyard came crashing down demolishing the churchyard gate and a corner of the roof of 3 Church Mews. The first intimation Penny and Andrew Simpson had of the impending disaster to their home was when a terrific flash of light illuminated the area. This was followed by a crash. At first they thought this was lightning but the interval before the thunder seemed to point to a storm further away than the noise indicated.

Although the Square was plunged into darkness they had not at this point lost their electricity. Just as well as what met their eyes would have been even worse by torchlight! On going into the bedroom they saw branches right up against the window and on entering the kitchen found a branch of the tree through their ceiling. Amazingly, no windows were broken. On going outside to investigate further they luckily returned for a torch as the electricity lines

were lying at neck height - the cause of the great flash. Jeff Roberts in the Village Shop had to work the following Monday by torchlight.

Bernard Jordan had only been in his house 7 minutes having just returned through those same gates from having locked up the church.

Our two trees were a landmark and from whatever vantage point in the village one looked they framed the church tower - how bare it now looks. Unfortunately the second one had to be removed and was taken down on Tuesday February 20th. Both trees had only been inspected in December and passed safe for another five or six years so their demise was a sad blow.'

Churchwarden, Mrs Molly Colwill, had been checking up and found out that they were 110 years old. They were planted when Tom Bromell's wife's mother (who was a Headon) was born, in 1880 (Tom Bromell was the former owner of Oaklands).

On the Night of March 9th, 1891[28]

With a less violent wind, there would have been a great fall of snow, as great probably as that of January, 1881, when difficulties and disasters painfully comparable with those of the present year were spread broadcast over not only the western portion, but the whole of England - it would have been a snowstorm and not a blizzard!

Bude was cut off from the outside world, except by telegraphic communication. In the roads around Bude the snow was quickly as high as the hedges, so that traffic, even on foot, was rendered impracticable.

Off Scilly, several accidents occurred, but they were neither so numerous nor attended with the same fatal results as those on the coast further east, The ketch 'Ant' Bude, was taken into Plymouth in a disabled condition, and with only two of the crew that remained severely ill from frostbites. On Saturday morning, 14th March, when about 233 miles S.SW. of Scilly, the 'Ant' was sighted some miles off, by the 'Astrea', with her sails down and flying a signal of distress. The 'Astrea' bore down upon her, and Captain Burton sent alongside a boat's crew, who found the captain, H. Hines, and a sailor named Jewell wrapped in the mainsail in a shocking state, and scarcely able to speak.

Their hands and legs were also so much swollen from frostbites and exposure that they could not handle anything or lift themselves up or stand. Brandy and medicine were administered to them, and after a time they sufficiently recovered to be able to inform their rescuers that the 'Ant' was ten days out from Saundersfoot with coals. Four days before a lad named Stapleton had died from exposure, and his body was thrown overboard.

Bude - The outside world and Bude were not so thoroughly estranged during the days succeeding the storm as was the case in some other instances, telegraphic communication remaining unbroken. All the other inconveniences of the blizzard - absence of mail, presence of immense drifts of snow, and similar discomforts - were freely experienced. There was an anxious time among the shipping interest in the port, many of the coasting vessels being at sea at the time the hurricane was raging. On the whole, the damage wrought to the shipping of Bude was not great.

1890 - The first heavy snowfall of the year occurred between the 25th and 28th November with heavy snow falling over England, especially Kent when up to 60 cm of snow was reported.

Another heavy fall of snow occurred in England and Wales between the 18th and 20th December. A snowfall of 45cm occurred at South Petherwin, Cornwall on the 20th.

1891 - 13th March, saw an easterly blizzard. Heavy, fine powdery snow and strong easterly winds raged across south west England, southern England and Wales, with over half a million trees being blown down, as well as a number of telegraph poles. On the 9th (and later?), a great snowstorm in the West of England, trains buried for days: east-north-east gale, shipwrecks, many lives lost, 220 people dead; 65 ships foundered in the English channel; 6000 sheep perished; countless trees uprooted; 14 trains stranded in Devon alone. Although the West Country was the worst affected, Southern England, the Midlands, and South Wales also suffered.

1946/47 - Winter: harsh, post Second World War winter - severe rationing. This was the coldest February on record, and coldest February at Edinburgh since 1764.

One of the harshest winters experienced in the British Isles, though there was little hint of severe weather until after mid January. Also regarded as the snowiest winter in the century, and for perhaps back to the middle of the previous century.

View down a snow-covered Week Green hill

The winter continued at its most savage in March, 1947, hitting particularly hard at a time of fuel and food shortages after the Second World War.

Some very heavy snowfall - a sequence of severe blizzards led to accumulations estimated at between 50 and 120 cm across the English lowlands, with drifts often in excess of 10 feet, and sometimes 15 feet.

The Second World War had been over for only 18 months, fuel was rationed, as well as food and clothing. Power cuts were common, frequent and widespread, and there was a shortage of coal (the main source of heat other than gas), due to transport problems, and the need to divert coal to the power stations. Mean temperature stayed below 0°C for 9 weeks. Bulldozers were diverted from bomb clearance to snow clearance. Ice-breakers had to be used in the River Medway. There were severe losses to agriculture; 2 million sheep died, and the frosts destroyed much of the late potato crop. The aftermath was equally severe, with widespread burst pipes, local flooding as snow melted: a winter of extreme misery.

1947 - The snowy winter of 1947: this event began late, as up until mid-January, although there had been cold spells, the weather was not particularly extreme. This is now thought to be the snowiest winter of the 20th century (and perhaps the snowiest since 1814), with some snow falling somewhere across the country between 22nd January and 17th March and the greater part of the UK had some form of snow cover continuously from 27th January to the 13th March. Level snow depths exceeded 2ft (circa 60cm) and there was much drifting. Much dislocation (railways particularly badly affected - a vital part of the infrastructure at this time) and great hardship emphasized the reduced circumstances the general population were enduring after the recent war.

1975/1976 - The famous drought of 1975/76 was memorable for its severity over most of the British Isles, and also for its exceptional persistence. It produced the highest values for a drought index for Southeast England in three hundred years. Not since 1749/50 had a period from one summer to the following spring been so dry in southern Britain. It was the driest 16-month period on record for England and Wales.

1976 - June/July: No previous heat wave in Britain, nor any since, has ever come close to the duration of this hot spell. From the 22nd June to 16th July, the temperature reached 80°F daily. Even more remarkable, from 23rd June to 7th July, a period of 15 consecutive days, the temperature exceeded 32°C somewhere or other in the country. It was easily the driest, sunniest and warmest summer in the 20th century.

I am sure we all have memories of the standpipes, scattered about the village. Carrying buckets of water back home to use for your essential needs. Several of the local residents, having their own private wells, have said that even through that prolonged dry period they did not see their wells completely dry up.

1978 - (18th/19th February): blizzards/heavy snowfalls experienced over South Western Britain. Ranking alongside the worst snowstorms of the century, particularly that of December 1927, this severe blizzard caused many people to be marooned on this Saturday night in places of entertainment.

Snow drifted well above 10 feet, and 7 lives are reported to have been lost. Winds reached storm-force at times, and snowfall was heavy and prolonged. On the 20th, as warm air encroached from the southwest, with further sleet, snow and freezing rain in places, a thaw of the lying snow led to local flooding.

Without a doubt this slow-moving front produced one of Britain's memorable blizzards comparable with those of 1963, 1947, 1891 and 1881. One major difference between 1891 and 1978 was that Cornwall, in the main, escaped this time, being in the warmer air.

2004 - August: the Boscastle storm. On the 16th, torrential rainfall fell on the headwaters of the two rivers that drain (in combination as the River Valency) through Boscastle. The highest (24hr) rainfall for this event is 200.4mm at Otterham (nr. Boscastle), which fell in under 5 hours.

At Lesnewth (also nr. Boscastle), 85.7mm fell in just one hour at the height of the storm (actually a series of heavy rain-producing cells). An estimate (radar and other evidence) has been made that at least 250mm fell from the storm-complex. Much damage was done in the town to buildings, bridges & vehicles - many of the latter being swept out into the harbour. All boats in the harbour were destroyed (or otherwise lost to the sea). Luckily, no-one lost their life. Flooding also occurred in other parts of N. Cornwall, including Crackington Haven (where structural damage was also evident) and Camelford.

Local recollections

Speaking to many of the more senior members of the village regarding changes in the weather, they echo each other in that the weather has changed dramatically over the past 50 years, or so. Perhaps this is the dreaded 'global warming' that is now being warned of.

Winters were more severe with periods of freezing conditions, whereas the summers were prolonged and consistently sunny. The story is that at the beginning of summer you put your coat somewhere, then as summer turned into autumn you had to go and search for your coat again!

The summer harvests were more regulated with the virtually guaranteed sunny, dry weather. Even I remember the fine summer periods spent riding on the combine harvester, manually bagging corn as it poured from the hoppers. Dusty, dry, and tiring work, although it was pleasing in a way to see, at the end of the day, all the bags of corn lying on the ground where once the corn had been standing. ■

The Village Green looking picturesque - Nov 2005

Cattle Market

The village has had a market, according to records, from around 1221. The permission to hold a market in the village was granted to a Richard de Wyke.

For most of us the market conjures up images of The Square and nearby roads bustling with cattle lorries, tractors and trailers, landrovers and cars with trailers, all with signs of having recently conveyed some kind of livestock.

It is understood that lorries were getting bigger and the amount of traffic in general was the downfall for a small village with narrow access roads. The market eventually closed and moved to the more-accessible market at Hallworthy.

Week St. Mary bids farewell to the Market

The hammer came down on 69 years of history at Week St. Mary on Saturday, 10th January 1987, when the weekly fatstock market closed down; a victim of its own success.

The market, which handles on average 120 cattle and 1200 sheep a week, has outgrown its site at Week St. Mary. Auctioneers Kittow's are transferring it to the larger Hallworthy premises.

Celebration mingled with sadness as farmers gathered for the final sale. Jack Ridgman, a former fatstock officer, recalled seeing the first Week St. Mary cattle market in 1918.

It started when two local farmers, Chris Venning and William Paynter, sold six cattle and sixteen sheep in the village square.

Said Mr. Ridgman: "I was seven years old. At those early markets the cattle were all Devons with loop horns. I saw the market start and now I will see it finish, but it's a sad day for Week St. Mary."

Mr. Cliff Orchard, the market Chairman for twenty-four years, has bought more stock there than anyone. He remembered the market closing for a time in 1947 because of a local outbreak of foot and mouth disease. The harsh winter of 1963 also prevented the market from operating.

But he also recalled happier moments: "About two years ago some sheep were being unloaded and they ran off across the village square, they got into a holiday chalets site where there was a cover over an outdoor swimming pool one of the sheep jumped onto the cover, went straight through it and ended up in the pool!"

Mr. Orchard said the market had been good for Week St. Mary, but people had to accept that change was inevitable. "Prosperity has brought us some problems, but at least we are going out on a high note," he added.

Week St. Mary sub-postmaster, Mr. Jeff Roberts, said the market closure was bad news, but he understood why it had to go. "Some villagers are pleased because it will be quieter here, but I think the majority are sad to see it close," he said.

The closure does not mean the end of work for Mr. Gerald Horrell, who has cleaned the market for more than thirty years. He will be dismantling the pens, many of which will go to Hallworthy. Kittow's became involved with the market in the 1920s when they acquired land adjacent to the square.

Senior partner, Mr. John Dennis, who has been coming to the market for thirty-eight years, was there on Saturday as his sons, Peter and Richard, carried out the last auction with Mr. Simon Alford. On offer were 88 cattle, 545 sheep and a solitary pig.

When the last graded animal was sold, Mr. John Dennis took the microphone and thanked farmers, the Ministry of Agriculture officials, hauliers and market staff for their help over the years.

He told 'The Post', "For sentimental reasons I am saddened to see the market close, but it is progress, we must have larger premises Week St. Mary market is a victim of its own success."

Mr. Dennis said that at Hallworthy the same strict market procedures would be carried out; cattle for grading would have to be on the premises by 10.30 am or they would be ineligible. The market will be missed at Week St. Mary's Green Inn, where landlady Mrs. Diane Hobbs cooked up to 30 meals each Saturday for farmers. Mrs. Hobbs penned a 20-line poem to mark the closure, which ended on an optimistic note: "We've had plenty of fun, now bidding is done, staff at the Green Inn can lay in till one".

Mrs. Hobbs said "We're very sad to see the market go, not just because of the business it brought, but because it's part of the village".

The Green Inn had a special market day licence extending its Saturday lunchtime session to 4 pm, but the pub will now close at the standard time of 2.30 pm.

Hallworthy, which already operates a market on Fridays, will hold its first Saturday market this week the only Saturday fatstock market between there and Taunton.[29] Reproduced by courtesy of the Cornish & Devon Post Series of Newspapers. ■

Charities

Like many villages in the land, local charities exist to further the needs of others less fortunate and our village is no exception. There are two significant charities in operation in the parish, one ancient and one modern.

Poor Man's Piece

An area of 2R 27P (2 Rods 27 Perches or Poles), managed by a body of Trustees, is to be let for the use of good husbandry and grazing only. The tenant is responsible for the upkeep of the hedges and ground.

From the recital in a feoffment, bearing the date 11th January 1710, it appears that a "little piece or quillet of land, containing by estimation half an acre, called the Poor Man's Piece, lying in the borough of Week St. Mary, given by John Clark, was conveyed, in trust, for the use of the poor, decayed, lame, impotent and decrepit people of the same parish for ever. The profits to be taken by the collectors and overseers of the poor for the uses of the aforesaid."

This land is let yearly and produces a rent of variable amounts which is then distributed among the poor, in small sums, by the churchwardens at Michaelmas and Christmas.

The rent in 1786 was £1 1s 0d (1 guinea); in 1835-6 was £5; in 1863-4 the income was down to £4 3s 0d and by the 1890s it was £2 10s 0d. The present rent is paid at Lady Day and varies slightly as the land is put out to tender every three years.

The records of the charity had been kept in the Parish Council Minute Book since its inception after the Local Government Act of 1894 until it was pointed out in 1969 that it was legally out of order to do so. From that time the records were entered into a separate book and the Parish Council were advised to nominate two members as Trustees of the charity, then they could continue to receive reports pertaining to the accounts of the said charity.

It is remarkable that the income from such a piece of land should continue to be made available for the poor for nearly 300 years but it must be noted that on more than one occasion discussions were made regarding the possible sale of the land. It has been noted that such a sale, if approved by the Charity Commission, could only be sanctioned if the funds received are only used to follow the basic philosophy as set out in the original terms of the founders wishes.

The 1985 Charity Act does allow a change of direction if the charity is considered to be obsolete and in such cases the new nature of the charity must still be considered to be in the spirit of the original gift.

A letter regarding the charity from the Charity Commissioners, dated 1919, states:

Charity Commission
Ryder Street
St. James', S.W.1
5th May 1919

County Cornwall
Place Week St. Mary
Charity Poor Man's Piece

Madam,

In reply to your letter of the 29th ultimo, I am to say that it appears from the Report of the Former Commissioners for Inquiring Concerning Charities, made in the early part of last century, that a piece of land containing about half an acre, called Poor Man's Piece, lying in Week St. Mary and given by John Clark, was conveyed in trust for the use of the poor, decayed, lame, impotent and decrepit people of the said Parish for ever. At that time the land was let yearly and produced a rent of about £5 which was distributed amongst the poor in small sums by the Churchwardens at Michaelmas and Christmas.

The Commissioners have little, if any, further information about the Charity and it is understood that the information contained in the Report was taken from a recital in a Deed dated 11th January, 1710. This Deed should be in the custody of the Trustees.

I am, etc.,

G.C. Bower

To: Miss E.J. Tuke
Clerk to the Parish Council
Week St. Mary
Holsworthy

Robert Johns Leukaemia Fund - Registered Charity No: 1050537
The R.J.L.F was formed in 1983 and is now run by three trustees. Namely, Bob Johns M.B.E (Roberts Father), Hazel Cartwright and Roy Cobbledick, in memory of Robert, son of Bob, who fought the disease for five long years but unfortunately lost the battle at age 11.

His treatment centres were the Leukaemia, Cancer, Ward 5 at Freedom Fields Hospital in Plymouth, Devon, for children; this has now been moved to Plymouth's main hospital, Derriford. Also, the Royal Marsden Hospital in Sutton, Surrey, where in later stages, he went for bone marrow and research.

Over the years Bob has raised money by various means; cycle rides, 'Kick Starts', Sinclair C5 round Cornwall and Fun Days. Even this year a small team of cyclists are riding from Land's End to John O'Groats to raise funds for the Leukaemia Fund.

The money raised by the fund is divided between these two centres every year. Few expenses are incurred, as they are mainly absorbed by the trustees.

It was announced in the 2002 New Years Honours list that Bob was to receive an M.B.E. for his tireless work in raising awareness for this childhood leukaemia, having raised in excess of £120,000 to date and showing no sign of slowing down!

Bob Johns was presented his M.B.E. by H.R.H. Prince Charles, Duke of Cornwall. Bob was dressed in traditional Cornish tartan kilt. It was said that Prince Charles instantly recognised the Cornish tartan and emblem as being 'his'!

Over the years Bob has organised many events varying from 'Kick Start' to 'Fun Day' with some amazing support acts.

Well done Bob! ■

Wild West display - Fun Day August 2003

A Walk To Week St. Mary

This article was composed by the following ladies of Week St. Mary Women's Institute; M. Hart, H. Hutchings, J. Uglow and C. Treleven. (circa: 1972)

The start of the walk:

The start of the walk looks like many hundreds of farm tracks throughout the county. It is not even signposted with a 'Public footpath' sign, merely bearing the name of the farm, North Broompark. It lies between the villages of Week St. Mary and Jacobstow, near the north Cornish coast at Widemouth Bay. Pause for a moment at the gate to the track and look over the field gate on the opposite side of the road. Here is a view of the typical countryside of the area, gently undulating farmland, with tree-filled valleys and the sea in the distance.

The track is of beaten earth and stone, with a grassy centre and is driveable as far as the farm. Until a few years ago visitors had to leave their cars at the gate and walk the four-tenths of a mile to the farm. Now history swings full circle and vehicles can use the road again. Less than fifty years ago this was a main route into Week St. Mary. Local inhabitants in their fifties can remember people driving along it with pony and trap to shop in the village. It had been used by generations of farmers taking their grain to the mill and bears the name of the Old Mill Road. Why did this more direct route into the village fall into disuse? The distance is only half that of the present road and the gradient of the hill no steeper than that of today's road. Did the coming of the motorcar, making it easier for farmers and their wives to travel longer distances to larger shopping centres sound its death knell?

The track is sheltered for the first part of its length, on the north side by a typical Cornish hedge or bush-topped bank, and on the other side is bordered by open fields. The hedge consists mainly of hawthorn, blackthorn, hazel, ash, oak and willow, which gives it, by Professor Hoskin's theory an age of approximately 600 years. Amongst the main varieties are odd specimens of mountain ash, alder and silver birch, the whole entwined with blackberry, wild rose and honeysuckle and fronted with gorse.

It is seen at its loveliest in the spring, with new green leaves appearing and the whole taking on its cloth of gold as the gorse bursts into full bloom, Halfway down the first field is a wild rose which differs from its neighbours, being a very dark pink, almost red.

All through the year a few flowers can be found in this sheltered hedge. Red campion, hawkbit and the odd daisy can be found even in the coldest weather. In their various seasons can be seen bluebells, buttercups, red campion, hawkbit, daisy, primrose, celandine, herb robert, stitchwort, knapweed, dandelion, silverweed, foxglove, barren strawberry, selfheal, ground ivy, woundwort, vetch and speedwell. Again, perhaps the loveliest time is spring when the bank is starred with clumps of primroses and large areas take on a blue haze as big patches of dog violets burst into flower. A single root of common toadflax flourishes just before the third gate. Halfway down the second field are several yellow broom bushes. The survivors perhaps of larger numbers from which the two farms took their names? This second field becomes a carpet of white clover in summer and the air resounds with the humming of the myriad of insects for which it becomes a happy hunting ground.

On a clear day Rough Tor and Brown Willy can be seen to the right, rising above their neighbours on Bodmin Moor. In front the slopes of Dartmoor are visible for a while. To see these clearly is not a good sign, it usually means rain will fall within a few hours. Westwood Common crowned with its Iron Age camp and the tower of Week St. Mary church can be seen immediately in front of us. The old track can be seen zig-zagging its way up the side of the hill.

The smaller ones made by mice, voles, weasels and stoats. Except for rabbits, which are numerous, these are seldom seen, but with the rare fall of snow their tracks are seen on its white surface.

The hedges are alive with the songs of birds, mainly of the more vocal varieties, hedge sparrow, thrush, robin, blackbird, bullfinch, chaffinch and yellow hammer. The quiet brown wren may be seen creeping about the bushes in search of food, while a lark sings overhead and in summer the swallows sweep over the meadows with their darting flight. Rooks, also occasional carrion crows search the fields for food and a member of the hawk family can usually be seen hovering in its quest for prey. These are usually sparrow hawks, with an odd kestrel and a pair of buzzards, which nest in the valley below us. The crows resent their presence and mob them in a daring attempt to drive them to hunting grounds further away. This pair of buzzards seem to hatch but one chick a year. In July a third and young bird appears, but by autumn the parents are alone again. A pair of ravens also nest in the valley and fly over with their distinguishing croak.

As we go through the third gate on the track the hedge is now on the south side, but it does not change in appearance. A few wild daffodils appear in this stretch in the spring. We pass the farmhouse, a small, traditional stone and cob cottage. Around it are more varieties of birds, mainly tits and wagtails. Sometimes one is fortunate enough to catch a glimpse of a green woodpecker, who disturbs the peace with his laughing cry. The field by the house is a favourite meeting place of magpies. As many as ten gather here at a time.

> One for sorrow, two for mirth
> Three for a wedding, four for a birth
> Five for silver, six for gold
> Seven for a secret, never to be told
> Eight for heaven, nine for hell
> And ten for the devil himsel'

Such was the rhyme told me by an old country woman.

This area too, is the meeting place for migratory birds. The telegraph and electricity wires sag in autumn with the weight of hundreds of starlings and swallows preparing for their long flight. In the second week of September a few goldfinches arrive. Their numbers gradually increase until a flock of at least two hundred can be seen feeding on the thistles and dancing through the air, a brightly coloured throng. In the first week of October they disappear overnight, not to be seen again until the following September. Jays scream in the wooded edges of the fields, but are seldom seen in the more open parts.

As we pass the farmhouse the track becomes less well defined. Our only indication is a slight depression in the ground by the hedge, just over the width of a cart, and a difference in the grass. The old stone track is still below the grass, only an inch or two beneath the surface. It can be felt quite easily if a stick is pushed into the ground. This means that water does not drain away so well here and the grass is usually greener than the rest of the field. Along the first stretch of hedge from the farm is a patch of bank where mushrooms are found in late autumn, growing on the bank and not, as would be expected, on the grass below it. We go through yet another gate.

In this field peacock butterflies are seen in great numbers in late summer. Butterflies, alas, seem to be getting scarcer, although a few can always be seen along the way in spring and summer. Brimstones are the first to appear, followed by the grizzled skipper, red admiral, painted lady, cabbage white and tortoiseshell. In some years they appear in great numbers. 1971 was an excellent year, but 1972 was a very poor one, probably due to the wet cold spring.

The next field has a lot of rushes growing in it and bears the name of Goosey Platt. Were the Michaelmas geese fattened here in years gone by? The boggy patch halfway down the field was once a clear running spring, the water supply for the farm we have just passed. What an effort it must have been to carry the water up the hill every day. A few new flowers appear in the field, ragged robin, devil's bit scabious, St. Johns wort, and purple loosestrife.

Within its sheltered hedges appear the earliest and juiciest blackberries. Sometimes a cock pheasant flies up from under one's feet, with its harsh 'korr-kok'. The track goes through another gate and on to a harder road. Here is a meeting-place of several track ways. Our path turns left and almost immediately right again, and then we have to ford a stream. The footbridge provided is not as wide as the stream and it is difficult to cross except in near drought conditions. In the stream which runs along the hedges to the left one might be fortunate to see a lamprey. They have been sighted, but only rarely, I was also lucky to see a ring-ousel here in the autumn.

The path now enters its most interesting stage historically. It goes into the yard of Burycourt, an old farmhouse with a few cob outbuildings. The house has been fortunate in finding an owner who has carefully restored the interior. It was the birthplace 400 years ago of Diggory Wheare.

He was the first Camden Professor at Oxford. Later he became the Principal of Gloucester Hall, now Worcester College. He wrote several scholarly works and on his death was buried in the chapel of Exeter College.

Leave the track here for a few moments to explore the 'dig' behind the present house. With the house on your left you will see a gap in front of you closed with sheep netting. It is easy to get round this and on to the 'dig'. The 'dig' is a 13th century manor house built of stone on the site of an earlier wooden building. It started as a large single hall and grew over the years into a sizeable complex of buildings. Excavation of the moat has been started recently and has revealed a double gatehouse, one on each side of the moat, with the site of the drawbridge in between the two. If you stand with your back to the present house the chapel is immediately to the left of the gatehouse. The altar site can be seen and the stone benches along the walls. To the left of the chapel is the original great hall that gradually extended round the site into the larger house. The mill stones used as hearths are still in place; the foundations of the outside staircase to the upper storey can be traced; the well is easily found and the two-tier toilets, the upstairs one originally jutting out further over the moat than the lower one. This year the site of wooden postholes of an earlier building have been found, indicating the existence of a wooden building prior to the stone one. As a result of this discovery further excavation will take place in the spring of 1973. Most of the stone from the old manor house was used in the building of Burycourt. The older house is believed to be the manor of Penhallam, mentioned in the Domesday Book. The name still exists in a farm a short distance away. There is some rivalry between the two owners as to who has the real Penhallam.

Various tales exist of buried treasure. There is a story of a crock of gold hidden at Burycourt, whilst the owner of Penhallam, an old man of 87, tells the tale of a king visiting the manor. He rode out for the day and whilst he was away some catastrophe overwhelmed the house, burying the king's treasure, which, according to my informant has never been recovered. If only us knew where to dig' he sighs, 'us ud find him'. I can hardly believe the king would ride away without making some attempt to recover his belongings. The old manor house of the dig was depopulated during the Black Death, 1348-9. Some two hundred years later Burycourt was built from its stones.

We go back into the yard of Burycourt and take the gate leading out of it and into a field. An old track goes up the hill, but disappears eventually. This field bears the name of the Bowling Green, with the one behind it being Town Place, indicating that at some time there was a settlement here. Perhaps the track once led to it. It is hoped that one day an exploratory trench may be dug across the area as it is believed to be the site of a Dark Ages village. Again local legend has a tale that this was where a battle was fought in the War. Was it a Civil War skirmish at the time of the Battle of Stratton? Or was it a Viking raid up the valley to the old settlement? Or was it an even older fight connected with the Iron Age camp on the hill we shall soon be climbing? Unless the proposed archaeological exploration comes up with the answer, we shall never know.

The present path runs along the bottom hedge of the field and crosses the wooded valley, recently reset with trees, by way of a wire-fenced path, with a gate at each end. It starts to climb the slopes of Westwood Common now.

The old road ran higher up the hill than the present path and could be seen zig-zagging its way up the slopes from the other side of the valley. The new path may have been originally made by the sheep, which roam the hill, but it is impossible to follow the old road now, for the patches of bracken, gorse and bog which encroach upon it.

There was once a large patch of woodland here, for this was the Westwood bought by Thomasine Bonaventure for the poor of Week St. Mary. Thomasine, daughter of a local farmer, was taken to London in 1463 by a rich London merchant, Richard Burnsby, who was impressed by her beauty, to become a servant to his wife. When his wife died he married Thomasine. His death left her a wealthy widow. She married again; on this marriage to Thomas Gall, she gave Westwood to the poor. 20 acres of woodland copse in the neighbourhood were bought and 'conveyed by the gracious lady, Dame Thomasine Gall, to feofees and trustees for the perpetual use of the poor of Week St. Mary, for fewel, to be hewn in pieces once a year, and finally and equally divided for evermore, on the vigil of St Thomas the twin'.

Once more widowed, she married a third time. This husband was John Percyval, goldsmith and usurer. He was a wealthy alderman who became Lord Mayor of London and was knighted by the king. Thomasine was presented to the king - Henry VII - who instructed her husband to make sure his wife was true - 'for she comes of the burly Cornish stock and they be ever rebels in blood and bone'.

The track continues through the wood, passing mainly through oak trees much smaller than usual, almost of the dwarf variety and holly bushes. On the top of the hill is an Iron Age camp. Little of this remains, an odd line of ditch and rampart being just visible in the present hedges. The track leaves the wooded slopes and climbs upwards into the farmyard of Ashbury. It curves to the left through the farmyard, although a bridle path goes straight on to Week Green. Unfortunately it has become so overgrown as to be impassable and the rather uninteresting track through two fields from the farm to the road must be taken. This brings us to the outskirts of Week St. Mary, where a few traces still remain of the college founded by Thomasine Bonaventure, who left the money for it in her will. The will has been recently saved from export to the USA. If a circular walk is required, turn left after leaving Ashbury instead of going into the village. The next left turn for Poundstock is taken. The road rapidly descends to Week Ford between high Cornish hedges. From the ford, now bridged, the hill climbs up through newly re-forested land. This wood has been mainly set with conifers. On the right hand side of the road a local beekeeper has a colony of hives. The road is completely canopied over by trees that keep the vegetation on the banks sparse, mainly ferns and lesser cowslips. At the top of the hill turn left for Jacobstow. On this stretch of the road widespread views of the coast and countryside can be seen.

Lundy Island is often visible -

> Lundy plain, sign of rain
> Lundy high, sign of dry
> Lundy low, sign of snow

So runs the old rhyme.

191

Bude and Stratton can be seen and on the higher ground above Bude, the two big dishes of the radar installations at Cleave camp can be seen, looking as though they have stepped out of the pages of a Science Fiction book. The road goes by three farms, Hele Barton on our right, Trehausa and Penhallym on our left. In summer the banks are full of wild strawberries. The last farm of Penhallym has been mentioned before. The present owner tells stories of a small village which once existed here. The family once possessed a map showing this, but unfortunately this was lost by a local bank - where it had been deposited for safety!

There was a row of houses on the opposite side of the road to the present farmhouse and a blacksmith's shop, whilst by the gate of the farm stood a cobbler's workshop. Nothing remains of these buildings. 'I remember my father ploughing in the last stones of the walls', I was told. In one of the farm fields is the site of the well from which the water for Christenings in Jacobstow church was drawn. Jacobstow church was once called St James of Penhallym, now the Penhallym has been dropped. In the field by the road to the left of the farmhouse a few remnants of very old cob wall can be seen. They are now so overgrown with brambles as to be barely discernable from the present hedges. And so round the last corner and to the gate where we started our walk. ■

Recollections

As part of the necessary research for this book I, along with my sister Linda, had the pleasure of speaking to several local people. They have kindly allowed me to publish some of their recollections about growing-up and life in the Week St. Mary area.

In alphabetical order of surname:

Glennys Baker

Born in Pyworthy around 1930, she remembers that they lived in rented accommodation. Her father had one of the first cars in Pyworthy and recalls visiting markets at Week St. Mary, Wainhouse Corner, Stratton and Holsworthy.

The family moved to Stewarts farmhouse in 1944. At that time it was partly rented accommodation and this is where George, originally from North Petherwin, was living. He was to become her husband.

In those early days at Stewarts House the men would go threshing during the winter whilst the women would look after the milking, etc., whereas the summer months would see up to 22 paying guests staying in the house while the men did the milking!

Because of WWI there was little meat available and they would shoot rabbits or kill chickens.

When married they moved into the house where Glennys still lives. George was a farmer, helping his brother before working for Unilever and BOCM. It was around this time that she recalls mains water coming through the village.

George, like so many, kept some stock and therefore couldn't leave the animals to go on holiday. They went to Blackpool once but George was 'as miserable as sin' until he could get back to his animals. Holidays were always difficult for those keeping animals.

Glennys warmly remembers the local carnivals - one entry was called 'Smiling Through' which she shared with Derek Brewer.

Like others spoken to, she often visited the many shops in the village, like Mrs Pooley's store, whose husband had a tailor's workshop upstairs and ran a taxi service, and Brewer's shop, mainly for groceries and sweets, but also had a showroom upstairs for dresses and hats.

Wartime rationing gradually eased after the war so Glennys went into Brewers and asked for some chocolate; being told they didn't have any she said that there was a bar in the shop window - the bar was presented to Glennys and she discovered that the contents were actually made of wood! Sweets were one of the last items to have rationing removed.

In the early days of television it was never turned on if the local preacher came to tea.

Pat Barriball

Although born in Plymouth during the blitz she moved to Marhayes by the time she was 1½ years old. Marhayes, in olden days, was a manor of Week St. Mary and traditionally was responsible for the right hand side of the church and when possible they still sit in the right hand pews.

One of a large family of girls, Pat recalls a good life of growing up on a farm. There was a pump in the kitchen and an open fire with a clome oven. Washing day was spent using copper boilers with cold-water tanks for rinsing the clothes.

Like most farmers offspring, growing up meant completing chores around the farm or house - Pat preferred the farm chores. As a young girl she had chickens to look after, then, from the age of about 9 years progressed to looking after the pigs.

Sundays was a hectic time for the family; chores to be done in the mornings like feeding the bullocks, then walking up to the village for the morning church service in their Sunday best. Preparations would be under way on the Saturday so as to save time in the mornings.

Her dad would clean out the van and put seats in the back to take them to the rectory for Sunday School in the afternoons, only to return and change clothes before finally changing into their best clothes for the Sunday evening service!

As the girls became older they would often cycle up to the village, including mid-week for bell ringing practice. The convoy would be led by the cycle fitted with a front light and followed by the bicycle sporting a rear light!

Pat often walked on her own up to the village - not something that many would feel safe doing in this modern age!

Although in Week St. Mary parish they attended Marhamchurch School and used a Bude doctor when necessary but in the main were good supporters of Week St. Mary activities.

Market days would often see the girls walking with bullocks whilst dad brought sheep up in the van; only to turn round and walk back, once there.

Once in the village they did not have much time for shopping as most essential things were delivered; groceries by Will Martin, meat by Coles and Sandercock's would leave bread in the milk churn to save driving up and down the lane. In the days of milk churns many things were placed in a churn for the farmer to collect later in the day, especially newspapers.

Main shopping was completed at Holsworthy, often by travelling to Bridgerule railway station and catching a train to the town, returning later in the day laden with goods. Pat recalls sitting on the back of her mum's bicycle both going and returning from the station.

To attract their father's attention when working outside they used to ring a bell - this bell came from Week St. Mary School.

The Rectory Room was responsible for Pat meeting her future husband and recalls the many dances, socials, concerts and parties held there. The dance floor would be sprinkled with Lux flakes to aid the ballroom dancing.

Bob Booker

Living in Clifton Tenement, Bob says it was some time before they fully realised what a gem the house was, until they started pulling it about. The most marvellous planking, forming a dividing wall from the location of the stairway, was found underneath many layers of packing and wallpaper. Now restored to its former glory it has added such atmosphere to the room and building alike.

The house is approximately 400 years old but may have been rebuilt about 200 years ago. This is supported by the fact that the 'modern' stairs are not wide enough to fill the original gap between the two opposing walls. It is possible that Clifton Tenement was a single story building before being continually modernised over the centuries.

Like many houses originally thatched Clifton Tenement was re-roofed with corrugated galvanised sheeting over the orginal thatch. When Bob investigated the roofing structure he removed the metal sheeting and had the thatch replaced.

Earlier this year Bob wrote in the Parish Magazine: "I consider it to have been a privilege to have represented you on the District Council for the past eight years. I would like to thank all the residents who voted for me and I apologise to you for not having succeeded for another term. I am of course disappointed that I am unable to continue to represent you in this capacity. On the 3rd of May I took a walk around the village and reflected on my time as a district councillor. After eight years of campaigning lobbying and debating, I felt that I had achieved some quite substantial benefits for my local community. Walking up the back lane to Week Green I used the 'not so new path'; the renovation of which I successfully negotiated, and prevented the cable company from ripping up the centre of the village. It is still there and used regularly. It remains a superb asset to our community. On reaching Week Green and walking past houses, I remembered my success 3 years ago in fighting the Valuation Office in St Austell and winning revaluations on a number of properties which had been incorrectly valued for property tax. This achieved a reduction in council tax and refunds for a number of residents who had been unfairly banded in 1991 some of whom had previously appealed and lost.

I descended the hill and passed Ashbury Grove. In 1993 this allocation of land for housing was recommended to NCDC by the Parish Council long before I became a councillor. I was one of only eight residents who responded to the initial consultations carried out! I voiced an opposition to the location of this particular housing allocation. The public local inquiry and inspectors report which followed produced only three responses! Two of these responses from residents requested a larger allocation for housing. Was this why I became a councillor? Building on this land was predetermined before I was ever elected as a district councillor. I was however extensively involved in improving the district's model 106 Agreement. This restricted a proportion of these houses to 'local need' housing which we have been so desperately short of. Just before the first occupancy, allocations were made on this site. After many years of lobbying I finally helped to achieve 'Local Priority' status for silver and gold band applicants with a local connection making it easier for youngsters to be housed in their own parish.

I have kept residents informed through the pages of the parish magazine on a wide range of issues. I did this first, as a Parish Councillor, then as District and finally as a County Councillor. I wrote my layman's guide to the planning system and serialised it over a number of issues. This was done to specifically help residents on a couple of issues at the time. I hope this still helps residents to understand the process and how to make representations when they have planning concerns.

Later on May 3rd when I entered the polling station and saw the name of our district ward 'Week St Mary and Whitstone', I remembered how I had worked with adjoining parishes both during the District Boundary Review and the County Boundary Review to ensure that both these decisions reflected our affinity with our neighbouring parishes. This lobbying of the Boundary Commission in London prevented us from being arbitrarily linked to the urban edges of Bude or Launceston as had been proposed. This has allowed our rural needs to be properly represented.

I arrived back in the square and looked across at the post office and wondered about the consultation which The Post Office Network recently carried out. I hope that my response along with others will help to keep this vital facility open.

There were of course disappointments like the lookout tower which I failed to get the funding for and the new entrances at Week Orchard and Higher Exe which were refused and subsequently granted after appeals! But contrary to the belief of some, councillors are not issued with a magic wand. I have never, and never will promise anything other than to work hard for the benefit of my local community. This I believe that I have done and I continue to do so (although in a more limited capacity) as your County Councillor."

David & Sheila Coles

David & Sheila, born in the same year, went to Week St. Mary school at the same time and have been together ever since. They both mention Miss Retallack who was quite firm with a ruler - Miss Retallack will be mentioned several times in this book!

His father learnt the butchers trade from Mr. Dennis of Lambley for 2/6 (two shillings and six pence or 'half-crown') per week.

While David went on to Bude Grammar School and learnt his trade as a butcher and farmer, Sheila worked at Sandercock's shop. He also recalls Sandercock's getting water from the village pump in the Square using a trolley upon which was placed a big tank, to take to the bakery, at the rear of the shop, for baking the bread.

Growing up saw David in the choir for many years while Sheila attended the chapel; he also started bell-ringing from about the age of 15 years.

Church and chapel outings were well attended and often found them at Salthouse, at Widemouth Bay, where they would sit on forms and have their meals.

During the war years 10 year-old David worked in his father's butcher's shop and was responsible for stamping the ration books. They used to go to Bude Meat Supply to get the rationed amounts for the village.

The evacuees arrived at the chapel and David can still see them crying, clutching their gas masks - everyone agrees it must have been a most traumatic time for the children, being forced to leave their loved ones and live with complete strangers.

Sheila remembers that they had two evacuees from Golders Green while David remembers that Colin Tarrant lived with his auntie whilst his sister Audrey was billeted with the Masters' at the Temperance Hotel.

Life was not all dull, at about 14 years he went to stay with an auntie in London and went to Wembley stadium - the entrance fee then was a massive 10 shillings (50p)!

David and Sheila both took part in village activities; like many parishioners they recall how the local carnival attracted many hundreds from outlying villages and towns. On one occasion David rode a horse wearing 'Pop' Martin's army uniform (my grandfather!). They also remember seeing silent films of Charlie Chaplin in the Rectory Room.

Den Colwill

One of the most senior members of Week St. Mary parish, Den was born at Week Green some 95 years ago. The family moved to Red Lion House before settling at Reeve House in the 1920s. The second eldest of 11 children Den and his siblings all attended Week St. Mary School.

Mr. Leggo, the teacher at that time, used to play football with the children and Den remembers accidentally kicking him in the leg - in those days shoes had steel section on the soles and it must have been quite a graze! Shoes were repaired by Mr. Higgins in the local shoe shop. Mr. Leggo was an old army man and you could tell what sort of mood he was in by the way he marched around.

Before attending school 10 year-old Den would have to milk 2 cows and like so many farmers sons would miss school to help with the harvests. He would go home for dinner and often could hear the school bell ringing before he got back so would have to run to avoid being too late!

Den's uncle Tom joined the army at 16 years of age by lying about his date of birth, as did so many, to fight in WWI. Tom was taken prisoner during the fighting in Turkey and nothing was heard for some time. Den remembers the great excitement when it was found that he was alive and well - that Christmas the family had a tremendous family party upon his return to Reeve House.

My grandfather (P.H.S. Martin) helped his family with the farm accounts. Den says that he was good at maths but didn't learn too much towards the end of his school life. His gran's family (Dennis) used to live at Lambley and on Sundays would walk as far as the junction together then would part for gran to attend chapel and grandfather to go to church.

During the First World War Den often saw the airships passing over the village (see chapter 12) and can remember going to Langford and watching about 20 men pulling down on ropes to bring the airship to the ground before tying it up to large weights.

He believes that Len Maddock, fresh out of the navy, had one of the first vehicles in the village, including a bus that was originally kept at Reeve House.

Den is one of only a few that can remember the blacksmith's forge being on the corner of the junction of the Bude road. At the age of 20 years he bought an AJS 500cc motorbike for £15. The policeman at Week St. Mary was all right but the policeman at Whitstone used to lie in wait for Den to pass, often catching him with no back light or poor brakes!

Despite Den's advanced years he still drives to various whist drives and occasionally plays skittles if the team are short of a player. He still tends his garden and bakes cakes; he prefers them to bought cakes!

Walter Colwill

Walter, the youngest of the Colwill children was actually born at Reeve House and can remember starting to work on the farm from about the age of 12 years. He just remembers rolling the soil using horses before tractors became available.

Whilst at school he says that some farmers would come in and ask the teacher for a number of boys to help pick potatoes, etc., for the war effort; sometimes they would pick fruit in Whitstone woods.

Like so many others he can still 'see' Miss Retallack holding up the back of her dress so as to warm her drawers at the stove.

When the evacuees arrived in the village there was a little rivalry between them and the local boys - the male evacuees would threaten to 'bash up' the village boys, except that they didn't even know what it meant! When the evacuees amalgamated with the children in the school it swelled the numbers to over 100.

Walter was in the Army Cadets, taught by my grandfather 'Captain Martin' and he said that he vividly recalls my grandfather driving around in his car with the silencer missing. Spares were hard to come by and you could hear him coming from miles away.

During the Second World War a family of entertainers used to live in the Rectory Room for a few weeks putting on plays for the locals

At the end of the war he remembers 'they' borrowed a wagon from Ken Uglow at Goscott Farm and that George Masters (village blacksmith) welded a bar on the front so that it could be pulled by a tractor, and collected wood for a large celebration bonfire at Delabole Head.

Rita came from Bridgerule and met Walter at a dance in the Rectory Room. Walter then spent many an hour cycling to Bridgerule!

Brenda Crocker-White

Born in 1934 Brenda's life was typical of so many families in which the children had to work at home to help before or after school. Her father worked for Cornwall County Council and kept some animals at Week Ford. Brenda can still remember having to 'lead the way' for the bullocks when taking them to market and being concerned that they might overtake her or just walk on over her, being so small.

Brenda was born in Clifton House and continued to live there, on and off, until this year when she moved into a smaller property.

The garden at Clifton House was raised by years of the blacksmith throwing ashes onto the ground at the rear of his shop. Also nearby was Coles' slaughter house and in those days was the source of several rats. As toilets were 'up the path' at that time there were usually 'gin traps' in evidence - she didn't stay too long either!

The kitchen had an earthen floor and a water pump and the house was lit by oil lamps until electric came to the village some years later then they had 1 light upstairs, one downstairs and two electric sockets. One socket was used with an electric Baby Belling cooker and the other for a radio set.

Her auntie ran the hardware shop next door and grandfather Higgins was the cobbler. Brenda was allowed to play in The Square, often playing rounders with the children from Week Green. She was not allowed to venture up to Week Green but on one occasion went up to see the Italian prisoners-of-war digging ditches. One of the prisoners plaited her hair - a bit of a giveaway for when she returned home; that got her in a spot of bother!

At school she was made to stand in the corner, by Miss Retallack, for not being able to remember The Lord's Prayer.

Soon after my grandfather arrived and became headmaster, Brenda's grandfather William Higgins (1857-1940) passed away; she was sent to school and was coping quite well until assembly demanded that she recite The Lord's Prayer, at which point she burst into tears. Brenda says my grandfather picked her up and comforted her for the rest of the prayer.

Brenda has vivid memories of the arrival of the evacuees; they had a young Cockney girl and she had obviously led a totally different life in London. On the first Sunday evening, bath night, she declared that she didn't want a bath, she'd had one before she came!

At school on a couple of occasions Brenda remembers seeing a Red Cross parcel arrive at the school. This was distributed amongst the children. Refreshment at the school was milk in a glass bottle with a cardboard top and a straw to drink it with.

Passing Brenda's house on their way to the blacksmith for shoeing she used to see two large carthorses walking in from Brendon, a couple of miles south of the village, in full regalia - ribbons and brasses; what a magnificent picture they made.

Brenda worked in Brewer's shop and received £1/16/4d and a 2oz bar of chocolate each week.

One very amusing story told by Brenda; her father was a regular exhibitor at the local flower and vegetable show, originally held in the school. Local policeman, Mr. McCall, had entered some runner beans into the show and Brenda's father kept saying to Mr. McCall, "You ain't growing no beans!" to which Mr. McCall would reply "You don't know what I'm growing!"

This banter went on for some time until the day of the show when her father and Mr. McCall placed their exhibit of runner beans side by side. Her dad could hardly contain himself when Mr. McCall was awarded the First Prize pushing him into second place.

Through the spluttering of disbelief Mr. McCall came up to her father and told him not to be too upset as they were actually his beans - he had picked them from her dad's garden just after he had left to attend the show! They did laugh about it afterwards.

Even though Brenda has travelled to Norway, Cyprus and Hong Kong she still, like so many of us, considers Week St. Mary to be 'home'.

Audrey Goodman

Audrey was born at Launcells and moved to Thinwood when about 2½ years-old, with her 4 brothers and 2 sisters.

Audrey, born in 1925, also had the 'pleasure' of being taught by Miss Retallack but does not recall the experience with too much delight. She was naturally left-handed but at school Miss Retallack would continually force her to use her right hand. This has had a long-lasting effect on Audrey.

There were quite small classes at that time, only 12 to 17 pupils. She and her brothers and sisters used to walk from Thinwood, up the back lane; occasionally they would walk back part way to meet their older sister who would present them with hot dinners before returning to the school.

Typical of farmers' families the children had to work on the farm; the girls would clean out the stables while the older boys would plough up to 1 acre a day with the horses.

Her mother used to post cream to visitors, sealed in tins, and produce up to 40lbs of butter per week to take to Holsworthy market. To keep the cream cold she used to hang pots of cream from crooks set in the top of the well, so they hung in the cold fresh water. This cold cream made excellent butter.

Like many others during those early years, she recalls walking up to the chapel for the morning service, then walking back home before walking back once more for the evening service.

During the war years Audrey was just one of several women that worked in Whitstone woods cutting up trees in order to make charcoal. Her brother would use a horse to pull out the felled trees to where they would trim and cut them up.

Talking to Audrey she made several references to a family group photograph. After producing the photograph she started to identify the dozen or so people, one of which was her uncle Walter Orchard, a regular in the Whitstone Male Voice Choir. When I saw his picture she then mentioned his son Norman - I was quite stunned really because she was referring to my wife's uncle and cousin! You just don't know who is related to whom; subsequent research has revealed that we are connected, through marriage, to almost half of the village!

Peter Gubbin

Peter's family came to Brendon in 1878 followed by a further 4 generations. He remembers having a governess for a year or two before attending Week St. Mary School.

He used to walk home accompanied by some other children who lived along the way to Brendon. Also remembering Miss Retallack he recalls her taking a school party out for a walk to Ashbury. This was one of the best days at school and was never repeated despite many requests. It became apparent when they returned that there had been the sorting out and shuffling around of desks because of the imminent integration of the evacuees - that was why they had been out for the walk!

Peter took an entrance exam for a boarding school at Truro. The examination was sent to my grandfather to arrange and officiate at Week St. Mary School. Peter said that he must have irritated my grandfather at some point because he was told that if he failed this exam my grandfather reckoned that he would end up being blamed and not Peter!

Living at Brendon, south of Week St. Mary village, his father used the blacksmith at Whitstone before coming to the village and using the services of Mr. Masters.

Living away from the village meant that deliveries were essential for food and other services but visits were always made on market days, also on the occasion of such annual events as the carnival and flower show. Early carnivals, he recalls, would have around 20 trailers pulled either by tractor or horses plus many walkers; hundreds would attend from the outlying area.

Like so many farmers' children, working on the farm was natural after leaving school. Although electric poles passed by Brendon cottages it was not for some time that electric was brought into the farm; not until the 1950s did this materialise - and many more years passed before a television set was purchased.

As many have stated, the weather was more seasonal in years gone by - summers were, in the main, longer and drier but not always kind during the winters.

Peter recalls one Christmas when freezing rain was experienced; possibly in the early 1960s. A car had driven from Saltash, bound for Poundstock, and had skidded off the road into a ditch near Brendon. It took some time to push the car back onto the road. The driver had never experienced such conditions before and was told that it was worse ahead - so he turned round and went homewards again!

I also remember, as a young child, travelling to Bude to visit my grandmother, auntie and uncle for Christmas, the car in which we were travelling spun completely around on a large sheet of ice near Flexbury Church, in Bude - we just bounced against the kerb, luckily. (David Martin)

Keith Hutchings

The Hutchings family lived in Week St. Mary village from the 1930s, Keith's grandfather having trained as a tailor living in Manciple House until they moved into Swannacott in 1919.

Keith was born in Swannacott in 1936. The family lived with his grandparents. Other than normal ailments Keith enjoyed good health and was never excused from school, to help with harvests, as both his father and grandfather were there to work on the farm. During the war years he says that he remembers prisoners-of-war working on the farm and an occasional land army girl helping during the harvest time.

His mother used to cycle to Bridgerule Station to catch a train either to Bude or Holsworthy for any major shopping events then cycle back home again, from Bridgerule, at the end of the day!

Although he walked up to the school in the mornings there was insufficient time to return home for dinner so he used to take his dinner with him and go to 'granny' Kinsman's, just below the school, to eat it.

Keith's father never drove on the road; they had a van but that was used only to take the milk out to the end of the lane.

The Rectory Room was a source of entertainment for Keith - it was here that he first met his wife, Enid, who had travelled from Pyworthy for the occasion. It was some time after that he next met her but the relationship blossomed.

Keith's great-grandfather, Bethuel Hutchings (1836-1926) was presented with a large imposing clock with the following engraved inscription: 'Presented to Mr. Bethuel Hutchings by friends of Week St. Mary in recognition of 58 years faithful service in the church choir. December 1906'

Although Keith cannot recall the circumstances under which these events happened, his grandfather was asked to present the 'goatskin mantle' on behalf of the manor of Week St. Mary to the Duke of Cornwall as part of the ancient 'feudal dues' ceremony. This he had the honour of doing twice, with Keith following in his footsteps in 1973, presenting the goatskin mantle to the present Duke of Cornwall, H.R.H. Prince Charles.

The original goatskin used by his grandfather was getting a bit ragged so Keith bought two new goatskins to be made into a mantle. The mantle along with other items presented to the Duke of Cornwall, when necessary, are housed in Launceston museum.

I found a report stating that Bethuel Hutchings (born 1871) and his wife (born 1874) recalled the arrival in Week St. Mary of the first bicycle - a homemade affair of wood and iron, built by a Mr. Elliott and ridden from Torquay. All went well apparently until arriving in the village when he was unceremoniously thrown off, much to the amusement of the villagers!

Bethuel also recorded that the village, at that time, had 14 carpenters, 3 tailors and 2 blacksmiths shops and that the school had around 120 pupils with just 1 teacher and 1 teaching assistant.

He also stated that there was a weekly horse-drawn bus to Launceston; the journey taking some 4 hours each way.

Pat Johns

Before 1915 part of Sea View Farm used to be Jo Ayres' workshop; he was a monumental stonemason and his name can be seen on many local headstones.

Pat's grandparents lived at Sea View Farm from 1915 and her father was born there. Pat, however, was born at Whitstone after a period of confinement at an aunts. Doctor Ward attended for the birth and as it was before the National Health Service, presented them with a bill!

When Jo Ayres retired and sold off his equipment Pat remembers Mrs Pooley, their neighbour, returning from the sale with the monumental trolley; Mr. Pooley was a tailor and ran a small taxi business.

During her younger years Pat used to walk up to the school in the company of the two eldest Gifford girls. She had dinner at the Temperance Hotel for a short time before going home for dinner.

A major recollection for Pat was the bus journey to Launceston to see Her Majesty The Queen on a tour of the nation, following her coronation.

It was quite handy for Pat and other children during the school years, having the lower green nearby on which to play.

The farmyard relied on well water to feed the animals but this supply was interrupted by the arrival of mains water going through the village. The trench cut through a supply vein and the well wouldn't hold water after that and was filled in.

Pat remembers the excitement of having electricity - a special offer at the time meant that if you had 5 lights installed you could have a free socket! A primitive offer by today's all-electric environment - 1 socket would not get you very far, what with computers, televisions, hi-fi equipment, let alone essential household equipment like washing machines, ovens or microwaves.

Like most farmers of that period horses were the everyday means of carrying goods or pulling implements and it was not until about 1956 that they purchased their first tractor. Harold Ridgman used to drive the tractor and it was featured soon afterwards in the Week St. Mary carnival. Later he also took some Women's Institute ladies to St. Gennys on the tractor!

Dorcas & Arthur Kinsman

Dorcas, born 1926 in Box Tree cottage, was brought up under what were normal living conditions of the day - oil lamps, candles, outside toilets and a 'black stove' for cooking on. She was lucky to have the lower green to play on with many of the local children from that end of the village.

She was collected by the Martyns of Kitleigh and taken to school at Week Green. There she recalls Miss Truscott as her first teacher with Mr. Sincock the headmaster. Eventually she had Miss Retallack as a teacher.

There were varying numbers of children attending the school, particularly as Lady Day and Michaelmas Day were changeover days for those living in rented accommodation and this would often mean some families departed from the area whilst others moved into the area and attended the school.

In the early days at Week St. Mary school there was no milk but Horlicks did make an appearance on particularly cold days; the large urn would stand on the stove to warm up.

Dorcas can just remember the Rev Hardy, prior to Rev Hambrook, and commented that there were always large congregations.

Arthur, who is a 2nd cousin to my wife, was born in Poundstock in 1920 and came to Week St. Mary to stay with his granny at Week Green. He never left after having met Dorcas who had been working indoors at Swannacott for sometime. She used to cycle to Swannacott daily.

Arthur's uncle John died at The Somme during WWI and is mentioned on the war memorial as is his father William and uncle Ambrose as being two 'who served' - his father was only 18 when the war ended as he had 'exaggerated' his age in order to enlist!

During the Second World War Dorcas had 3 evacuees living with them for a while from Plymouth. She also heard that some Belgium refugees spent some time in the Rectory Room.

Arthur had a motorbike by the early 1950s and after spending sometime cutting down trees in the local forests with an axe and crosscut had employment at a wood mill near Halwill, riding his motorbike daily - he says that the main roads were mostly covered in tarmac but the side roads were still loose stones or chippings.

Across the road from Dorcas' house was the shop of Mrs Pooley. Some of the children used to go upstairs where Mr. Pooley worked as a tailor and play with some toys. Dorcas also remembers being told to go to Mr. Pooley for a haircut, costing a mere 2d (two old pennies).

They both recall visiting fairs to the lower green, with the main vehicles parking outside their house whilst the swing boats and merry-go-round was on the village green.

Arthur then worked for many years for the council looking after the hedges and ditches around the parish. He also helped to build the bridges at Whiteleigh and Hendra.

When the mains water and sewage pipes were laid down through the village they recalled that the trench, as it passed through the lower village green area, was some fifteen feet in depth to allow for the rise in the land whilst still maintaining a downhill gradient for the pipes.

Arthur & Ruth Martyn

Arthur, born at Kitleigh in 1925, had three older sisters. Like so many from farming backgrounds they had to undertake various chores around the farm. These chores varied according to their age and ability. Often jobs were to be completed before going to school in the mornings and more to be done upon their return later in the afternoon.

Arthur recalls having to walk to the village many times a week - not just on schooldays but frequently twice on Sundays. Leo Pooley used to pump the air for the church organ for the morning service and Arthur would do it for the evening service.

At that time Arthur says there were about 60 children attending the school. Mr. Sincock was the headmaster and was well liked, and there was Miss Retallack!

Leaving school in 1939, as the war started, they had 2 boy evacuees, from Bristol. He was in the Home Guard and recalls being in a group of nearly 60 men, using a field behind the old Rectory Room, for rifle practice twice a week.

When the possibility of an invasion was announced it was serious enough for Den Treleven to spend the whole night at the top of the church tower on sentry duty.

Arthur met his wife, Ruth, when at the age of 23 years he and George Baker attended a dance at Egloskerry. He later met her again at Peters Fair, Holsworthy, and, as they say, the rest is history - they have been married for nearly 53 years. As a married couple they moved to Kitleigh.

For electricity, like so many farms, they relied on a 'startamatic'. This was a diesel generator which started up automatically when it sensed that something had been switched on, usually a light. After some moments the bulb would light. This was very disconcerting for visitors for if they switched on a light and the bulb did not come on almost immediately they perceived that the bulb had gone and like most people would operate the light switch several times - the poor generator kept trying to start, then stop, then start and so on.

The farm received deliveries by Sandercock's and Martins but generally went to Holsworthy on market days for the main shopping.

Although horses were in use for many years he remembers with affection the arrival of their 1950 Fordson Major. This tractor was used in many Week St. Mary carnivals, pulling floats as necessary.

The local hunts took place around Kitleigh, often finding foxes in nearby Whitstone Woods. There was no sign of deer in those days.

Mary Medland

Mary's mother, Lillian Cook, trained in London as a Nurse, passing her exams in 1923. After moving to St. Gennys, to work as a nurse, she had to cycle everywhere to visit her patients. Lillian then met her future husband, William Stephens, and Mary was her first child.

Lillian did not work until Mary was 4 years old then the family moved to Week St. Mary, living in rented accommodation at Lambley Park, above the garage. She was then the Nurse to Dr Ledgerwood. Mary's mother learnt to drive and had a car to allow her to visit patients in the parish. After a while they moved from Lambley Park up to Week Green, in Mr. Woodley's cottage.

Mary attended the school for no more than one year, having contracted measles, though does remember Miss Retallack!

Her attack of measles left her with terrible pains in her leg and subsequently spent four years in various hospitals.

In her younger days, Mary remarked, she still remembers her grandfather taking her to Launceston in a pony and trap, going by the backroads until nearing the town, then using the main road.

After Mary's marriage to husband Ken, they moved out of the village to Exworthy Farm - she still recalls that their local postman at that time was Horace Hooper who lived at Tor View.

Joyce & Den Orchard

Joyce and Den had strong connections with Whitstone in their early years, both attending Whitstone School. They walked to school together and had such a strong relationship from that time. Married over 50 years ago they moved into the 400 year-old house they still occupy - such a peaceful rural place, next to the forests, often visited by young deer. Den said he remembers that they went on honeymoon with £40 and came back with £20 - you wouldn't get very far on that amount today!

Den had a bicycle for 2 years before he bought a motorbike. He did take Joyce as pillion passenger on the motorbike but she wasn't too keen on that mode of transport!

Both Den and I have a similar recollection, although some years apart - he was travelling out of the village on his bike went he met Alfred Sandercock returning from making some deliveries.

A short while before a herd of cows had walked along the road and they had duly deposited their 'stuff' all along the road. Alfred drove straight through it spraying it right across the road, covering Den and his bike! Den appreciates that it was not intentional but that it was just unfortunate timing!

I had exactly the same thing happen to me when as a young boy I was walking home, just a few yards before turning off the road into our driveway - it was a lovely sunny day and I had my shirt undone with the sleeves rolled up, when I met Mrs Kaluzinski driving into the village in her little A30 car. She was not a very tall person and just managed to peer out over the steering wheel. Like Den, I know she did not do it intentionally, but drove through a fresh line of cows 'stuff' only deposited there a short while ago! It went everywhere - all up my side, in my hair, and well inside my shirt - I think that was when I learnt to swear! (DM)

As a youngster Den recalls being paid 2/- (two shillings) for helping to drive bullocks up to Week St. Mary market. He also said he recalls the days when the cattle were driven to Bridgerule railway station; they would collect more animals along the way. Den used to walk with the animals at first before he had a bicycle while some went on horses, making it so much easier to control the animals - he says it was far better to cycle back home than to walk.

In Den's youth his father decided to concrete out the shippen. This task cost 6 guineas (£6 and 6 shillings) and to pay for it he had to sell his best cow and calf at Week St. Mary market for which he got £17/10/0.

When Joyce arrived in the village the Women's Institute was some 11 years old; she was proud to be later elected President and still supports the community in so many ways.

She remembers Granny Ridgman regularly winning prizes at the village's Flower Show for her entry of sweet peas.

Alfred Parnell

Alfie was born 1920 in the little cottage on the end of the row of buildings in Stewarts Road when the Ridgman's lived in my sisters' house. Alfie was also amazed to learn that we, like him, had been taught by Miss Retallack.

When his mother married Charlie Goodman in 1934, Alfie used to go back down to his gran's house and stay. Within a couple of years he joined the Territorial Army then 'call-up' for the outbreak of war saw him travelling to Bude for onward travel to Launceston and Plymouth. Although he went abroad briefly in 1944 he was back in London when the blitz was on.

He remembers a military exercise under way just north of London which saw a large convoy of vehicles pulling guns travelling through the city. It was slow going and his driver said he reckoned they would never get out of London. He then promptly drove their lorry into the end of the barrel of the gun being towed in front of them. This damaged their radiator and they had to stay there for a day or two until repaired - that was when he found that the driver's family lived just round the corner from where the accident happened. What a lucky co-incidence that was!

He tried to come home as often as possible, usually every three or four months. He would travel by train with a ticket issued to Bude but alight at Bridgerule station.

Unfortunately Alfie suffered a wartime injury in France and was sent back to Wolverhampton for treatment prior to convalescence near Exeter. Once recovered he rejoined his unit at Dorchester until February 1946.

Back at Week St. Mary he stayed with granny for a while until moving up to the council houses at Broadclose, living with his sister and brother-in-law. Initially the council houses had to rely on wells for their water supply, there being 3 wells for the six houses, one well at 2, 4 and 6 Broadclose, but mains water was installed soon afterwards.

Alfie returned to working at Kitleigh after the war and one day (June 1949) recalls hearing a fire engine heading towards the village. This was my grandfather's hayrick in what is now the pub car park. It also housed various outbuildings and was very close to the old chapel but no buildings were lost despite the firemen having to use water from some distance away.

During his younger days he would cycle to Cherry Cross and catch a bus to Plymouth to watch Plymouth Argyle play at home, returning much later back to collect his bicycle at Cherry Cross, and all for no more than 10 shillings (50p).

Most local people associate Alfie with Sunday paper deliveries. Apparently he used to cycle to Bridgerule on a Sunday morning to visit a distant relative. Sunday papers started to arrive later and later at Week St. Mary so Alfie used to bring one back from his visit. Others in the village soon caught on that as Alfie was able to bring back a newspaper from Bridgerule, before the papers got to the village, then he might as well bring one back for them!

Alfie cycled at first, starting his deliveries in 1955, then once retirement was reached he had lifts there and back, finally stopping the deliveries in 2004.

The other main activity associated with Alfie was cutting the grass in the churchyard. This started around 1978 and continued for over 35 years when Alfie reached 84 years old.

He has vivid memories of the original blacksmith's shop at the Bude road junction. He said the council cut back the corners of the small, square-shaped junction as there was not enough room for a vehicle to pass when the horses and traps were outside.

The garage at Week Green was built just before the war when Len Maddock had a coach. This coach was originally housed at Reeve House until the garage was built, finally disposed of at the beginning of the war when fuel supplies were severely restricted.

Just before the garage, on the right hand side, there used to be carpenter's shop with a wood store opposite, operated by Frank Parnell. Tom Pauling learnt his trade as a carpenter at Whitstone and took over the business from Mr. Parnell, building a new workshop opposite the school at the entrance to back lane.

Les Parnell

Although born in Jacobstow Les came to Week St. Mary as a baby some 85 years ago, living in Stewarts Road. As a youth he kept pigeons in what is now my sisters front room!

School time was generally uneventful for Les, remembering teachers Landrey, Sincock and Miss Retallack (of course!). Gardening was one of the classes and Les was appointed head gardener.

He remembers when the local bobby, who he thinks was called Fradd, came into the school to warn the children not to enter the churchyard after the lightning had caused one of the pinnacles to crash through the church roof.

Les and a neighbour, Leo Pooley, used to help pump the air for the church organ. Wearing his best boots he would be sent to church where he spent some time in the choir.

Week Green hill was made of crushed stone and a 'dust' covering when Les was a child, with horse-drawn carts having to use a 'shoe' slid under one wheel to slow the cart down as they descended the hill. Some carts had a chain to completely 'lock' one wheel from turning but this method was not generally favoured as it wore down the metal rim of the wheel and that cost money if it had to be replaced.

Les was the only person interviewed that mentioned the early days of the market site. It originally was an area used for cracking stones. Large stones were brought up from Week Ford quarry and broken into much smaller 'road-sized' pieces.

Like David Coles, Les recalls Sandercock's filling a large container with water from the pump in the Square for the bread making at the rear of their shop. They had a large wood-burning furnace, the wood being kept down 'kennels' - although we know that 'kennels' refers to the area down by the then blacksmith's shop, beside Market Place, no-one knows exactly why it was called that. Les commented that the holly tree in the garden of Tinghamscott is well over 100 years old.

Les' family moved from Stewarts Road, the house owned by Mr. Benoy, to a couple of other houses until residing in the new Council houses two up from our family. Les said that his uncle was a carpenter with a workshop at Week Green where he used to make wagon wheels. He recalls that his uncle bought a bull-nosed Morris car and used to jack up one wheel and use that wheel to turn a belt-driven saw for cutting logs.

Leaving school at 14 years old it wasn't long before war came and he joined the R.A.F., spending two winters in Iceland when darkness prevailed for nearly the whole day. Iceland was a strategic place during the war, preventing the Germans from establishing a base from which to launch raids on Britain. Leaving the Air Force Les then joined the Army. Upon being asked which regiment he would like to be in, he said 'a Cornish one please' - typical Army, they put him in a Scottish regiment! After undertaking commando training Les travelled through North Africa, India and onto Java. When his de-mob time arrived it took him three months to return to the UK. Les was not impressed with his offering of civvy clothes so came back to Week St. Mary in uniform.

After army life he, and some colleagues, used to go digging drains - 3 feet down at 3/- a foot, also digging wells at £2 a foot. He remembers digging one well when his colleague said to the landowner that he had found water and invited him to go down and measure the depth. The man said there was no way he was going down a well so Les's colleague said that he would go down - the measuring tape was 'accidentally' pulled down an extra few feet!

For those that think that people well past retirement age should only be seen to sit in a chair by the fire and sleep can also take a lesson from Les who still works in his son's workshop every day.

Joseph Paynter

Born at Winsdon, North Petherwin, Joseph came to Week St. Mary at the young age of just three weeks old, to live at Kilbroney with his grandparents and Aunty Evelyn. Kilbroney was built around 1903 for a German doctor, Dr. Rench(?), who bought the plot for £1,000. Above the garage was accommodation for his driver. The Paynters took over occupation of Kilbroney in 1912.

The Paynters were strict Methodists and followed their beliefs all their lives. Their ancestors were responsible for turning the Tree Inn into the Temperance Hotel. It was felt that in those times of great hardship it was adding to the poverty of those families whose menfolk spent money on drink. Joseph's grandfather was usually preaching somewhere, if not at Week St. Mary, on a Sunday, and attendance was essential for morning and evening services, in addition to Sunday School lessons during the afternoon. At home, Sundays meant no toys or books - even the Farmers Weekly was put away and replaced by the Methodist Recorder.

Methodist Christmas parties were held in the Sunday School room and on one occasion they were treated to a black and white cowboy film - quite a novelty in those days.

Joseph remembers his first day at the nearby school. He had to knock the door to be let in! Only a short walking distance from Kilbroney he did not have to go down to the Temperance Hotel for school dinners with the others. Miss Retallack did exercise discipline - guess who was made to stand in the corner for throwing a snowball over the wall into the girls' toilets. The toilets were outside the main building and somewhat primitive.

He says that he recalls that when Nurse Jones left the village, to be replaced by Nurse Weiss and Nurse Piper, she left her dog with them.

The proudest day for Joseph was accompanying his grandparents to Buckingham Palace. His grandfather, a long-standing County Councillor and Justice of the Peace, was presented with the MBE, by H.M. Queen Elizabeth II; this was for services to agriculture during wartime.

Leo Pooley

Leo's parents used to live in Manciple House, where his brother and sister were born, before moving to Sea View (Red Lion House). Sea View had once been a hostelry, and Leo recalls the pipe that brought the beer into the kitchen. His father continued his tailoring whilst his mother ran the shop, selling a mixture of drapery, grocery, fuel and sweets. Using a pony and trap when living in Manciple House, then by motor car when at Sea View, his father would go on his rounds taking orders for clothes or suits. Once completed the items would be delivered. One of the popular lines was 'farmer's britches'.

Around 1935 Leo and another young boy swapped bicycles for the dash down Week Green Hill in order to go home for dinner. The intention was for the one getting there first to stop by the war memorial and wait for the other. Unfortunately it had been raining and when he got to The Square the brakes didn't work. He shot past the war memorial at speed crashing right through Sandercock's shop doorway and ended up leaning against the counter!

Reg & Lorna Risdon

Reg went to Whitstone School, as did his older sister, but unlike his sister managed to avoid being taught by Miss Retallack. She had spent a short period of time as a relief teacher from Week St. Mary.

Reg related his memories regarding the aircraft that crash-landed at the back of their farmhouse, when he was around 6 years old. Neighbour Norman Orchard, at Froxton, had also noticed the aircraft flying round, barely missing the tops of the trees, with smoke pouring from the fuselage.

The pilot, Flight Sergeant W. F. Tollworthy R.A.F.V.R., tried to land in their big field but overshot and landed in the next, much smaller field, crashing into the solid hedge. This field was occupied by sheep at the time, killing several as it landed. In the previous field was the farm's horses - they were terrified and ran straight through the wooden gate, back into their stables.

Mary, Reg's sister, arrived at the wreckage first, closely followed by their father and neighbour Jack Colwill. The pilot had managed to clamber from the plane, escaping with minor injuries. They took the pilot into the farmhouse. Some distance away, at the lookout post, it is believed that the plane was seen to go down and the emergency services were alerted. An engine from Bude's Fire Service arrived as the plane was well on fire. Reg remembers seeing them lay hoses from the tender into their pond - the pond was sucked up in seconds!

R.A.F. officers arrived to survey the accident scene and a guard party was arranged to keep an eye on the wreckage until it could be recovered. The men used to come into the house during the evenings and play darts; though one night they were surprised by the arrival of a sergeant - they quickly ran out the back of the farmhouse, up into the nearest field. They explained to the sergeant that they were investigating some nearby noises!

The plane was chopped up with axes and the pieces brought to the end of their farm lane when they were placed onto an articulated lorry and taken away.

Reg attended Titson Chapel where he was in the choir for a while; his mother played the organ and sister Mary was a Sunday School teacher.

Some time was spent away from school as Reg's father had bad feet and subsequently purchased a tractor, with steel wheels, from Hambley's at Whitstone. His dad told them to show 11 year-old Reg how it worked, so Reg spent many a day driving the tractor and learning how to plough and use other bits of machinery with the tractor. Being a young lad he was not able to start the tractor by turning the starting handle, so dad did that bit until he was older and stronger.

Although Lorna lived at Boyton and Maxworthy, it did not stop Reg from cycling miles to see her, finally getting married in 1959 and moving to Bowdah Farm.

Like most places, at that time, they relied on well water; she had to pump up to 17 gallons of water a day for various purposes.

Lorna and her nearest neighbour, Cherry Sainton, were members of Week St. Mary Women's Institute and used to drive along Steele lane to pick up Christine Treleven before entering the village at the lower green.

Regular trips to Week St. Mary market were made, often by a collection of farmers, each adding a few animals to the convoy as it passed their property. Upon arrival at the market, in the early days, there were no pens and the cattle were placed in a small field at the back of the market.

In the later years he recalls having his bicycle run over by a cattle lorry as he went to secure his cattle in some pens - that meant having to walk home!

Gordon & Pearl Rogers

The youngest of eight children, Gordon was born at Trefrouse in 1927, along with his 6 sisters and 1 brother John.

He recalls vividly the walk from Trefrouse to Week St. Mary School - it was only during the dry summers that they could walk up back lane, from Lambley corner.

Like so many people in and around the village he was taught by Miss Retallack. Although many ex-pupils have unkind things to say about Miss Retallack and her style of discipline, Gordon remembers that she also had a good side. During heavy showers, should any of the children walking in from the distant farms or houses arrived soaked, she would see to it that they had dry clothes and were cared for before returning home at the end of the day.

The school, by this time, had three full classrooms. A partition was used to make an additional room - this room was used for any examinations. Gordon remembers Mr. Paynter from Kilbroney and Mr. Gubbin from Brendon acting as adjudicators, as part of their responsibility as school governors.

During the war each farm had to grow varied amounts of potatoes as part of the war effort. Trefrouse grew about 1½ acres of potatoes. Farms that did not specialise in growing potatoes had no option but to manually plant and therefore pick potatoes by hand. This was one time when children were often away from school, helping harvest the potatoes.

Gordon recalls the 'lookout post' being erected, first in wood, then of brick. His father and George Masters (the village blacksmith of the day) were the top shooters in the Week St. Mary Home Guard and of the whole Bude area. They would go to Northcott Mouth on a Sunday morning to practice shooting and grenade throwing.

Some time after war was declared Gordon clearly remembers hearing some bombs being dropped on Cleave Camp. It was a Sunday morning and he had gone down to a field to bring up the horses to do some work and heard the noise. The enemy aircraft came back again in the afternoon but by this time they had anti-aircraft guns ready and drove the plane away!

The army made a small camp in one of the fields in Trefrouse and he recalls that one night there was tremendous rain and the officers went off to Bude for the night, leaving the men to camp out. Gordon's dad invited the men down to the house where they stayed, warm and dry!

A short while later they moved from the field a few hundred yards away into a field belonging to Owen Smale. It was here that they had a searchlight. They were operational for some eighteen months before shifting the complete camp out to a field south of the village - forever to be known as 'Camp Field'. When they were near Trefrouse, Gordon's mother used to bake pasties for the men on Sundays.

When the church tower was damaged by lightning, in 1935, Gordon says he remembers looking out of the school window towards Tom Pauling's workshop, seeing it bathed in sunshine. The other side of the school, towards Whitstone, was as black as anything. Then, all of a sudden, a tremendous bang shook the building!

Gordon's father was a true church supporter, being churchwarden for around 50 years and captain of the bells for 25 years.

By about 1950 they had their first vehicle. Gordon was learning to drive when he, and two friends, went to Launceston and on to Davidstow before returning home via the A39. Passing through Davidstow they saw some young ladies walking along the road so stopped to 'have a chat'. One of these young girls was Pearl and they married in 1954.

Gordon recalls that his first wage from Duchy Bakeries was £8 2s 4d with their rent costing 25 shillings. They did manage to save enough to buy a Ford Popular car costing around £300.

Eventually Gordon and Pearl moved to Bude, where Gordon became manager of the Co-op for many years. He also had the distinction of being Mayor of Bude.

Jo Shipton

Although not Cornish, but almost a life-long resident of the village, Jo Shipton has been a valued supporter of Week St. Mary for many years.

She and her late husband, George, came to Sladdacott over 50 years ago after their marriage; this was their first home. They had looked at so many farms and the nearer they went towards Exeter the dearer the farm property got. When Jo visited Sladdacott, with her future mother-in-law she fell in love with the place, even though it was a miserable rainy day, hoping that George would also see the beauty in the place - this he did and the purchase went through.

The farm allegedly goes back into the 1500's and may have been part of an ancient inheritance by a prominent family in the Egloskerry area.

Jo used to cycle regularly into the village before learning to drive. It was a ruling that if you had children attending a school in excess of 2 miles you could get assistance with travelling; needless to say, upon enquiring, Sladdacott was 'just' under the 2-mile limit! Jo learnt to drive as she knew her husband would not be able to stop work at various times of the day in order to take the children to school or go shopping. Their son also had the distinction of being taught by Miss Retallack but their daughter went to school after she had finally retired.

The farm was visited by both Sandercock's van weekly and Brewer's van fortnightly from the village, other than that they regularly visited the village for clothes or hardware supplies. Main purchases were undertaken in Holsworthy.

As a dairy farm they had no sheep or pigs other than a large friendly sow called 'pig'. This animal used to get everywhere and much time was spent trying to get it out of sheds or barns until it was decided she would have to go!

213

George was at the market awaiting delivery of the sow but it never turned up. Jo could just not persuade it to get in the lorry, despite there being the driver and a resident student to help her. The following week a more masterly effort was successful. They also had 2 geese that used to terrify Jo and one day enough was enough - they too left the farm!

In over 50 years attendance at Week St. Mary church Jo has seen many changes and has had the pleasure of being a churchwarden for over 15 years.

Jeanette Turner

Although the youngest person in this chapter, just a couple of months older than me, Jeanette had such wonderful memories of living at Thinwood and later Trefrouse, from 1953. When her mum and dad moved into Trefrouse, her grandparents moved out into one of the new council houses by the school.

She can still remember her first day at Week St. Mary School, meeting Miss Retallack - she can't remember many other days but the first sticks in her mind.

Jeanette needed a doctor once, in her early days, and Dr Ward refused to come down the lane to see her as the National Health Service had been introduced and he only wanted private patients so they had to use a Holsworthy doctor.

Growing up on a farm, like so many others, she had to learn various jobs around the farm. Learning to milk a cow, by hand, she started by trying to fill a cup before progressing onto a jug, then finally using a bucket.

Although they did not have mains water at Trefrouse until 1976 they had always been used to a flush toilet operated by collected rainwater.

Jeanette's mother, Ivy, was able to dowse water and she found a place in a nearby field that suggested a good supply of water. Ivy and husband John dug the well by hand, going down some 20 feet. A bucket was filled and wound up to the top by means of a windlass. It was not easy digging and Jeanette still remembers the 'arguments' when Ivy would tip the bucket too early when pulling it to the side at the top of the well, tipping water down over John. After much shouting they would swap over until the same thing happened to Ivy when John tried to retrieve the bucket. Ivy had a hole in one Wellington boot and had to stand with one foot up the side of the well which didn't help at all. The well was finally dug and proved to be a good source of water for many years.

Electricity arrived by means of a generator in 1978. Jeanette recalls that they built a concrete slab but could not fit the generator until the concrete was fully hardened, however they quickly tried it out and Jeanette had an electric bulb in her bedroom. It was so bright but had to be turned off until the generator had been fitted properly onto the slab. Jeanette was ever so disappointed to have to go back to using candles.

Although living fairly close to the village they had most things delivered by the local traders; Sandercock's for bread, Martin's for general groceries, Mr. Woodley left the meat order in one of the churns for collection to save driving up and down the lane. Truscott's came from Bude with gas; Ken Yelland came to the farm with the clothes van and Corona was delivered regularly. ■

The Past Fifty Years

My sister, Linda Cobbledick, recently gave a talk at the Women's Institute about the changes that Week St. Mary has undergone during the past 50 years. The talk was well received and attended by one of the largest numbers of members and visitors seen for a long time.[30]

With the help of my drawings and some old photographs, suitably enlarged, she enlightened many with a virtual 'walk' from the southern end of the village, down Week Green hill, around The Square and through to the Lower Green and out to the north of the village.

Many of those attending were local residents but there were also quite a few 'recent' arrivals to the area that were quite unaware of the rich history the village held.

1. School Gardens: These were cared for by the older children there was a boys and girls garden; the flowerbeds either side of the school porch were also kept tidy by the children.

2. Water Tank: This was a large water tank on stilts in the field behind Broadclose council houses, filled from a borehole, to supplement the water supply.

3. Maddock's Garage: This was a wonderful place especially for us children who happened to have a problem with our bicycles or had a flat tyre, as Eric Brown who lived with the Maddocks would easily repair this. Len Maddock ran a taxi business and when our Grandfather arrived in Bude with the evacuees, they came to Week St. Mary in a bus owned by him. You could buy petrol, have repairs done or even have your accumulator batteries charged at the garage, in their tiny little kiosk you could buy batteries, cigarettes, puncture repair kits or torch bulbs.

4. Martins: This was a grocery shop run by William Martin, his wife and son Terry. The shop was really old-fashioned, almost like Arkwrights shop in 'Open All Hours'.

Daily patrols (by bicycle!) at Maddock's Garage!   Just checking on things at Maddock's Garage!

You could buy any general groceries - everything was in sacks; flour, dried fruit, tea, sugar and other dry items. As children we would be mesmerised watching Mr. Martin measuring the goods into paper bags and folding the top of the bag so meticulously into neat little packages. Mr Martin also ran a delivery service and mobile store.

3, Broadclose: 'home' for many years, from around 1947 - 1979. So many memories!

He had great difficulty in talking which, for young children, was quite frightening in a way - as children it meant very little to learn that he was a victim of Mustard Gas during the First World War.

5. The Beeches: Most people would know this as the Green Inn but around fifty years ago it was the School headmaster's home where my Grandfather and family lived. It was also a smallholding with several beech trees, hence the name. I remember when the bulldozer was called in to remove the massive roots of the trees when making the yard into a car parking area for the new public house.

6. Chapel Caretakers house: Formerly the Bible Christian Chapel, this became the house of the Chapel Caretaker and at that time was the home of 'Granny Cobbledick'.

7. Maddocks: (Doctors) The house of Mr. & Mrs Maddock was used as the doctor's surgery for many years. For a brief spell Regent House was used until the Parish Hall was built. Many villagers will recall Dr. Ward and Dr. Wright conducting their surgeries in the village three times a week.

8. District Nurses: No. 1 Broadclose was the home and surgery of the District Nurses; Nurse Piper and Nurse Weiss. Also living with them was Nurse Weiss' mother who spoke no English. The young children of those Council houses would go Carol singing outside their house and as a reward would get asked in and be given little bags of sweets. The nurses gave our mother some of their old black woollen stockings for us children to use as Christmas stockings. Characteristically the stockings stretched longer each year and you had to really delve in to get to your orange and nuts from the toe of the stockings! Our Dad always told a story of Nurse Weiss, a fairly short bespectacled lady, who drove a little black Morris 1000, and had asked dad to ride with her in case of difficulties during a spell of bad snow and ice on the roads. Her being very small meant she could only look through the top half of the steering wheel and as they approached Week Orchard dad was shouting for her to watch out for the cows in the road - she replied, "What cows?" but by the time she stopped they were almost in the middle of the herd.

9. Brock's Wood: Opposite Broadclose is a field that belonged to Mr. Brock. It was a very steep field leading down to 'Brock's Wood'. This made a wonderful playground when it snowed; we use to be straight across the road with our tin trays and spend hours walking back up the hill to have a few seconds fun sliding down it. The woods were a really magical place for small children - the good thing was that there were no worries about letting us go there to play, a far cry from the worries of protecting children in today's society.

10. Tom Pauling's Workshop: At the junction of the back lane to Lambley stood Tom Pauling's carpentry workshop. He was a general carpenter, wheelwright, barber and undertaker; you knew if there was a light on after hours that he was making a coffin. When you reached the classroom for older children you could see him across the road, working away in his workshop.

11. Eggs: A little further down from Tom Pauling's workshop was the home of Olive Pethick and her sister Agnes Smale and it was here that we would be sent by our mum to buy eggs.

12. The School: The centre of our childhood memories; especially of Miss Retallack who seemed to teach here forever!

13. The Parson's Walk: Nobody actually knows why it was so called but a walkway ran along the hedge top from the end of the row of houses where Mr. Martin had his shop down to the Rectory (now Wentworth House). When the council houses opposite the school were built the parsons walk was reduced by that amount, then, when the Glebe was created the walk was reduced even more. Where the entrance to the Glebe was there was a wide grass verge and a sycamore tree on the hedge - it had a very large branch overhanging the grass and made an ideal place for a swing. Most of the children of Week Green, at one time or another, either played on this swing or climbed the tree.

14. Rectory and Rectory Room: Fetes on the lawn spring to mind especially the one where my sister was supposed to give her strawberries to the vicar but cried her eyes out instead, much to the annoyance of Miss Retallack. Following the path up to the Rectory Room you would have found the wooden parish hall. Everything took place there from socials, concerts, teas, parties and the most wonderful dances; Eric Brown was often MC for this and the band was usually 'The Black and Whites' with George Masters (blacksmith) on the drums. I don't think anyone could forget the toilets - good job there was no health and safety in those days as it was a bucket under a hole in a wooden seat. At Socials or parties everyone joined in with the games, even the vicar, and we can still recall the time when Revd. Simpson was blindfolded, playing 'Blind Mans Buff' and sat on Ivy Horrell's lap, saying 'ducky ducky'. Ivy was quite plump and started to laugh; once Ivy started to laugh there was no stopping her and she was not able to say 'quack quack'. There are so many happy memories about times in the Rectory Room to those of us who frequented the building.

15. Orchard's Shop: 'Bespoke Tailors' the sign said that hung on the wall for many years. For young children it was quite a climb up the granite steps with the slate slabs either side of the doorway. Inside was an Aladdin's cave; you could have a suit made, leave clothes to go to Millbay's dry cleaners, buy knitting wool, greeting cards, toys, haberdashery, underwear and many other things. Run by Geoffrey and his brother Russell. Geoffrey used to go out in his car, house-to-house around the district. He was a very rotund man almost as wide as tall but extremely smart in his suits. His big black car would be packed so high with things to sell that at times he must have struggled to see out of the side windows. In the cottage next door to the shop lived their sisters Nellie and Louie, this was where I, and my sisters Susan and Linda, went for piano lessons, over the years, but sadly none of us pursued it for long. Next door to them in the other cottage lived Granny and Granfer Ridgman. Granfer Ridgman dressed up every year at Christmas to play the part of Father Christmas for the Sunday school or Christmas parties in the Rectory Room. For many years Granny Ridgman carried buckets of water up the path to the Rectory Room, the hall having no mains services other than electricity.

16. Barbers Builders: The buildings just below the Rectory were originally the stables for the resident vicar but were sold many years previously. Although Mr. Barber, a builder, had the property as a workshop it was later sold to Mr. Bate and became known as 'Honey Stores'. It was then that some fine honey was bottled.

17. Chapel: Fifty years ago families were either known for attending the church or the chapel except for weddings or funerals whereas today there is far greater harmony with a sharing of religious activities.

18. Post Office and Telephone Kiosk: This was in the bungalow opposite the chapel and owned by Mr. and Mrs Donald Sandercock. The phone box was at the top of the long flight of steps; to the left was the door straight into the little Post Office adjoining their living quarters.

19. Brewer's: A wonderful grocery store, also having a delivery service - all the sweets were on the left of the shop and all the grocery items on the right.

20. Butcher (Fred) Colwill: As you turn at the junction, onto the Bude road, the first house on the right was their home and butchers shop. He at one time had his 'slaughter house' where the bungalows are, opposite the parish hall.

21. Clifton House: Turning left, back at the junction, towards the Square, brings you to the first house on the left. The garden is so very much higher than the roadway; this is because the original blacksmith's shop backed onto the garden and all the ash was thrown back onto the ground.

22. Higgins' shoeshop: The next house was a cobblers and shoe shop but was the first of the local shops to close down.

23. Ridgman's: Opposite Clifton House you can still see the raised plinth where the petrol pumps stood. What is now the bakery was the ironmongers shop. You could buy anything from a pound of nails to a bone china tea set. Mrs Ridgman also ran a taxi service.

24. Butcher Coles: Following on round to the left, into the Square, was another butchers shop owned by David Coles' grandfather, then by Reg Colwill for many years. Reg used to have a van and visited houses in and around the parish.

25. Temperance Hotel: on the right hand side of the square, Doris and Jack Edwards owned this first building. The school children staying for school dinners walked down in pairs with the teachers to have their meal. This was also the busiest place on a Saturday as Doris cooked meals for the farmers attending the market.

26. Cattle Market: The site of the new development 'Market Place' was very busy and a vibrant hub of the village on a Saturday, many walking their animals through the village to market. This was one of the few remaining village markets in North Cornwall. The village would have a queue of lorries and animals waiting to be checked into their pens. This congestion remained until the afternoon when they were either taken away by their new owners or driven off to the slaughterhouse. It was wonderful to go and climb the bars of the pens to be part of things, enjoying the sounds but not necessarily the smell! Sadly, the market outgrew the village and the number of lorries, tractors and trailers had become a problem, often parking a long way up Week Green hill. It was the end of a tradition when the market closed and the business moved to Hallworthy.

27. Blacksmith's Shop: The now thatched cottage on the right of the Square was the home of George and Edna Masters. His smithy was just down the lane behind the house.

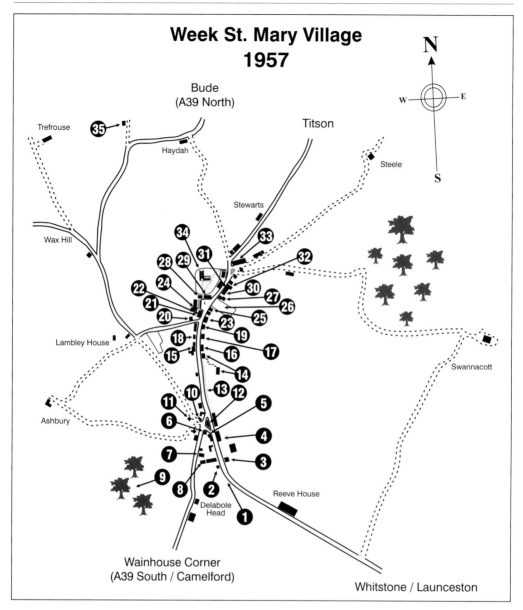

**Week St. Mary Village
1957**

N

Bude
(A39 North)

Titson

W   E

Trefrouse ③⑤

Haydah

Steele

S

Stewarts

Wax Hill

③④   ③③

③⑧ ③⑨ ③①   ③②

②② ②④   ③⓪

②① ②⑦ ②⑥

②⓪   ②⑤

Lambley House   ②③

①⑧   ①⑨

①⑤ ①⑥ ①⑦

①④

①⓪ ①③ ①②

①① ⑤

Ashbury   ⑥

④

⑦   ③

⑨

⑧ ②   Reeve House

Delabole
Head   ①

Swannacott

Wainhouse Corner
(A39 South / Camelford)

Whitstone / Launceston

It was a welcoming place and George never minded us children watching him shoe a horse or making something. George was a very clever man in his profession and used to judge at county shows.

28. Tom Bromell's: Go to the other corner of the square and this was a smallholding where we used to be sent by our mother to collect milk in an aluminium can. Where his barn and orchard was is now the site of the 'Church Mews' houses.

29. Sandercock's: Sitting central in the Square, the site of the current shop and post office, the business was in the hands of the Sandercock's for many years. Another very busy general grocer having delivery vans going to the outlying farms and villages.

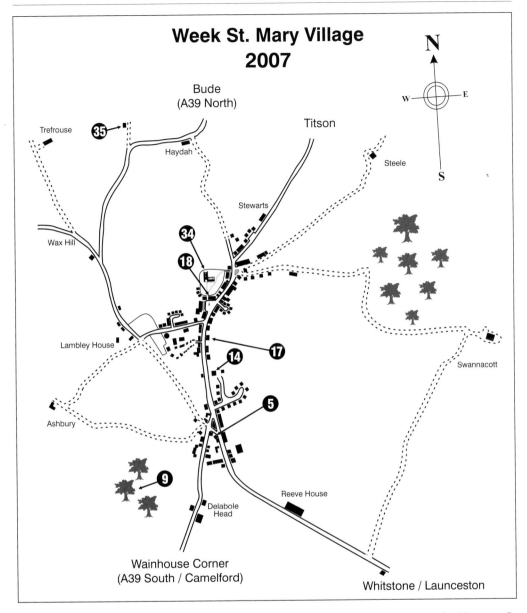

Week St. Mary Village
2007

N

W — E

S

Bude
(A39 North)

Titson

Trefrouse

(35)

Haydah

Steele

Stewarts

(34)

(18)

Wax Hill

Lambley House

(14)

(17)

Swannacott

(5)

Ashbury

(9)

Reeve House

Delabole
Head

Wainhouse Corner
(A39 South / Camelford)

Whitstone / Launceston

30. Sandercock's Store: This was at what is now called Manciple House. It was their storeroom and upstairs in the flat lived Miss Retallack.

31. Police House: Now called Hayescott, but fifty years ago was simply, the Police House. You knew if you did something naughty in the village that the police would get to hear of it and then your parents would as well! What a shame that the villages no longer have their own bobby.

32. Merchants: This was in the Old College and owned by Reggie 'Butt' Colwill. Here you could buy anything from coal to feedstuff for animals.

33. Granny Pooley's: Entering the Lower Square you would know this as Red Lion House. Long ago it had a very high hedge almost hiding the front of the house and you had to go through a small gate to get to the front door.

Some children would go there after school dinners, unbeknown to the teachers, as they were supposed to go straight back up the hill. Shaking the door, to ring the bell, granny Pooley would open up to sell us some mints. In her shop were tobacco, cigarettes and sweets, the chocolate bars even stored in glass jars with lids screwed on. She was an elderly lady who dressed in long black skirts and had a shawl so this made some children think of her as a witch (of course she wasn't). Above the shop Mr. Pooley was a tailor and had his workshop.

34. Parish Church: The main focal point of the village. It was very much a place of worship and not like today where churches and chapels are used for various public events.

35. Lookout Tower: Go out of the village onto the Bude road and you can see the landmark of the Royal Observers Corp's Observation Tower. Sadly this is now suffering from neglect and has become a dangerous building, but fifty years ago was a place to go for the best view of the coast and countryside. We would love nothing better than to take a picnic out there on a nice day.

• **County Council roadmen:** Frank Martin, Harold Ridgman, Bill Marks and Arthur Kinsman spent many years working on the roads. We never had a problem with drains becoming choked; the sides of the roads were kept neat and tidy with a cut through for the rain to run into the ditches. The men looked after the whole parish. How times have changed, now they work from a lorry and don't worry about cleaning drains and ditches.

• **Postmen:** The village had their own postmen, Jim Cobbledick, Arthur Cobbledick, John Horrell and Harry Morrish; they knew everybody and knew instantly if something was amiss.

• **Transport:** Twice a week you could get the bus to Bude. On Tuesdays and Fridays it left the village at dinnertime and teatime. If you went to the cinema whilst in Bude you had to leave before the national anthem to make sure that you did not miss the last bus back home at 9pm - if you were lucky you would have just enough time to buy a bag of chips from Mrs Darch's chip shop and run across the road to the bus stop.

We have no idea on how the next fifty years will change Week St. Mary - the spread of 100 years between the above recollections of around 1950 and 2050 will produce dramatic changes if the past is anything to go by.

As a child I know that, like so many other households, the house was frequently left unlocked when unoccupied. My mother would leave money and shopping instructions, along with premiums and the insurance books, for those likely to call that particular day. They would deposit the appropriate goods and take the money, leaving any change as necessary, and shut the door behind them.

These days most houses are locked, bolted, protected by burglar alarms and watched by neighbours. Oh, how we often pray for a return of the 'good old days'. Whether future changes will see a closer-knit community or just a collection of people doing their independent things will not be something that I shall be around to see, but let's hope that the community spirit lives on in Week St. Mary for many years to come. ■

Clubs & Groups

Week St. Mary is a thriving community, shown by the number of groups, clubs and organisations, each playing their part in combining a common interest, unity, strength, companionship and camaraderie; all in all, an important social bonding structure.

No one club is more important than any other, I believe each plays a part in the overall plan of community togetherness. Some belong to more than one club or group and that 'overlapping' is sufficient to ensure a genuine community bonding.

Week St. Mary Responders

In the first year of operation Week St. Mary Responders have responded 30 times to Emergency calls both inside the Village and within about a 5 mile radius of the village centre. They currently have three qualified responders and three who have yet to complete their ambulance experience Sessions. They have completed several training sessions with the help of the Ambulance Service and Peter Juniper who is one of their members and a Red Cross trainer.

On 15th March over £3,500 was handed over to the South West Ambulance Trust, this being the sum raised by the Parish to set up the scheme.

They now have their own Responder Liaison officer, an Ambulance Technician, who provides the support they need and organises their training.

At present the Responders that are available are nowhere near enough to cover 24 hours a day, 7 days a week. They all have busy lives and commitments. The Responder group needs more Volunteers to train in Basic Life Support and to learn to use the defibrillator. Then with plenty of man power they will be able to more nearly cover all day every day.

As more people receive the help of the Responders group the value of the scheme becomes clearer. It is a great comfort to anyone in distress to know that there is someone to help them while they wait for an ambulance to come to them. In this area the wait is seldom less than 20 minutes but their local Responders can be with them inside 5 minutes. Even neighbouring villages are within the vital 8 minutes that we have in which to make a difference to someone whose heart has stopped.

Week St. Mary Conservation Group

A group only formed a couple of years ago when changes were threatened to the village green that would have meant a loss of some of the green.

The group is available to help parishioners preserve local characteristics that might be in danger of being lost due to development.

Week St. Mary Youth Club

The Youth Club has been running in excess of 25 years, catering for both groups of Seniors and Juniors.

Week St. Mary Book Club

The village even boasts a 'book club'. They read one book a month and currently meet on a Tuesday evening at the Chapel schoolroom. All books are provided, free of charge, by the Cornwall Library Service and are picked up at the meeting. The group has now been going for just over a year and would like to increase its membership. Like all good meetings tea/coffee and biscuits are provided.

Week St. Mary Community Web Site

Started by myself and my sister, Linda, the web site hopefully brings up-to-date information to local residents and ex-pats. People regularly visit the web site from all round the world, especially since the introduction of the transcriptions of all the headstones in the churchyard and cemetery.

Week St. Mary Football Clubs

The village has a long history of having a football team - now the village boasts two male teams and even a ladies team. The First Team, under the guidance of Tom Hannaford, became Duchy League Division 5 Champions.

Week St. Mary Parish Church & Methodist Chapel

Recent years has seen the church and chapel communities combining their resources more often in a show of unity and strength. Both the church and chapel have demonstrated great changes to the structure and fabric of these religions to ensure that these institutions continue to thrive and increase awareness of God's presence and to celebrate God's love.

Week St. Mary Playing Fields

To have a play area was something that the village never had for many years. The introduction of the field and playing equipment means that there is no reason for children to play out in the road.

The field and equipment continue to be monitored on a weekly basis for any unsafe occurrences or failures. These inspections are recorded and our thanks are extended to Sue Booker for carrying out this onerous task so conscientiously. Two trees were donated last year by the Bude and District Forum, an Ash and an Oak. These were planted by members of the village youth club and seem to be doing very well. They are positioned alongside the fence below the play equipment area.

Week St. Mary Women's Institute

As I have mentioned earlier in this book, the W.I. has continued to grow and demonstrates an exciting time for its members with a range of guest speakers covering the most diverse subjects (including me and my diverse subject!).

NO LACK OF TALENT AT WEEK ST. MARY (circa 1950)
W.I. EXCELS IN FIRST PUBLIC STAGE ENTERTAINMENT

It is not a rare thing to discover talent. What is rare is to discover the exact kind of talent required, not only ready at hand but in abundance. Such was, however, the experience of the Women's Institute, of Week St. Mary, when it presented for the first time since its formation in 1945, a full evenings Stage-entertainment to a public audience.

On Saturday the Rectory Room was crowded with an audience that rewarded its entertainers with generous applause, unrestrained laughter and - truest of all rewards - the silence of absorbed attention. After a gramophone overture the curtains parted to reveal the W.I. Choir ready to give their first number: "You Can Smile" was accompanied by Miss E. Paynter who then gave place to Miss A. L. Orchard for "O Can We Sew Cushions".

Conducting, Miss Teague gathered her choir to its effort, and the Choir responded with a controlled enthusiasm, delightful to experience. A welcome, and most amusing discourse, was given by Mrs. N. Gubbin (Chairman).

Then came the Minuet, arranged by Mrs Vedrenne to the music of Beethoven, and dances by Mrs W. Petherick and Misses I. Colwill, P. Jones and B. Pooley, this stately memory of an age long bygone so pleased its audience that an encore was demanded and given. The next item, a duet, "Whispering Hope" was sung by Mrs A. Martin and Mrs D. Treleven.

The first of two plays, produced by Mrs Vedrenne, was "A Dust-up at Madame's" by Ida P. Parfitt, a light comedy taking place in a hat-shop in the West End of London. Played by Mrs F. Charlick, Mrs S. Ridgman, Miss I Fishleigh and Miss A. Parsons, it drew constant ripples of laughter.

Mrs. R Orchard read Jan Stewer's "Lumbago Cure" and the first half of the concert was rounded off by Miss Teague and her Choir giving "Country Gardens."

After an Interval, the Choir continued with "Ye Banks and Braes" with Miss May Cobbledick at the piano. A double-duet "Come to the Fair," was sung by Mrs L. Hutchings, Mrs A. Martin, Mrs R. Orchard and Mrs D. Treleven.

The second play, Essex Dane's "Wrong Numbers," was played by Mrs M. J. M. Annett, Mrs J. Lamerton and Miss B. Pooley. Its comedy was as telling as its thrill - a threat endorsed by an automatic pistol - was convincing. Mrs N. A. P. Townend then read from Hilaire Belloc's most witty "Cautionary Tales for Children" which was followed by the Choir's finale, "Brother James's Air" and Brahm's "Lullaby."

Bouquets were presented, on behalf of the Institute, to Miss Teague by Mrs D. Treleven; to Mrs Vedrenne by Miss B. Pooley; and to the President (Mrs D. Treleven) by Miss I. Colwill. The President thanked Miss Teague and Mrs Vedrenne; Mrs W. Ridgman who had given her invaluable services throughout rehearsals and performance; the door stewards and all others who had helped, including Messrs D. Brewer and P. Gubbin (electrical equipment), and L. W. Vedrenne (properties). The curtains were then rung down upon a stage which had been faultlessly managed by Mrs. G. Masters.

Week St. Mary Skittles Club

It is likely that the game of 'skittles' has been around for many centuries in one form or another.

There are four men's teams playing in the Holsworthy and District Skittles League - WSM "B" won Div. 2 and were 'Runners up' in the John Hockin Front Pin Cup. They were also 'Runners Up' in the D. & I. Bridgman Cup which gave them and the winners of that cup (Holsworthy A) entry to play in the 'Devon Area Finals' which Week St. Mary B won beating Barnstaple in the final. The team consisted of:- I. Cobbledick, I. Braund, G. Braund, P. Coles, S. Cox and A. Hill.

Of the four men's teams Den Colwill is one of the original players and still helps the teams out, if required, at the age of 94. It's not just the men that play skittles - the women also enjoy the game with four teams.

There are several other groups that help to support the structure of the village and each help in their own way; these include:

Week St. Mary Quilting Group

Examples of the group's work has even travelled abroad - the group made a large quilt that was presented to The Venerable Vuyani Buso, Archdeacon of Umzimvubu in South Africa and his wife Mrs Phyllis Buso when they visited the parish in November 2006.

Week St. Mary Coffee Pot Club

Currently meeting in the Methodist School Room it is an ideal opportunity for carers, parents and grand-parents to get together and have a chat over a cup of tea or coffee and a biscuit, and for the children to socialise and play in safety.

Lay Ministry Teams

Over the past few years the financial constraints experienced by the Diocese of Truro has required incumbents to be accountable for an ever increasing number of parishes. Week St Mary has been one of those to feel the 'pinch', becoming first a benefice of two church communities, then four and, most recently, eight. Subsequently, although Week St Mary has always been a very sociable and supportive community, it has been of additional benefit to the village that some members of the church congregation have been prepared to undergo appropriate training and become Lay Pastoral Ministers and Worship Leaders.

The first of these were 'commissioned' under the direction of Bishop Bill in 2004 and the teams have been growing steadily ever since. Members of the Pastoral Team voluntarily visit and support, amongst others, the sick, the housebound, the disabled and the lonely with a consistency that could now never be exercised by the clergy; whilst the Worship Leaders enable a full and regular timetable of services to continue by assisting in the planning and leading of worship.

C.A.M.E.O. (Come And Meet Each Other)

Once a month, at Week St Mary Rectory, people from across its benefice Come And Meet Each Other to drink tea, catch up with local chit-chat and generally relax in the company of other sociable friends and neighbours from the eight church communities.

This is of particular value to people who might not otherwise have the opportunity to meet with old friends, or to make new ones, and some of whom are transported to CAMEO by members of the Pastoral Team. ■

Open air 'Songs of Praise' on the village green - 2006

'Dog Show' - Revel 2006

Miscellaneous Snippets

Flush Brackets

2GL Brackets: Flush brackets were first used during the 2nd Geodetic Levelling of England & Wales between 1912 and 1921. The 2GL series were numbered from 1 to 3000 and did not have a prefix letter. The vast majority of the flush brackets in the 2GL series were placed on walls and buildings, but a small number were used on triangulation pillars. There are 46 examples of these listed in the database, all in the range 2943 to 2999.[31]

Such are the flush brackets placed at Reeve House and Week Green with another sited at Creddacott Farm.

The flush bracket at Week Green is very close to where we lived as children and when trying to find this particular bracket I was absolutely amazed to find it in such a place that we had walked past it many thousands of times and never noticed it!

The flush bracket at Reeve House was used during the Second and Third geodetic levelling sessions, England & Wales, and was levelled with a height of 547.531 feet [166.887 metres] above mean sea level and the second Flush Bracket was levelled with a height of 539.070 feet [164.309 metres] above mean sea level.

Police Constables

PC52 Thomas Henry Hosken (Enlisted:15/1/1859)
PC Warne
Sgt James Fuller (Hillside, 1901 census)
PC Tresidder
PC Lamerton
PC McCall

Recollections from some show that one of the policemen used to live at Hillside. In 1939 the Police House had moved to Hayescott. This was the Policeman's residence until the 60's when the Police Authority bought two new houses at Whitstone - Week St. Mary then lost its Police presence!

Transatlantic Cable

Travelling to Stratton School on the school bus, along the coast road of Widemouth, I recall seeing the first cable-laying ship standing just off the Cornish coast.

It was well-reported at the time as the cable was buried deep in the sand, running towards a bungalow-shaped building that housed the main connection with the British telephone system.

The third transatlantic telephone cable (TAT 3) was opened between Tuckerton, New Jersey, United States and Widemouth Bay, Britain. It was taken out of service in 1986 after 23 years of service.

Berry Comb

Berry Comb, in Jacobstow, was once the residence of Thomasine Bonaventure, and it was given at her death to the poor of St. Mary Week.

Sir Nicholas Slanning (1606-1643)

Sir Nicholas Slanning and his men had a brief sojourn at Saltash before rejoining the rest in a rendezvous with Grenville's foot.

They brushed aside a small force at Week St. Mary on May 13th and at 5.00a.m. on the 16th attacked the forces on Stratton (now Stamford) Hill, Stratton. This produced their most spectacular victory when, after ten hours of fighting uphill against twice their number of much better equipped enemy with a dug-in battery, they gained the position, killing 300 and capturing 1,700 with fourteen guns, £300 and plentiful provisions, at a cost of 80 men. Slanning and Trevanion commanded the westernmost of the four columns.

Goscott Farm

Goscott

There was formerly a chapel at Goscote, dedicated to St. Lawrence. The chapel of St. Lawrence at Goscote was licensed in 1380.

Ashbury Camp

Ashbury is an earthwork in the form of a parallelogram of about four acres. At Swannacott there is a smaller oval entrenchment 150 feet by 130 feet. Swannacott was a manor.

The Beeches / The Green Inn

A short while after the death of my grandfather in March 1953, 'The Beeches', the headmaster's residence, was sold. When on February 17th 1956 Mr. Trengrove was granted a full liquor licence, the property then became known as The Green Inn. Despite a regular change of landlords the pub has been running continually since that date.

I can just remember, as a very young child around 1952-3, sitting on the patio at the rear of the premises eating 'afternoon tea' in the sunshine.

Treetops Leisure Cabins

The arrival of retired Squadron Leader 'Jimmy' Douglas and his family to the village saw the construction of 'Treetops Leisure Cabins' with the erection of a series of Swedish-style wooden chalets.

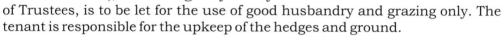

Poor Man's Piece

This is an area of 2R 27P (2 Rods 27 Perches or Poles), still managed by a body of Trustees, is to be let for the use of good husbandry and grazing only. The tenant is responsible for the upkeep of the hedges and ground.

Red Lion House

Red Lion House, Lower Square, was formerly an Inn, as was New House.

Market House

Lower Square was once the site of the ancient Market House, but there is currently no evidence of its previous existence.

Burdenwell Manor

This Manor dates back to the 16th century and was once owned by the Granville family. Despite rumours, it has never been proven that a tunnel actually existed from Burdenwell to the church. Such a tunnel was believed to have acted as a possible means of escape, should this have been necessary, to avoid capture or death from an enemy.

Penhallam

Grass-covered ruins of a medieval manor house, surrounded by a protective moat, are to be found in a delightful woodland setting. One particular example of the form such building might take, during the 13th century, is the manor house at Jacobstow, formerly the manor of Penhallam and held by the Cardinhams and the Champernownes, two of Cornwall's richest families. The manor was abandoned by the middle of the 14th century and has been preserved at foundation level ever since.

Newspapers

The main local newspaper for Week St. Mary is the Cornish & Devon Post, based in Launceston, part of the Tindle Newspapers Ltd group, owned by Sir Ray Tindle CBE DL, Honorary Vice-President of the Newspaper Society.

The paper, along with the Tavistock Times Gazette and Cornish Times, all part of Tindle Newspapers, celebrates its 150th anniversary during 2007 and as part of the celebration was visited by their Royal Highnesses, Charles and Camilla, Duke and Duchess of Cornwall.

I am indebted to this newspaper for the support given by way of references and contributions from their archives.

Ambulance

The Parish Council organised (1927) a collection for the Launceston and District Motor Ambulance.

River Tamar

It was decided to support Cornwall County Council in their endeavour to make the River Tamar the boundary between the two counties

Week St. Mary Youth Club

October 24th 1981 saw the newly formed Youth Club at Week St. Mary opened under the management of Mr. M. Goodman at the Parish Hall when 34 young people were enrolled.

Chipney Lake

It was brought to the attention of the Parish Council of the state of the 2 bridges on the WSM to Launceston main road, namely at Chipney Lake and Greenamoor Bridge.

Electric Lights

January 13th 1936 the Parish Council decided to enquire as to the cost of placing some lights in the village now that the electric light was available.

At a parish meeting on June 14th 1937, a vote was taken on the matter, resulting in the following: for electric lights 17, against 89. This was the end of the matter.

The installation of lights finally being accepted during 1976 and after some minor objections to the siting of light poles the installation finally went ahead and the County Council took over responsibility on 19th October 1976.

Council Housing - Week Green

The name "Broadclose" was proposed by the Parish Council and accepted by the District Council. Number '3' is where, as a family, we all grew up, until the untimely death of our mother in December 1978. So many memories of times long gone, but that's another story!

Water Unusable in The Square

1955 Workmen had contaminated the well in the Square making the water virtually unusable.

Well Doors Damaged

Week Green well doors damaged in 1957 but soon repaired

The Cliftons of Week St. Mary

Many old properties have names that reflect their original occupants. One such name is 'Clifton' being recorded within the village confines from as early as the mid-1500's. Records show that it was a fairly large family and occupied more than one property over the years.

One such Clifton was Richard, born in the village and christened on April 26, 1725. He was the son of John Clifton and Patience (Ryder) and moved to Camborne some time before September 9, 1751. This started the growth of the Clifton family in that area.

References to the Clifton name appear in Week St. Mary church records, Hearth Tax Returns of 1664 and the 1569 Muster Roll. In Palm Beach, Florida, U.S.A., descendant John W. Clifton, is responsible for amassing a vast amount of genealogical information and corresponds regularly to a number of Clifton supporters.[32]

Bridge Required at Whiteleigh

During 1961 heavy rain caused the road at Whiteleigh to become impassable and it was said that a bridge was needed urgently.

Long before the days of concern about pollutants entering the streams and rivers, I recall my dad taking me to this ford in his lorry in order to wash the vehicle. We would throw buckets of water at it and scrub the flatbed with brooms.

Village Pump Moved From The Square

In 1962 it was proposed that the pump in the Square be removed as it fallen into disuse.

Telephone Service

On the 2nd July 1923 it was decided by the Parish Council that it was desirable to accept the conditions upon which the Post Master General would permit a Public Telephone Service to be installed in the village. The GPO required a guarantee of £11 for seven years. Apparently a discussion ensued as to why they would require an extra 3½ miles of cable as the wires from Bude to Whitstone passed through the village!

The kiosk was originally positioned outside the then Post Office, by the church entrance, and was moved next to the bungalow of Mr. and Mrs Donald Sandercock (opposite the chapel) when they took over as Postmaster and Postmistress. Upon their retirement it was moved next to the market and the Post Office services were incorporated in Sandercock's shop.

As many of us will recall, operators - not direct-dial, in the main, controlled the old telephone system. As our mother had asthma it often fell upon me to walk down to the kiosk to make a phone call on mother's behalf. I was entrusted with 4 pennies for the call that were inserted into the slot when instructed. When the call was answered you had to press button 'A' before they could hear you. If there was no answer you pressed button 'B' and your 4 pennies would drop out into a half-cup shaped tray for your retrieval.

I used to be terrified of losing a coin - no four coins, therefore no phone call and it was a long walk!

When passing a phone box it was a regular activity for the children to pop in and press button 'B' to see if any money would drop out of the box.

West Week Close

Naming of new Council development in 1981

Stand Pipes

Stand Pipes in use around the village due to drought conditions during late summer 1976.

Water Tank

Erection of the water tank, opposite the garage at Week Green, sometime around 1955, was finally disposed of in 1977.

Parish Nurses

Nurse Piper & Nurse Weiss moved into the new Broadclose Council Houses - the only Council House with a garage! (circa 1950-55)

Week Green - Lambley Footpath

In 2000 MK International laid a digital data cable down through Back Lane (common land) on condition it laid a footpath and gates, thus avoiding digging right through the village.

Cory of Week St. Mary

William Cory (1783-1862), the founder of William Cory & Sons, a farmer's son born at Week St. Mary in Cornwall, left for London sometime before 1810. By the time he retired he was a respected gentleman of Bloomsbury.

Village Co-ordinates

Latitude: 50°45'2.10"N Longitude: 4°30'2.24"W Elevation: 150m

Cornish Translation

Week St. Mary = 'Gwigvaria'

Doctors

Over the past century Week St. Mary has boasted a good selection of doctors, including:

> Dr Curtis
> Dr May Frederick (Surgeon & M.O.)
> Dr Coates (Stewarts House)
> Dr Ledgerwood
> Dr Freeth
> Dr Ward
> Dr Wright (for over 36 years)

Although Dr Ward lived at Widemouth Bay he conducted local surgeries in some of the surrounding villages - Week St. Mary, Kilkhampton and Morwenstow.

The Week St. Mary surgery was held in Mrs Maddock's house on Monday, Thursday and Saturday of each week. The small waiting room, I recall, had stuffed birds in glass cases. It was always very dark in the small room - the electric light was never turned on as far as I can recall.

If any of us in our family needed to visit the surgery we could easily see when the doctor had arrived, by looking out of our back door, over the hedge at the bottom of next doors garden and seeing his car, then we would walk round the corner to the waiting room.

After surgery hours the doctor would make any necessary house calls around the village. When Dr Ward retired Dr Wright took on the practice. He continued the local surgery at Mrs Maddock's until the new Parish Hall was completed when one of the rooms was allocated as a consulting room.

When Dr Wright retired the villagers were informed that medical cover would be taken over by The Medical Centre, at Stratton. Initially, the medical cover was provided by one of the doctors visiting each village, once covered by Dr Wright, using a purpose-built mobile surgery. This vehicle cost in excess of £100,000 to be specially designed and equipped, plus annual running costs.

Our local doctors were quite used to getting urgent calls in the middle of the night, but once Dr Wright retired we had to make use of the night-time cover supplied by a countywide scheme of mobile doctors.

Unfortunately, this mobile service is very much influenced by such matters as performance figures, financial restrictions, response times, as indeed is the support given by the ambulance service. It can happen that in an emergency one might have to wait in excess of half an hour for an ambulance to arrive from a distant town - the local ambulance being at Plymouth or Barnstaple hospitals with some other emergency.

Cost of Living

We know that the cost of living, and dying for that matter, has risen dramatically over the years but even so, the day-to-day living expenses were relevant to the level of income and outgoings experienced at that time.

1940 Dec		£	s	d	Dec	Expenditure	£	s	d
28	Commence month with	6	15	11		1st week			
28 - JAN 4	1st week spent	1	7	11	30 Jan 2	Batteries 9/10, Stamp 2½		10	0½
		5	8	0		meat 7/-, Baker 4/2½		11	2½
11	Third Party Ins	2	1	3		P in £1 2/2, Brown bread		2	7
		3	6	9		Sea Fet. 2/9, 2 wks papers 1/4		4	1
4-11	2nd week spent		14	3½			1	7	11
		2	12	5½		2ND WEEK			
	2 days Threshing		4	0	6	S. 1/-, Baker 1/9		2	9
		2	16	5½		Carol singers, Baker 3/2		3	8
11-18	3rd week housekeeping	2	11	3		meat 6/9, Bread 4½		7	1½
			5	2½	11	Papers			9
22	Wages	9	14	10				14	3½
	Petrol		2	1		3rd week			
		10	2	1½	13	Batteries 1/6, Bread 9?		2	3
18-25	Housekeeping etc	5	1	10½		S. 3/2, Fitz £1. 7.10	1	11	0
		5	0	3	16	meat 6/-, Garland 1/9		7	9
						Sandereck		3	1½
						Paper 1/5, Col.?		1	6
						1 oz. wool 1½, Brush 4/-		4	7½
						Bread		1	0
						£	2	11	3

$\underline{1950}$ Paid out

£ . s . d

Jan 2nd Petrol   9. 2 -
  3.200 T V. O.   11. 9. 2
  4. Wireless Licence 1. 0. 0
  6. Pethich Bros. corn. 4. 4. 6
  19. Fire Insurance -3. 14. 6
  19 Land Tax   -1. 11. 7
  19. Pearl Insurance   9. 12. 4
  11. Whitlocks repairs tractor ~4. 18.. 7
  13. Mr. Martin Corn Bill -4. 18. 0
  21. Mr H. Martin 3 pigs 3.10.0 each 10. 10. 0
  7. Woodall. 3 ton novel -6. 10. 0
  17.   Bath   ~17. 6
  11. Lantern & Derris Root ~18. 6
  28. Pethich corn bill + 22. 7. 01.
  28   Petrol   9. 2
Feb. 4th Pethich Bros. corn ~8. 14. 6
  7   calor Gas   -1. 2. 4½
Jan 13th "   "   *1. 2. 4½
Feb 9 Fowls House }   29. 15. 0
  9th (Hoover cover)   12. 6
  13th Viel & nails   5. 6
  24   Petrol   9. 2

235

Rectors of the Parish Church

1278	Richard De Grangiis	----	Joseph Ferdinand
1342-3	William De Helperby	1716	John Turner
1348	Robert	1772	Thomas Bedford
1349	John De Alkyngton	1781	Edward Baynes
1362-3	Richard Bolham	1821	William Galter Gee
1376	William Aylsham	1852	James Saunders
1382	Ralph De Pylaton	1876	George Hanslip Hopkins
1387	John Grey	1886	John Dawson Peake
1387	John Gorwelle, LL.D.	1895	William Wilkinson
1404	William Hals	1900	Samuel Holker Haslam
1406	John Gorwelle, Jnr. LL.B.	1919	Charles Thomas Whitmell
1433	William Collyne	1921	Maurice Victor Hardy
1434-5	John Hawke	1931	Arthur Hambrook
1460	William Wase	1947	Noel Alexander F. Townend
----	George Sydnam	1955	William Thomas Soper
1502	John Halt	1959	William Thomas Simpson
----	Robert Peech	1981	John Gregory Edwards
1509	John Mulsworth	1995	Ivan Meads
1558	John Greynefylde	1998	Robin C. W. Dickenson
1580	John Kerslake		
1625	William Langford		
1642	John Biston		
1643-4	Isaac Rouse		
1680-1	Joseph Trewinnard		

Week St. Mary Church:
from an enchanting
watercolour by John Lynch

Week St. Mary Church Bells

No.	Note	Inscription	Weight		
			Cwt.	Qrs.	Lbs.
		THE RING OF SIX BELLS IN THIS TOWER WAS RECAST AND REHUNG IN 1950 BY GILLETT & JOHNSTON, CROYDON			
1	F#	MEARS & STAINBANK, FOUNDERS, LONDON GIVEN BY COSMO NEVILL PEAKE IN MEMORY OF KING EDWARD VII R et I 1910 RECAST 1950 BY GILLETT & JOHNSTON FOUNDERS, CROYDON	4	1	2
2	E	CAST BY JOHN WARNER & SONS, LONDON PEACE AND GOOD NEIGHBOURHOOD RECAST 1887 RECAST 1950 BY GILLETT & JOHNSTON FOUNDERS, CROYDON	4	2	23
3	D	PROSPERITY TO THIS PARISH A 🔔 R 1731 RECAST 1950 BY GILLETT & JOHNSTON FOUNDERS, CROYDON	5	1	5
4	C#	PROSPERITY TO THE CHURCH OF ENGLAND 1731 RECAST 1950 BY GILLETT & JOHNSTON FOUNDERS, CROYDON	5	3	2
5	B	ABR RVDHAL OF GLOCESTER CAST VS ALL 1731 RECAST 1950 BY GILLETT & JOHNSTON FOUNDERS, CROYDON	6	2	18
6	A	I TO THE CHURCH THE LIVING CALL AND TO THE GRAVE DO SUMMON ALL RECAST 1887 J. D. PEAKE - RECTOR T. WALKEY - CHURCHWARDEN B. HUTCHINGS - CHURCHWARDEN CAST BY JOHN WARNER & SONS LONDON 1887 RECAST 1950 BY GILLETT & JOHNSTON FOUNDERS, CROYDON	8	3	0
		THE REVEREND N. A. F. TOWNEND, M. A. - RECTOR J. H. ROGERS - CHURCHWARDEN T. ROGERS - CHURCHWARDEN	**35**	**1**	**22**
		E. ASHMORE (WRITER), CROYDON	GILLETT & JOHNSTON LTD, CROYDON BELLFOUNDERS & CLOCKMAKERS		

Notes from the Church Register

S ome of the more interesting snippets pertaining to the church between 1688 and 1971 are reported here and it is interesting to note that a constant flow of activities relating to the church and its administration goes to show the strength of the church in a rural environment.

1688 North East pinnacle struck by lightning.

1812 North East pinnacle again struck by lightning.

1843 South East pinnacle struck by lightning.

1865 South West pinnacle struck by lightning.

1876 The Reverend James Saunders died in April. The Benefice was presented to George H. Hopkins, M.A., Fellow of Sidney Sussex College, who was inducted in September. The condition of the Church was such that the drainage from roof gutters poured through into the Church.

1877 First meeting held for the necessary steps for restoring the Church early in 1878 - the year previously the fabric was thoroughly investigated by Mr. J.P. St. Aubyn.

1877 Friday July 13th - Confirmation was held by the Bishop of Truro. 6 candidates in all, 5 from Week St. Mary and 1 from Jacobstow. There had been no confirmations in the parish for 70 years - an old man, John Fry, remembered it.

1878 March 7th, Meeting of parishioners to support the movement for restoring the Church.

1878 Nov. 8th - South West pinnacle struck by lightning at 6.45 am. The Tower had been struck, during the winter months, on previous occasions: 1688 - NE pinnacle, 1812 - NE pinnacle, 1843 - SE pinnacle and 1865 - SW pinnacle.

1879 July 6th, last services in the Church prior to restoration. There were 8 communicants and the offerings totalled 4/-. Services were subsequently held in the Board School Room from July 13th to July 4th 1880.

1879 July 7th - work on the Church commenced.

1880 July 8th Church re-opened. Expenses to that date were £1,502.16s.9d. Morning prayer and sermon by the Bishop of Truro, Evening prayer and sermon by Canon Cornish, the total offerings collected on the day were £24.7s.9d. After the opening, eleven windows were filled with granite tracery and mullions at a cost of £313, the gift of Mr. C. Winbolt. They were completed in 1883.

1881 March 22nd, Confirmation by the Bishop of Truro, 19 candidates, 15 from Week St. Mary and 4 from Jacobstow.

1885 This Benefice was presented to Rev. J.D. Peake, Rector of Pitchcolt, Bucks.

1887 The Tower was restored with new roof and new floors throughout and the basement pointed. The bells were re-hung in a new oak bell cage and two were re-cast by Messrs. Warner & Co. This work was done at a cost of £170. A handsome stained glass window by Kempe was given by Mr. Nash, in memory of his daughter, the wife of the late Rector Rev. G.H. Hopkins, who died in 1884.

1889 A handsome window with granite mullions and tracery and filled with Cathedral glass was given by Mr. C. Winbolt. A portion of new flooring was put in inside the South entrance door.

1895 The Rev. W. Wilkinson of Leicestershire exchanged Livings with the Rev. J.D. Peake and was inducted on December 2nd by the Archdeacon of Bodmin. The high winds stripped off some 18 or 20 roof slates and damaged the lightning conductor.

During the year a tea was given to the children of the Board School, by the Rector and twice to the Sunday School. The Church tower needs pointing, the rain beats on the bricks and then drains through the joints making the walls inside very wet. The work must be done soon or the tower will suffer.

1896 A subscription list has been opened for repairing and pointing the tower. On 21st September the offertories on Revel Sunday and at the Harvest Thanksgiving the next day amounted to £2.7s.3d. besides which a Sale of Work realised £6.0s.0d. and the sale of the old organ made another £6.0s.0d.

1896 October - The Parish Room in the Rectory Yard was opened for games, reading and amusement for men and adults during the winter months - and a very good number attends, Popular lectures and tea parties are occasionally given by way of change, instruction and sociability.

1896 November - A new public road has been made and opened from the Tavistock road to the one leading to Bude, coming out by Haydah so that going down and up those steeps by Haydah are avoided.

1897 May 25th, the Tower is now finished and looks well able to withstand the storms once more - a fitting memorial of the Queen's Diamond Jubilee.

1897 June 1st, to celebrate the completion of the restoration work a public tea was held in the Rectory Room and about 80 people sat down to tea. At 7.30 pm there was a service of thanksgiving in the Church. The tower was opened entirely free from debt and a statement of accounts was printed and sent to each of the subscribers to the fund.

1897 June 20th, by Royal Command special services were held to commemorate Her Majesty's reign of 60 years. On the actual Jubilee Day there were great rejoicings all over the country; here, there was a free tea for all parishioners and a mug given to each child. Sports were held later in the day and a church service.

1899 June 30th. Rev. W. Wilkinson passed away after an illness lasting a week.

1899 July. Owing to the kindness of the Rector's family and other friends, the Church bells have lately been re-hung. The living is now vacant.

1899 August, during the vacancy the Rev. H.R. Jennings (Vice-Chancellor of Truro Cathedral) now vicar of Millbrook took charge of the Parish from August 12th to October 23rtd and from October 23rd until the arrival of the Rev. S.H. Haslam, the Rev. H. Edwards (of the Bishop of Truro's Staff) took charge.

1899 In August weekly and Holy Day celebrations of Holy Communion were re-established. In October, Matins and Evensong were said daily at 10am and 6pm in the Church.

1900 The Rev. Samuel H. Haslam, M.A. was inducted to this Living on 22nd January, by the Archdeacon of Bodmin.

1901 Queen Victoria died January 22nd and a memorial service was held in the crowded Church on Saturday February 2nd.

1901 March 18th. A Confirmation was held in this Church by the Bishop of the Diocese, the following were confirmed: Michael Thomas Treleven (aged 52), William James Rundle (aged 19), Joanna Wickett (46) and Elizabeth Ann Hooper (35).

1903 A new two manual organ by Messrs. Bevington & Sons, Charing Cross Road, London, was built in the Church on the south side-aisle, to replace the old organ which stood on the north side. The original estimate for this organ was £223.10s. This sum was raised by voluntary contributions, concerts, etc and the old organ was sold to Bradford Church, Brandis Corner, N. Devon for £30.

1906 March 31st. The Bishop of St. Germans confirmed 25 candidates in Week St. Mary Church today, Jacobstow 13, St. Gennys 5, Whitstone 2, Week St. Mary 5.

1906 A surpliced Choir consisting of 11 boys and 5 men was instituted on Whit Sunday, June 3rd. The extensive restoration & improvement of the Rectory was begun April 18th and were completed in 1907. The old kitchen was converted into the Dining Room, the Hall was enlarged, the old Dining Room became the Study, the old Study became the new Kitchen. Bathroom, lavatories etc. were provided. New windows were supplied throughout and a new back entrance and steps leading from the road was made, the old tumbledown cob buildings at the back were removed and a new stonewall built. The out buildings were also restored and improved. The total cost was defrayed by money from private sources.

The old dial was found at the Rectory, it was used as a step to the old Schoolroom. It was repaired and erected over the Church door.

1909 November 26th. A confirmation was held at St. Anne's Church, Whitstone on this date and 5 candidates were from Week St. Mary: Mary Constance Colwill (aged 16), Mary Margaretta Coles (15), Esther Mahala Coles (14), Ada Bertha Coles (14) and Bessie Winifred Coles (13).

1910 A clock was placed in the Church Tower early this year. Mr. N.F.A. Cobbald obtained the clock for a small sum and he and S.H. Haslam made the face, hands and connecting parts and erected it in the tower. It has been going steadily and keeping good time for several months.

1910 King Edward VII died May 6th and was buried May 20th. A united memorial service was held at the Church according to the authorized form at 1pm, the time appointed for the interment, the Church was crowded with representation from every house in the parish.

1911 The Lord Bishop held a Confirmation here on this date. The following were confirmed: John Duke (aged 26), Ellen Cordelia Marshall (18), Elizabeth Trease Sandercock (28), Edith Cornish (16) and Beatrice Annie Lyle (28).

1912 The new Tower Screen was dedicated. It was made by John Northcott & Co. of Ashwater, Devon. The total cost was £35.10s.

1913 The following were confirmed at Whitstone Church on March 10th: Charles Pooley (aged 27), Albert Pengelly Rowland (22), Horace William Hooper (20), James Congdon (19), Frank Rogers (18), Frederick Thomas Colwill (17), David Nathaniel Coles (14) and Mary Jane Parnell (39).

1915 The following were confirmed at Week St. Mary by the Lord Bishop of the Diocese on March 23rd: Edwin Gerald Coles (14), Robert Cecil Coles (13), Edward John Sheldrake (15), Ethel Alice Lyle (13), Joy Jane Chidley (13), Hazel Andrew (14), Annie Beatrice Alberta Cobbledick (14) and Florence Elizabeth Jane Parnell (13).

1917 The following were confirmed at Week St. Mary, on March 19th: Joy Clarissa Dennis (22), Gwendoline Rose Mary Rowland (22) and Mary Elizabeth Kinsman (21).

1919 The Rev. H.S. Haslem resigned on July 1st, owing to ill health. On October 15th Rev. Charles Thomas Whitmell was inducted.

1921 Early in 1921 Rev. C.J. Whitmell became unwell and resigned on 1st April. Rev. M.V. Hardy came into residence for Sunday September 11th and was inducted on November 5th. The Rectory Room, built by Rev. Haslem and bought from him by Rev. Whitmell has now been purchased by the Church, for £150.

1922 March 20th Confirmations by the Bishop of the Diocese at Week St. Mary: William Henry Parnell (19), Leonard Charles Hutchings (18), Ena Anne Catherine Badcock (14) and Winifred Mary Lyle (15). On July 6th the first Garden Fete was held: £25. October 3rd: Canon Haslam died at Paignton.

1923 Rectory Room, new stove bought. Boiler house built. New stoves were put in the Church at Revel, when the total amount of cost was raised (£25). The new stoves were made like the old ones, the wisdom of this is doubtful as they are very small, but supplemented with two Perfection heaters, they give a fair result.

1923 The Church Army[d11] visited the Parish in October.

1924 New lamps were put in the Church at a cost of £40. Some of the old lamps were put in the Rectory Room.

1925 On March 22nd the following were confirmed in Week St. Mary Church by the Lord Bishop of the Diocese: Richard John Barkwell (34), Dennis William Colwill (12), Hampton Henry Hicks (17), William Lyle (45), Thomas Bertram Lyle (12), William Ridgman (38), John Henry Ridgman (13), Doris

Beatrice Colwill (14), Jane Edwards (55), Winifred Retallack (26), Mary Ann Ridgman (34) and Hilda Annie Rowland (26). The Rectory Room was painted on the outside by voluntary helpers led by Mr. Rowland.

1926 As the chairs in the Church are all very old, worm-eaten and gradually collapsing it was necessary to re-seat the Church. £48 was raised on Easter Day to start the re-seating fund. There has been a very successful Flower & Vegetable Show and Garden Fete during this year.

1926 The Church Army van visited the parish in November and there were some very good services.

1927 On November 25th the Bishop held a confirmation at Week St. Mary, when the following were confirmed: Roy Ivan Pooley (12), Marion Christine Badcock (13), Irene Chidley (15), Hazel Valentine Lyle (13) and Ida Morwenna Pooley (14).

1929 In July the organ was taken apart and cleaned and slight renovations made, by Hele & Co. of Plymouth at a cost of £32.10s.

1930 March 31st - The following were confirmed by the Bishop: James Henry Tresidder (39), Phyllis Katherine Mary Rogers (16), Audrey Philippa Rogers (14), Margery Coles (15) and Beatrice Mary Martin (13).

1931 The Rectory Room was enlarged by the addition of a room for refreshments and a gentlemen's cloakroom.

1931 July 3rd - Rev. A. Hambrook, formerly of St. Bartholomews, Nottingham, inducted, having exchanged livings with Rev. Hardy.

1932 Confirmed at Poundstock Church on Monday March 7th, by the Bishop of the Diocese: William Thomas Congdon of Kitsham and Thomas Rogers of Haydah.

1932 June: Death watch beetle - the first years treatment with Presolini carried out on all necessary Church timbers.

1933 March 27th. Confirmed at Week St. Mary, by the Bishop of the Diocese: W.A. Brend of Lower Square, H.M. Treleven of Steele Farm, R. Toms and N.M. Williams of Langford Hill and John Colwill of Reeve House.

1934 Death watch beetle treatment - completed with its third annual application by workmen of the village. During the year new sets of Churchyard gates and posts have been supplied and fitted.

1935 Thursday 21st February: The S.E. pinnacle and centre of the Church Tower were struck by lightning, after a hailstorm lasting around 2 hours, causing large pieces of masonry to fall through the Church roof and resulting in a great deal of damage to the building.

The following telegram was sent to the Ecclesiastical Insurance Office, 11 Norfolk Street, London WC2, from Bude at 4 pm., the local telephone service being dislocated by the storm: "Church struck by lightning; seriously damaged; immediate inspection suggested; writing." A reply telegram arrived from Bude 6pm, stating that their assessor, Messrs. Ware & Co., Beaford Circus, Exeter, would visit the Church at once. Mr. Ware arrived the following day at 12 noon and took charge of the Church on behalf of the Insurance Office. Services took place in the Rectory Rooms until January 12th 1936.

1936 Re-opening services were held on Thursday 16th January, the Bishop of the Diocese preaching and holding a Confirmation. The following were confirmed on this occasion: E.J. Westlake of Kitsham, F.H. Martin of Marhays, I.C. Colwill and J.M. Colwill of Reeve House, M.E. Ridgman of Hillside, J. Martyn of Kitleigh and M. Stacey of Tower Hill.

1936 March 15th, the following were Confirmed at Stratton Church: H.H. Ridgman of Hillside and H. Stacy of Tower Hill.

1937 Photographs of the Church 1) Whole Interior, 2) High Altar, 3) St. Johns Chapel, 4) Exterior, were taken at Easter in this Coronation Year of George VI and copies, together with photographs of the Church damaged by lightning, were put in the Registers Safe. The copyright of the first four at Knights Studio, Bude, was bought with the first photographs. A new piano was bought for the Rectory Room and the exterior of the building was painted.

1938 The Nave walls were re-pointed outside.

1939 Confirmed March 30th at St. Stephens, Launceston, by the Bishop of Truro: H.M. Congdon of The Green, B. J. Martin of Marhayes and M. R. Rogers of Haydah.

1939 March - the Church walls were washed down with brown lime.

1939 At 11 am on Sunday September 3rd, War was declared against Germany at its aggression on Poland.

1939 September 17th Sunday Services of Feast of Dedication held as usual, on Revel Monday the Foxhounds Meet 8.30 am, Tea 4 pm, Evensong 6 pm, Social 7.30 - 10 pm, the sports etc. having been omitted. Future evensong 3 pm, Air-raid Signal: two bells, All-clear: Tenor bell.

1940 The Church walls show no sign of darkening by dampness this year for the first time for many years. After the exposure to the weather in 1935, years were needed for the walls to dry out and this did not become possible until they were re-pointed in 1938. Revel was held, as last year, with no children's sports or tea.

1941 Revel, as last year, no children's sports or tea.

1942 Revel, as last year, no children's sports or tea. The Church walls show darkening by damp only on the West side, due to the overflowing of the gutter trough on the South side and to the lower gutter overflow on the North side.

1943 Confirmed at Marhamchurch on Midlent Sunday, April 4th 1943, by Bishop Hunkin: E.V. Coles of The Square, J. Stacey of Corner House, The Village, M.D. Rogers of Greathills Cottage and M. Cobbledick of Stewarts Road.

1945 Confirmations at Poundstock Midlent, Sunday March 11th, by Bishop Hunkin: Mr. & Mrs. S. Ridgman of Goscott Cottage and D. Treleven of Lower Square.

1945 On Tuesday May 8th Victory was won and proclaimed in Europe against Germany. The Service of Thanksgiving was Festal Evensong at 7.30 pm attended by a crowded congregation, greatly moved at so great an occasion.

1945 Thursday July 5th: Labour Government declared, Mr. Attlee (Prime Minister), whose brother Mr. T.S. Attlee is one of the chief laymen of the diocese.

1945 Wednesday August 5th Victory was proclaimed in the Far East against Japan and the Great War ended. The Service of Thanksgiving was Festal Evensong and similar to that held in May.

1946 In considering a stained glass window at the high altar, the Rector called attention to the fact that all three East end windows are out of centre to the North, while the lower arch is out of centre to the South. Apparently no one had ever noticed this before.

1947 The Reverend A. Hambrook resigned on May 1st. The Reverend Townend M.A., R.A.F. Chaplain was inducted in the Parish Church on July 4th at 7.00 pm by the Bishop of Truro and the Service was followed by a social evening in the Rectory Room.

1947 In the autumn a Sunday School and a Choir were formed. A Parish Magazine, to be called "The Beacon" was begun at Advent. An electric boiler was installed at the Rectory Room at a cost of £11.

1948 On February 29th a Confirmation Service was held in Week St. Mary Church by the Bishop of Truro, at which Candidates were from Kilkhampton, Launceston, Bude, Stratton and Whitstone. The following were confirmed from Week St. Mary: G. M. Gifford, M. R. Gifford, C. I. Horrell, J. I. Mallin, D. Coles, E. A. Mills and J. H. Pearce. The candidates were afterwards entertained to tea at the Rectory. A new set of bell ropes were obtained from John Taylor & Co. and were dedicated at Evensong on Sunday May 30th. The cost of the ropes was £20.12s.6d. The money was raised by the ringers by means of dances and socials.

1949 Electric lighting and organ blowing was installed in the Church in March at a total cost of £200. A grant of £70 was made by the Rural Churches Fund and the rest of the money was raised in the parish over a number of years.

1949 A very successful Garden Fete was held in the Rectory grounds on June 16th, the first one to be held for some years. The sum of £45.8s.1d. was raised towards the Church Thanksgiving Fund. The Churchyard paths were re-laid with tar by voluntary labour at a cost of £30.

The exterior of the Rectory Room was repainted by Mr. S. Barber during July and August and some necessary repairs were done at the same time, at a total cost of £47.10s.0d. The money was withdrawn from the Rectory Room repair fund. A new stove was also installed at the end of the year, £9.5s.6d.

1950 A new Churchyard gate was made by Mr. T. Pauling and the rest were repaired and painted. The coal shed was also repaired. Total cost came to £17.17s.9d. The Church Army Mission Van visited the parish from January 22nd to February 9th; Capt. Usher held mighty services in the Rectory Room which were well attended. He preached in the Church on Sundays.

The following were confirmed by the Bishop of the Diocese at Kilkhampton, on March 19th: S. Petherick, R. Warne and P. Gifford.

1950 A successful Fete was held in the Rectory grounds on June 22nd. It included a "Pageant of Week St. Mary". The sum of £31.5s.7d. was raised towards the Cornish Church Thanksgiving Fund.

The six bells were recast and re-hung on ball bearings by Messrs. Gillett & Johnston of Croydon. The frame was secured more strongly to the beams, which were reset and the girders repainted. The Bishop of Truro re-dedicated the bells on Sunday September 17th, the Dedication Festival.

1951 A camellia, given to the parish by the Cornish branch of the Council for the Preservation of Rural England, in memory of Bishop Hunkin, was planted on the south side of the Church, near the vestry door, on the afternoon of Palm Sunday, by Mr. J.H. Rogers, Rector's Warden.

1951 On June 21st a Garden Fete in the Rectory grounds raised £40 for the Cornish Church Thanksgiving Fund.

1952 The following were Confirmed by the Bishop at Kilkhampton on March 23rd: E. Masters, H. Pauling, W. Jones, J. Lamerton, S. Lamerton, V. Colwill, Y. Crofts, R. Crofts, D. Gifford, V. Ellis and M. Ellis.

1952 Some necessary repairs done to the foundations and floor of the Rectory Room, under the Ladies Cloakroom, at a cost of £22. The work was done by Mr. Barber of Week St. Mary and was consequent on extensive rotting of the main floor beams through faulty pillars and lack of free passage of air beneath the building.

1947 - 1952 During the past five years the following improvements have been made to the Rectory and paid for by the Cornish Church Thanksgiving Fund: Boiler in the kitchen, washing up basin in the pantry and electric light in those rooms before unsupplied and electric pump for the water supply from the well to the house.

The Glebe Farm buildings in the lower yard were sold; these buildings originally housed the stables. The old schoolroom was excepted from this sale as it might be of use in the future and was not subject to dilapidations.

1952 On June 26th a Garden Fete was held in the Rectory grounds, raising £34. The cost of recasting and re-hanging of the bells was finally paid off on June 12th.

1952 On February 15th, the day of King George VI Funeral, a Requiem was said at 8.00 am and a combined Memorial Service was held at the Parish Church in the evening - a full Church.

1953 The Coronation of Queen Elizabeth II was marked by a broadcast of the Service in Westminster Abbey, in the Parish Church. The broadcast was most successful and the congregation, although small, took all opportunities of joining in with the Service. The rest of the day was spent enjoying sports, public teas and a bonfire.

1953 On October 22nd a most successful Bazaar was held in the place of the usual garden fete, which would have clashed with the Coronation. A ladies working party had been in operation since March and it provided the bulk of the goods for sale. As a result over £60 was raised for the C.C.T.F.

1954 The Bishop of the Diocese held his Visitation in St. Mary's, Launceston, on 3rd June, on which occasion the Rector of Week St. Mary was admitted as Rural Dean of Stratton. The Bishop of North Queensland, Australia, who was visiting the Rector, preached on Revel Monday.

1954 A successful Bazaar was held on October 21st in aid of the C.C.T.F. and over £60 was raised. On the departure of the Reverend Townend, the Christmas Crib, which had been in use in the Church for the past eight years, was left by him to the Church for future use. This crib was made in 1945 by German P.O.W's, at R.A.F. Station Upper Heyford.

1955 The Reverend Townend resigned the living on January 8th. The Rev. W.T. Soper was inducted on Saturday May 14th, at 3 pm, by the Bishop of Truro. The Service was followed by tea in the Rectory Room and a Social in the evening.

1955 A successful Garden Fete was held in the Rectory Grounds on July 7th and the proceeds amounted to £35 were towards the Church Heating Fund.

1955 A very successful Revel this year in perfect weather. The Revel sermon on Monday September 19th at Evensong was preached by the Rev. Canon L.M. Andrews, C.V.O., M.C., M.A., Chaplain to H.M. the Queen and Rector of Stoke Climsland.

1955 The carol mime "Nativity" was presented in costume, in the Church, on Thursday December 22nd, at 7.30 pm, by the Sunday School children. It was also presented in Whitstone Church on the following Thursday and again in Week St. Mary Church on Sunday January 1st 1956.

1956 Five candidates from this parish were confirmed at Poughill Church on Sunday March 4th, by the Lord Bishop of the Diocese. They were: P. B. Colwill, B. Hutchings, H. I. Ridgman, J. S. Jones and M. Hutchings.

1956 A Garden Fete was held on the Rectory Lawn on Saturday June 23rd, proceeds were in aid of the Church Heating Fund and the sum of £44.12s.11d. was realised.

1956 Dedication Festival, Sunday September 16th, Church full at Evensong.

1956 Harvest Festival and Revel, Monday September 17th: The Lord Bishop of Truro preached at Evensong, when again there was a full congregation.

Heavy rain had led to cancellation of the sporting events, though it cleared sufficiently for the comic football match to be held. Unfortunate absence from the Revel was that of Church Warden, John Henry Rogers, in hospital in Plymouth, after breaking his leg by falling from a ladder, in August.

1956 The Annual Bazaar was held on Thursday December 6th. Proceeds amounting to £50 were donated to the Church Heating Fund this year, as the C.C.T.F. account had enough balance to meet our obligations for 1956. The electrical heating system installed in the Church by Messrs. Woolacott of Stratton, was switched on for the first time on Sunday December 23rd.

1957 An inaugural service was held for officially opening the heating system, on Thursday January 11th, when a Blessing was given and the Rector of Whitstone, Rev. R.E. Underwood, gave the address.

1957 A Garden Fete was held on June 22nd on the Rectory Lawn. The proceeds for the C.C.T.F. were approximately £60.

1957 The Feast of Dedication and Harvest Thanksgiving were held on September 22nd and 23rd. The Revel preacher at Evensong was the Ven. The Archdeacon of Bodmin.

1957 The Autumn Bazaar was held on November 30th when £35 was raised for Church Funds.

At a Confirmation Service in Stratton Church on Sunday December 15th the following were confirmed by the Lord Bishop of Truro: J. Colwill, D. Horrell, D. Petherick, J. Ellis, C. Jones and M. Jones.

1958 The Annual Garden Fete was held on Rectory Lawn on Saturday May 31st. A Social in the Rectory Room in the evening concluded the days events. £42.4s.0d. was realised for Church Funds.

1958 Dedication Festival, Harvest Thanksgiving and Revel were on Sunday September 21st and Monday 22nd. The preacher on Monday evening was the Rev. Canon Bowden, Chancellor of Truro Cathedral. £33.17s.8d. was raised.

1958 The Autumn Bazaar was held in the Rectory Room on Thursday November 20th, a Social followed in the evening and over £50 was raised towards the Organ Restoration Fund.

The restoration work on the organ was carried out by Mr. E. Sergeant, of Launceston, at a cost of £178.15s.0d. and a re-dedication service was held on Friday December 19th when a short recital by Rev. W. Allwood Evans, Rector of Marhamchurch, followed.

1959 August - The wife of the Revd. W. T. Soper died in Greenbank Hospital, following an operation. The Memorial Service and Committal of the ashes took place on 20th August. The service was conducted by the Rev. Walter Prest, R.D., assisted by Rev. R. Underwood, Rector of Whitstone. The Archdeacon of Bodmin took the Committal in the Churchyard.

1959 Rogation Sunday - The Revd. W.T. Soper died suddenly after Evensong, having taken full services all day, including a Baptism. The Funeral service was taken by Rev. W. Attwood-Evans, Rector of Marhamchurch, at Plymouth Crematorium, on the following Wednesday and the Memorial Service took place at the parish evensong at Week St. Mary, conducted by the Rector of Marhamchurch, assisted by the Rural Dean, Revd. Walter Prest. The address was given by the Archdeacon of Bodmin, Ven. W.H. Prior, who also officiated at the committal of the casket in the Churchyard.

1970 The Rector's announcement from the pulpit of his decision to deny access to the Rectory Room because of a health and safety risk caused some aggravation amongst many parishioners. It was felt that the decision to close the Rectory Room should have been delayed until the building of the new Parish Hall was complete so as to continue to offer a meeting place for the parishioners.

1971 January 1st: The Rectory Room was sold by the P.C.C., Week St. Mary to the Rector for the sum of £60. (This was signed by the Rector, W.T. Simpson and by the Treasurer, M. Cobbledick).

A letter in the parish Magazine 'The Beacon' dated May 1957 contained this letter to the parishioners from the Rector, W. T. Soper:

Dear People,

It was a joyous Easter. The Church was beautifully decorated, thanks to those who worked so hard to make it so. We were blessed with fine weather over the weekend and congregations at all services were good. A full choir added to the 'wholeness' of our worship and the beauty of the services. Reference to the choir reminds me that I must say how very grateful we are to Miss Chidley for renovating some of the surplices and to Mrs Cobbledick for washing and ironing them. It has made a great improvement.

I am writing just at the end of the schools' Easter holidays and the children will be back at school again when this issue of the magazine is circulated. I wish them all a happy summer term and good progress, especially asking God's Blessing on the five-year-olds who begin their school life at this time. The summer months will soon be with us. We are going ahead with preparations for our Annual Garden Fete to be held on Saturday, June 22nd. Then there is the Parish Outing to Exmouth on Saturday July 27th for which Mrs Frank Martin will be taking bookings from now on. The cost will be 12/6.
With good wishes to you all,

Your friend and Rector

W. T. SOPER

Events relating to
Thomasine Bonaventure

c.1437 Thomasine Bonaventure probably born about this time

c.1450 John Percival became a merchant tailor

c.1458 John Percival became a freeman of London

1485-96 John Percival alderman of Vintry Ward

1486 John Percival became master of the merchant tailors

1486-7 John Percival sheriff of London

1487 John Percival knighted

c.1487 Living with his wife Dame Thomasine at 71 Lombard Street, London

19 April 1503 Death of Sir John Percival

1504-5 Dame Thomasine bought houses in London to found a further chantry (in addition to Sir John Percival's chantry) at St Mary Wolnoth

15 May 1506 Sir John Lisle of Thruxton, Hants., sold the Manor of Simpson in Holsworthy to Dame Thomasine Percival

10 July 1506 Dame Thomasine's deed of endowment to found a chantry, obit and Grammar school at Week St. Mary

1 Aug 1506 The three trustees conveyed the endowment to 19 footees (names also in endowment deed of 10th July 1506)

12 Aug 1506 Seisin of estates given by Sir John Lisle's attorneys to four of the feofees on behalf of all the feofees

9 Nov 1507 Henry Thorne conveyed to Dame Thomasine Percival the manor of Bradworthy in Devon

6 Nov 1508 Royal licence to alienate lands for the endowment of the chantry of Thomasine Percival at Week St. Mary

Between 10 April and 30 July 1512 Death of Dame Thomasine Percival

10 May 1539 Thomas Row's lease of part of the manor of Simpson

1536 Thomas Row occurs as schoolmaster

1536 Dispute with the Bishop of Exeter about the tithes of WSM School

1546 Chantry school at WSM a "great comfort to all the country" who sent their children to board there for free education

1548 Week St. Mary School utterly decayed

1548 School transferred to Launceston. William Cholwell may have gone to Launceston. The usher at Week St Mary, George Spry and his wife Alice, the laundress, remained at Week.

1555 John Spry "minister of the chantry of St John the Baptist at Week St Mary" in receipt of a pension of £3.6.8d.

1570 Stephen Gourge ex-schoolmaster of Launceston and incumbent of St Mary Magdalene (and formerly sub-prior of Launceston Priory) still living at St Thomas by Launceston with two former canons of the Priory.

1725 John Prideaux sold the manor of Simpson to Thomas Pitt, first Lord Londonderry, his sister carried the estate to James Stanhope in marriage.

1910 Holsworthy estate (including the manor of Simpson) sold by the 7th Earl Stanhope.

1971 Deed of endowment of Week St Mary School acquired by Sotheby's

10 July 1972 Deed of endowment sold at Sotheby's

13 Oct 1972 Decision of the Reviewing Committee on the Export of Works of Art prevented its export to the USA

16 Nov 1972 Deed of endowment was purchased by Cornwall County Record Office with the aid of a grant from the Friends of the National Libraries

1841 Census Analysis

Agricultural Labourer	53	Miller	2
Apprentice	6	Pauper	19
Blacksmith	1	Pensioner	2
Butcher	1	Saddler	2
Carpenter	6	Schoolmaster	1
Carpet Weaver	1	Schoolmistress	1
Char Woman	3	Shoemaker	2
Cheese Dealer	1	Shopkeeper	1
Cordwainer (Cobbler)	1	Silk Weaver	1
Draper	3	Surgeon	1
Dressmaker	1	Tailor	4
Excise Office	1	Tinplate Worker	1
Farmer	47	Unclassified	465
Female Servant	32		
Gardener	1	AGES:	
Glover	1	0 - 13 years	271
House Keeper	2	14 - 19 years	93
Independent Means	24	20 - 29 years	118
Innkeeper	3	30 - 39 years	84
Labourer	2	40 - 49 years	72
Leatherseller	1	50 - 59 years	71
Male Servant	68	60 - 69 years	49
Maltster	2	70 - 79 years	23
Mason	5	80 - 89 years	5
Merchant	1	90 - 99 years	0

1856 Post Office Directory

Gentry:
Saunder, Rev James, BD
Tuke, James, Esq

Traders:
Badcock, Daniel Dennis; farmer
Baker, Henry jnr; farmer
Baker, John; farmer
Baker, Thomas; farmer
Balhatchet, John; blacksmith
Balhatchet, John; farmer
Bickford, William; mason
Braund, John; shopkeeper, maltster, brewer
Bray, Daniel; butcher
Broad, John; tailor
Colwill, William; carpenter
Congdon, Daniel; farmer
Cundy, William; blacksmith
Cundy, William; grocer & draper
Dalgleish, Henry; revenue officer
Featherstone, Michael; grocer & draper

Fry, Henry; New Inn
Hart, William; mason
Hoskin, Henry; tree ?
Hutchings, Richard; carpenter
Hutchings Richard; grocer & draper
Hutchings, Thomas; tailor & draper
Mason, Isaac; farmer
Orchard, John; Kings Arms
Perkin, John sen.; farmer
Perkin, John; blacksmith
Prower, Thomas; builder
Prower, William; farmer
Read, Nathaniel; farmer
Runnalls, Joseph; boot & shoe manf.
Smeethe, John; beer retailer & carpenter
Smith, William; boot & shoe maker
Tuke, James; surgeon
Webb, James; butcher

National School:
Samuel Balhatchet; master
Miss Mary Jane Balhatchet; mistress

Week St. Mary School Record Book

29th November 1875 Week St. Mary School Board has been held in a room (hired by the Board for the same purpose) since this date.

30th October 1876 The school was opened by the Rev. G. H. Hopkins. There were just 10 children admitted during the first week.

4th May 1877 Still no blackboard!

14th September 1877 One boy sent to Stratton Workhouse[d12] (an orphan or pauper) for truancy, not returning to Week St. Mary until 21st September 1877.

22nd March 1878 17 Children absent from school suffering from whooping cough.

26th May 1878 School closed for 3 weeks due to number of pupils suffering from Measles.

3rd October 1878 School closed for 3 weeks due to number of pupils suffering from Scarlet Fever.

24th October 1882 School closed owing to a Bazaar in connection with the 'Dissenters of the Parish School'.

8th June 1885 There are now 85 pupils listed in the School Register.

15th December 1885 Because of a Measles epidemic the school is closed until 5th January 1886.

1888 Only a slight rise in pupils in 3½ years - There are now 89 pupils listed in the School Register.

20th April 1888 Whooping Cough is making it very noisy in class!

11th January 1889 There are now 95 pupils listed in the School Register.

1st October 1889 27 Children absent from school. Mostly boys out digging and storing potatoes.

20th May 1890 Several children away because of a Sunday School Tea at the Bible Christian Chapel.

3rd March 1891 Week St. Mary School closed due to blizzards.

26th June 1891 Closed for some weeks due to outbreak of Scarletina (It was recorded on 22nd April 1892 that the Scarletina had almost gone).

19th September 1892 School closed for Revel Day.

21st December 1895 Week St. Mary School closed for 2 weeks for the Christmas holidays.

7th January 1896 The Doctor ordered the School closed due to an epidemic of Whooping Cough.

25th March 1896 Whooping Cough returned to the school.

3rd June 1896 Week St. Mary School closed for 3 weeks due to epidemic of Measles.

14th May 1897 There are now 115 pupils listed in the School Register.

9th September 1898 Half the school away due to blackberry picking and potato digging.

25th April 1898 Military Drill today well executed but some of the smaller fry are rather a bother with their wrong motions.

14th June 1899 Several children gone to Widemouth at the invitation of the Vicar and his wife! (Rev. William Wilkinson)

13th July 1899 There are now 120 pupils listed in the School Register.

8th October 1900 Week St. Mary School closed as required for use as Polling Station.

13th November 1900 Poor attendance during the afternoon as several boys away because of a demonstration in the village on 'turf hedging'.

28th March 1901 Ground covered in snow; poor attendance.

2nd April 1902 Snow, only 9 children present!

27th July 1903 Two-thirds of the children at a Seaside Picnic.

15th February 1904 Work of week vigorous and accurate. Average 96.8 attendance; this is the highest average since the school has been built.

23rd February 1904 Over 100 children present today.

15th March 1904 Over 110 children present today. There are not enough desks and work is cramped.

26th May 1904 Gloomy sultry day. Temperature registers 72°F at 2.45 p.m. and there are 80 children crowded in large classroom and 34 infants in their classroom. Children are listless and restless. Air is unhealthy.

24th June 1904 Average attendance for the week is 110 out of 135 on the books.

8th July 1904 The school is poorly attended this afternoon. 87 out of 136; this is owing to haymaking.

5th May 1905 School Inspector's Report states that children are over-crowded by 25% with some 120 children crowded in the small school.

19th September 1905 Week St. Mary School to be closed on the orders of Dr. Reutroch(?) owing to Scarlet Fever in the village.

23rd October 1905 Discipline is falling owing to great overcrowding.

12th June 1906 A young person of the parish is to be buried today so several children away.

29th June 1906 School extension well under way; very noisy and dusty.

26th September 1906 Large numbers of children away. Potatoes are being lifted so children kept at home.

5th November 1906 School Inspector's Report says that necessary enlargement of building nearing completion.

7th January 1907 Epidemic of Measles so School closed for 3 weeks by Medical Certificate. School re-opened eventually 18th February. Low attendance.

1st May 1907 (Several reports over previous 5 months). Whooping Cough prevalent again.

November 1907 Stratton Fair today. Several children gone with parents to help drive cattle.

29th January 1908 A daughter of Mr. J. Badcock, former resident of this parish, is to be buried today in the village churchyard. They have asked for 10 or 12 boys to hold the horses at 3 p.m.

1st May 1908 A very poor attendance this afternoon as there is a May Day concert at the Rectory and the children are away at the practice.

25th June 1908 Several children away on account of the Free Methodist Anniversary.

22nd September 1908 A. W. Rablen commenced work today as headmaster.

28th September 1908 Miss Squire commenced work as Assistant Mistress.

15th March 1909 Week St. Mary 'Fair Day' today. Snow is falling and is lying inches deep on the ground.

13th May 1909 By consent of Manager's, School will open at 1 p.m. and close at 3 p.m. in order to allow Bible Christian children to attend funeral of woman connected to Sunday School.

6th July 1909 Medical examination today, 40 children examined. 4 were pronounced mentally defective, 2 advised to take medicine and 1 told to visit eye doctor as soon as possible.

20th September 1909 School closed on account of Week St. Mary Revel.

20th May 1910 School will not open today on account of the funeral of King Edward VII.

26th October 1910 Nellie Cobbledick is frequently late, especially in the mornings. This afternoon she arrived at 1.55 p.m. and as the register had been closed for 20 minutes I sent her home.

9th January 1911 Managers decided school could not open owing to work connected with new folding partition.

26th June 1911 School closed for Coronation of King George V.

18th July 1911 School closed for Choral and Temperance Festivals.

1913 Repeated entries saying the School closed today for Church Outings, Choral Festivals, Band of Hope Festival, trips to Widemouth, etc.

1914 No mention of WW1.

29th January 1915 Influenza, ringworm and scab amongst the children. School to be closed for 2 weeks by order of the Medical Officer.

7th June 1915 At the Music Competition held at Wadebridge on 21st May Week St. Mary School won Trefusis Banner, scoring 98/100 for sight singing and 183/200 for songs of all grades of competition, this School won the highest marks in both sections.

30th March 1917 Today I resign charge of this school due to my failing eyesight (A.W. Rablen).

2nd April 1917 I took temporary charge of the School today (W. J. Whittaker).

5th May 1917 W. J. Whittaker resigned temporary duty.

21st November 1917 George Reed has to stay away from School, having Scarletina. Florence Reed, his sister, also must stay away.

11th December 1917 The capture of Jerusalem has been announced and at the request of the Vicar the School will close at 3.30 p.m. to enable children to attend Thanksgiving Service in the Church at 3.45 p.m.

21st January 1918 Visit by Rev. Haslam in connection with proposed presentation to be made to Miss Jones who is leaving at the end of February.

12th February 1918 We are having a weekly collection of eggs for wounded soldiers and sailors. 52 eggs have been brought in today and sent to Launceston.

15th March 1918 Miss McMerkin from Liskeard commenced duty as supply teacher today.

6th May 1918 Miss Mellor appointed Assistant Mistress has declined the post.

27th May 1918 Mrs. Williams has commenced duty as Assistant Mistress.

5th June 1918 Have to proceed to Plymouth tomorrow to join the Army and I now resign charge of the School. (E. J. Leggo).

6th June 1918 Miss Bettison commenced work as Assistant Mistress.

10th June 1918 I take charge today (E. M. Hawking).

5th July 1918 Resigned charge of School (E. M. Hawking).

8th July 1918 Took charge of School (J. E. Dean).

17th September 1918 A new cooking stove was placed in Infants room today.

9th October 1918 Received instruction from Managers to close School next week for potato lifting.

25th November 1918 Only 25 of our 80 children present. School closed until 9th December. A lot of sickness in the village.

14th February 1919 The egg collection for wounded soldiers has now ceased. 1,591 eggs have been sent since 12th February, 1918.

24th February 1919 Have returned to take charge of School after being absent on Military Service. (E. J. Leggo).

23rd May 1919 Visited by Mrs. Curtis who talked to children about Empire Day and the proposed village War Memorial.

18th June 1919 A School Library has been started.

30th June 1919 Peace was signed on Saturday so the Union Jack was flown today from one of the trees in the playground.

5th February 1920 School closed until 12th February, owing to Scabies.

27th February 1920 74 children on the register and every child present all week.

8th March 1920 Miss Barbary commenced as Certified Assistant Mistress.

25th February 1921 The playground has been covered with a layer of stones which have not been rolled into the ground. The result is that children are unable to play any games and it is impossible to do Physical Exercises as the stones are so sharp.

23rd June 1921 School closed for birthday of Prince of Wales.

28th February 1922 Week St. Mary School closed for marriage of Princess Mary.

26th June 1922 Word from District Clerk that Doris Colwill has been successful in passing Minor Scholarship Examination held at Bude on 27th May.

24th November 1922 Received load of farmyard manure for School garden from Mr. W. Smale of Week Green.

6th March 1923 Received word from Bude Secondary School that the body of the wheelbarrow for the school garden is complete, but that they have difficulty in getting a wheel!

24th May 1923 Empire Day. A cross of flowers and wreaths were placed on the War Memorial by the children. Sports were afterwards held in a field lent by Mr. W. Smale.

1st October 1923 I take charge of School (D. Pearce).

8th January 1924 (First mention of...) Miss Retallack as Supply Teacher.

23rd January 1924 Being fine weather the opportunity was taken of carrying out operations in the school garden.

15th February 1924 A boy was excluded today as he has ringworm. Notified County Medical Officer.

18th February 1924 New gates fitted at the entrance to the playground.

31st March 1924 Miss Best absent today so Miss Retallack took charge.

4th April 1924 Miss Best Certificated Assistant, finished duty here today.

7th April 1924 Miss Isabel Trembach, the new Assistant, will not commence duty until later in the week. Miss Retallack took over lower department and I took the upper section.

29th April 1924 The Headmaster is absent (sick). Dr. King, local MOH visited the school and recommended its closure.

1st May 1924 Received order by telephone to close school at once. This was done 3.50 p.m.

2nd May 1924 Received covering letter about school closure School will re-open 26th May.

10th June 1924 Miss Retallack absent today for purpose of being medically inspected at Bude. The prefect system was explained to upper class today. Those chosen were John Stacey, Dennis Treleven, Christine Masters and Olive Leach.

15th September 1924 Miss Retallack is acting as supply teacher at Whitstone until September 18th.

22nd September 1924 School closed Week St. Mary Revel.

29th October 1924 School closed, being used as Polling Station.

11th November 1924 Armistice Day School marched to War Memorial and there observed two minutes silence.

17th February 1925 Received two coal buckets and one iron mat from Mrs. Martyn.

26th May 1925 Empire Day Sports were held in a field adjoining the school, kindly lent by Mr. W. Smale.

8th June 1925 An extract from report by H.M. Inspector, Mr. W. Page, states, "The Headmaster began duty in October 1923 and conducts the School in a capable manner. The order is good and the children show a keen interest in their work. Entertainments by children have secured about £20 for Provident, a Library and Apparatus. The teaching of Gardening is on good lines...."

25th June 1925 School closed in afternoon by consent of Managers owing to Anniversary at Week Green Chapel.

25th October 1925 Received notification that Cookery classes commence at this school.

27th October 1925 Received Horticultural Superintendent's Report on school gardens. Week St. Mary is again awarded First Class Certificate.

10th June 1926 School closed this afternoon on account of Royal Cornwall Show at Launceston.

22nd July 1926 School closed today, Flower Show and Fete at The Rectory.

18th February 1927 The stove in the Infant Room is smoking badly. I have reported same to District Clerk. I am getting the blacksmith to see to it.

3rd June 1927 School closed. 20 children and staff visited the 'Education Week' exhibition at Truro.

15th July 1927 Three children awarded book prizes for essays in connection with Beethoven Centennial Celebrations (Ida Pooley, Freda Prouse and Cyril Petherick).

3rd March 1928 School piano is being delivered.

4th May 1928 The county has approved a £5 grant for a school library the school has raised equal amount.

30th October 1928 Attendance for week 72.2% due to large amount of sickness.

18th February 1929 Michael Treleven has been awarded a scholarship at Bude.

15th April 1929 Owing to measles the county M.O. has advised exclusion of under 5's for at least one week.

11th November 1929 Armistice Day, lessons given and children listened to wireless service from the Cenotaph.

23rd January 1930 School closed this afternoon on account of Dedication Services at the church.

10th June 1930 Sir Donald Maclean, M.P. visited the School this afternoon.

13th October 1930 Miss Retallack sent to Jacobstow as Temporary Supply Teacher.

27th October 1930 Miss Retallack returned to Week St. Mary.

28th May 1930 Miss Retallack assigned to Whitstone School permanently.

15th January 1932 Mumps and Jaundice widespread.

3rd March 1932 New stove fitted in small classroom. 72 children on the Register.

20th June 1933 School closed. Rechabite outing.

11th July 1933 Cookery classes started under Miss William. Mr. Jeffery called to take measurements for a plan of school and playground.

11th September 1933 There are now 77 children listed in the school register.

20th October 1933 18 children absent through Measles and sickness.

1st November 1933 Miss Winifred Retallack here as supplementary teacher.

8th November 1933 Scarlet Fever. One child infected and two contacts excluded.

17th November 1933 Seven children absent with Scarlet Fever.

20th November 1933 School closed due to Scarlet Fever.

18th December 1933 School re-opens.

15th January 1934 Severe storm overnight; loose tiles and broken roof lights.

17th April 1934 Received new rake and spade from Gillbard's, Launceston and plans for coke house.

10th September 1934 There are now 72 children listed in the school register.

30th October 1934 Mrs. M. J. Martin *(no relation: Author)*, caretaker, has died.

29th November 1934 School closed due to wedding of Duke of Kent and Princess Marina.

11th March 1935 Heavy snowstorm. 31 children attended in the morning and 36 in the afternoon out of a total of 70 children on the books.

24th June 1935 No-one to take Miss Truscott's place, for the time being Miss Retallack taking classes 2 and 3 together.

3rd December 1935 Received six tables and six dual table desks. One inkwell and one table leg broken.

21st January 1936 King George V died last night. Suitable lessons and remarks made to children.

28th January 1936 School closed for funeral of King George V.

7th September 1936 There are now 65 children listed in the school register.

30th November 1936 Much sickness prevails (colds and Whooping Cough).

1st March 1937 Heavy snow showers, only 30 children attended in the morning and 32 in the afternoon.

18th March 1937 Received 12 dual desks and 24 chairs. One chair broken, has been returned.

1st July 1937 Replacement chair received.

6th September 1937 Playground unsatisfactory due to demolition of old lavatories and erection of new.

1st December 1937 School closed. H.M. King George VI visiting Launceston, 46 children taken to see him.

26th March 1938 18/9d to District Clerk from selling needlework.

30th March 1938 Playground levelling begun.

18th May 1938 Miss Retallack absent. Gone to Plymouth to present a purse to Queen Mary on behalf of L.H.F. (?).

2nd March 1939 All children measured for gas masks by district ARP officer.

14-15th June 1939 Headmaster absent, acting as Steward at Royal Cornwall Show at Bude.

4th October 1939 Work on resurfacing yard begun.

16th October 1939 Miss Retallack sent to Kilkhampton school.

18th October 1939 Miss Retallack returns to Week St. Mary.

17th June 1940 About 50 evacuees have arrived from Croydon. Their teacher has been given permission to use the school building if they wish to get the children together.

4th July 1940 Evacuees using Methodist Sunday School for teaching purposes.

12th November 1940 Boy fell in the yard today and broke a finger. Sent to doctor and finger set.

12th December 1940 Highly successful concert given by scholars of this school in conjunction with Sydenham evacuees.

14th March 1941 Consenting children inoculated against Diphtheria.

10th April 1941 Harold Sincock resigns as Headmaster.

20th April 1941 Under instructions from Truro P.H.S. Martin takes charge of this school. Eighteen evacuees from Bristol admitted.

14th May 1941 Twenty evacuees from Plymouth admitted.

4th December 1941 Fry's Cocoa Film Unit gave a display at the school.

29th June 1942 First Aid and Home Nursing Course held at school under Dr. Freeth.

31st March 1943 School closed under 'Invasion Exercise'.

20th December 1943 Sgt. Richards (Police) came and talked on the 'butterfly bomb'.

21st December 1944 School party in the Rectory Room; juniors at 3.30pm and seniors at 7.30pm organised by troops from Cleave Camp.

5th July 1945 Evacuees returned home and teaching divided between P.H.S. Martin and Miss Retallack.

28th June 1946 Only 13 children out of 45 were in attendance, due to an epidemic of Measles.

15th July 1946 Brenda Pooley wins scholarship to Bude Grammar School and Michael Martin wins boarding scholarship to Launceston College.

5th July 1947 Garfield Higgins and Catherine Congdon win scholarship to Bude Grammar School.

19th November 1947 Headmaster absent, taking his wife to Plymouth hospital for urgent operation.

15th April 1948 Miss Retallack off with broken ankle.

13th October 1948 Piano tuner called.

28th March 1949 By arrangement with Mr. & Mrs. Charlick a canteen has been started in the Temperance Hotel.

28th January 1950 Eight children taken the first test for transfer to Grammar School.

12th June 1950 P.H.S. Martin handed over to Miss Lane. "...in view of the condition of my health, it is unlikely that I shall again have charge of this school".

12th July 1950 School holiday for Royal Cornwall Show.

14th February 1951 Milk (bulk) to be boiled.

29th June 1951 Miss Lane leaving, Miss Mosely will take over on 1st July 1951.

10th January 1952 Milk was delivered from Mr. Martin's farm at Sea View.

6th February 1952 News of death of King George VI.

28th February 1952 Miss Mosely resigned and Miss Retallack appointed.

11th December 1952 School nurse (Piper) visited.

20th March 1953 Received news that P.H.S. Martin passed away this morning.

23rd March 1953 9am, children lined up outside school as the coffin was loaded into the hearse, bearing our wreath.

29th January 1954 Heavy snow and roads blocked. Snow level with school walls in places.

16th December 1954 School party. Progress prizes won by Pat Martin, John Ellis, Jeanette Rogers and David Martin.

8th February 1955 Mr. Parsons, plumber, called to inspect sinks, etc. with a view to connecting to mains water supply going down the main road of the village.

24th February 1955 Heavy snow and frost, all frozen!

3rd February 1956 Cold, only 31°F all morning.

9th May 1956 School closed. Children taken to Launceston to see Queen Elizabeth and Duke of Edinburgh.

30th January 1957 Gave Mrs. Harris (caretaker) new coal bucket from stock.

11th December 1957 Mr. & Mrs. Vedrenne presented prizes: Progress Prizes to Susan Martin and Mark Wadge, in the infant class and Mervyn Colwill and Jennifer Orchard from junior class. Most popular boy and girl was Tessa Wadge and Joseph Paynter.

8th January 1958 Owing to death of Miss Mosely I take charge now (Ruth Saltern).

6th May 1958 Ruth Saltern confirmed as Head Teacher.

25th October 1958 Boys urinal pipe leaky.

25th November 1958 Record player delivered.

15th December 1958 Annual prize giving: Silver Cup presented to David Martin and Owen Booker; Progress Awards to Arthur McCall, Barbara Harris, Joanna Kaluzenska, Susan Martin, Mark Wadge, Susan Deans, Ivor Cobbledick and Elaine McCall.

30th January 1959 Robert Booker tripped over a step and cut his head. Nurse dressed it for him.

29th April 1959 Susan Martin slipped in the classroom, fell on her wrist and fractured a bone. Dr. Ward contacted and he ordered her removal to Stratton Hospital. I took her and her mother to Stratton where Dr. Ward examined it and sent her to Plymouth.

25th May 1959 Susan Martin had plaster removed today.

29th July 1959 Mrs. Deans appointed caretaker.

16th December 1959 Prize giving: Miss E. Paynter gave prizes to David Martin, Susan Martin, Margaret Cobbledick, Margaret Venning (juniors); Samuel Boundy, Ivor Cobbledick, Mary Deans and Linda Martin (infants). Cups to Barbara Harris and Mark Wadge.

11th March 1960 Test papers received for one child (David Martin).

17th March 1960 Test taken by David Martin today.

30th September 1960 Severe flooding on many roads. Mrs. Saltern and several children were late arriving.

18th July 1961 Two cases Measles confirmed.

18th June 1962 School floors have been sanded and sealed.

19th September 1962 Miss Retallack heard today she has been given a one year extension of service as she will be 65 at Christmas, up to 31st December 1963.

8th January 1963 38 children on school register. All present despite roads covered with packed snow and ice. 44°F in class.

25th September 1963 Health Office (Truro) says milk will come from Davidstow milk factory.

1-3rd October 1963 Milk arriving too late for use and milk has been cancelled.

19th December 1963 Miss Retallack presented with £28 and bouquet from pupils.

11th June 1964 Diane Smeeth reported for supply duty.

9th September 1964 There are now 27 children on the school register.

15th December 1964 Diane Smeeth confirmed as infant teacher at this school.

8th April 1965 Prizes awarded to the following children from Messrs. Brooke Bond: Valerie Baker, Ann Harwood, Alison Sandercock, Terry Harris, John Sandercock and Julie Martin.

11th May 1966 Two children received prizes in a Children's Art Exhibition in Launceston: Ian Horrell (2nd) and Julie Martin (3rd).

11th July 1966 Two children absent with Chicken Pox.

17th January 1967 One child absent with Measles.

20th March 1968 Sgt. Scott addressed the children on road safety.

4th July 1968 Telephone installed by G.P.O. (Week St. Mary 370).

18th September 1968 Messrs. Woolacott's installed new radio.

19th September 1968 Messrs. Woolacott's installed new aerial.

2nd November 1968 Harvest Supper held in school for Parish Hall Committee.

7th January 1969 There are now 23 children on school register.

2nd June 1969 Julie Martin received notification of place at Bude Grammar School.

1st July 1969 Investiture of H.R.H. Prince Charles as Prince of Wales shown on T.V. Juniors to Temperance Hotel and infants to Mrs. Baker's to watch.

16th July 1969 Juniors to Temperance Hotel to see the launch of Apollo 12 on T.V., the first men on the moon.

7th January 1970 Roof put over boys' urinal.

27th April 1970 Three children confirmed with German Measles.

20th May 1970 Susan Drouet (7yrs); school painting, has won a prize in Cann Medland's car competition and Wendy Horrell (7yrs) was highly commended.

18th December 1970 School Party after tea each child was presented with a gift by the youngest pupils, Stephen Martin and Andrew Cobbledick.

9th September 1971 There are now 19 children on the school register.

13th October 1971 Managers Meeting our school, Poundstock and St. Gennys will close and all children will go to new school around January 1973.

16th February 1972 Owing to power crisis we are not using any lights or water heater.

1st March 1972 Two cases of Whooping Cough reported.

7th March 1972 Mr. Law (Head of Bude Grammar School) and Mr. Rayner called at 2.30pm to interview 2 girls.

13th March 1972 The County Library van visited today and exchanged 100 books.

5th June 1972 Three children, Patricia Gubbin, Jill Hutchings and Peter Prust have been selected for Bude Grammar School.

18th October 1972 Both classes and teachers went to Boyton Church Hall for a puppet show by the Da Silva Puppet Co.

20th November 1972 One day's holiday on the occasion of the Silver Wedding on H.M. Queen Elizabeth II and H.R.H. Prince Philip.

9th January 1973 School re-opened after Christmas with all 24 pupils present.

15th February 1973 Roads covered with frozen snow.

3rd April 1973 Dr. Patterson carried out full medical examination today.

11th April 1973 Mr. Henchley took photo of the children walking down to dinner at the Temperance Hotel and at the playground for the local teacher centre. Mr. Hunn called and took wireless and record player away.

Week St. Mary County Primary School now **CLOSED** and all pupils transferred to the new school at Jacobstow.

Week St. Mary children with Mr Bill Gordon and his mini-bus, starting out for Jacobstow School - Summer 1976

Lasting Impressions

As with all collections there are items that duplicate, items that are not quite up to the required specification and some that don't quite fit into any exact category. In some cases you find that you have a vast number of items falling into just one or two sections. This has not put me off - I have decided not to disappoint anyone by excluding such images but to try and include as many photographs as possible in this last section of the Appendix.

I hope that each of you will find something to smile at or just be excited as you recall similar scenes or events from your own past. Whilst some of the pictures are self-explanatory and therefore will have no captions, others are quite important in their way and I will add any notes that may have been provided by the contributors.

Farming in the Week St. Mary area using techniques long gone, even the combine harvester (above) is looking rather dated by today's standards of machinery

A fine set of footballers; men -v- women, or is it the other way round?

Some feudal dues as presented to the Duke of Cornwall
(Left) Petrol pumps at Maddocks Garage

1921.

A meeting was held in the Rectory room on Monday Aug 15= at 8 o'clock, to do about the purchasing of the room as Mr Whitmell wanted a definite offer by the Tuesday morning of £150 or he would have to take some other means to dispose of the room, after it was proposed that we purchase the room. the sum pro. Dr Coates seconded Mr Badcock. of £11· 0· 6 was promised at the meeting. and the churchwardens. H Rogers & N Coles. was asked to see Messers Peter & Son. whom Mr Whitmell had appointed as agent for the sale of the room,

An extract of the minutes regarding the sale of the Rectory Room

On a calm day it needed 25 men to grab the three guy ropes but more if the weather was bad.

Once hauled down they were attached to very large concrete balls

Stephen Henry Broomhead who joined the RFC in 1915, and after an air communications course at Cranwell, joined RNAS.

Looking every inch an aviator - dressed in leather coat, goggles and boots - he was photographed at Langford Woods

50-mile walkers:
Roy Barriball, David Martin, Rodney Duke, Graham Axford
Mavis Colwill, Esther Colwill, Hester Barriball, Monica Jones
Maureen Axford, Ivor Barber, Jackie Colwill, Marcel Ellacott

Evacuees on a field trip to pick daffodils to send home, but the 4th girl from the right (front row) is not too happy... she had fallen in the water!

Week St. Mary Band outside Burdenwell
Barrie Haslam, Bert Rowland, John Horrell, Tom Sandercock, Len Maddock, Hartley Orchard
John Lyle, Ern Higgins, Owen Smale, Mr Goodman [drum] of Whitstone

Looking south, towards Week Green Hill, from Blacksmith's Corner

The Square as viewed from the church tower - note the market has gone
and new buildings are under way

Crowning of the Harvest Queen
on the Village Green

Week St. Mary Parish Hall - a unique
and innovative design, pictured upon
completion

A garden fete on the Rectory lawn

The Rev Simpson bringing up the rear of a 'training' session - Revel circa 1963

The schoolchildren, accompanied by headmistress Mrs Saltern, processing to
The Square for the commencement of the Revel celebrations

...and another fine example of 'men -v- women' or is it?

The Tree Inn - 1905

Audrey Tarrant says: This was taken on a later visit with my friend Molly Perry (neé Tarvin) on one horse, Mr. Rogers from Trefrouse on the other and Owen Smale from Waxhill walking with his dog

Some of the clearly defined ruins at Penhallam

WEEK ST. MARY,

Painting Rectory Dec. 1925.

Church Room .... Room with voluntary help.

Dr. to R. P. ROWLAND & SON,

Builders, Wheelwrights & Undertakers.

1925		£	s	d
June	56 lbs purple brown @ 6d.	1	8	.
	2 gals 1 pt linseed oil		9	7
	2 qt 1 pt terebine		11	7
	42 lbs light Slate paint @ 10°	1	5	.
	14 lbs white paint @ 10°		11	8
		£ 4	15	10.

Paid 25

Accounts from John Wesley's Journal

Tuesday 18th June 1745

Being invited by the Rector of St. Mary Week, (about seven miles from St. Ginny's,) to preach in his church, we went thither in the afternoon. I had not seen in these parts of Cornwall, either so large a church or so large a congregation.

Tuesday 16th July 1745

About three I preached in St. Mary Week church, on "Repent ye, and believe the Gospel" (Mark 1.15).

Monday 15th September 1746

A guide, meeting us at Camelford, conducted us to St. Mary Week. It was the time of the yearly revel, which obliged me to speak very plain.

Sunday 26th July 1747

I preached at Tamerton church in the morning; Mary Week, in the afternoon, and St. Ginny's in the evening.

Sunday 1st September 1751

We were well buffeted both with wind and rain, in riding from thence (Tresmere) to John Turner's, where the congregation was waiting for me; and we had another season of solemn joy in the Lord.

Sunday 2nd October 1757

I rode to Mary-Week. A large congregation was gathered there, many of whom came seven or eight miles. The house stands in the midst of orchards and meadows, surrounded by gentle rising hills. I preached on the side of a meadow newly mown, to a deeply attentive people.

Monday 29th September 1760

Being invited, by the Minister of Mary Week, to preach in his church, I crossed over the country, and came thither about four in the afternoon. The congregation was large, considering the weather, and quite attentive and unconcerned.

Monday 27th September 1762

I rode to Mary Week. It was a kind of fair-day; "Tend the people were come far and near for wrestling and other diversions; but they found a better way of employing their time, for young and old flocked to church from all quarters."

1569 Muster of Weeke Mary

John Moris: gent doblet bill pr.splints
John Colwill: bow sh. arr scull bill
George Roll: armiger light gelding for light horseman
with requisite harness and weapons corslet pike bow
sh.arr haqbut scull
Degorie Harvy: bill
(blank) Palmer:
R. Mylton:
Ric Clifton: bow 4 arr
James Trewyn: bow 6 arr
Willm Morfill: bow sh.arr
Humfry Morfill:
John Colwyll deThinwood: bill salett hagabut
John Trewyn: bow 12 arr bill
Robert Colwyll: bow
John Perse:
John Wheare: bow 6 arr sallet
John Wheare (jun): bill
Alexander Wheare: bill
Thomas Mylton: bow 12 arr sallet
Edward Mylton:
John Orchard de Melhowse: bill
Willm Sutcott: bill scull
Edmound Orchard: gorget dagger bill
Willm Orchard:
Thomas Sutcott: 6 arrows
Walter Hore: bow 12 arr jack
Thomas Barnepole:
John Sutcott: bow 12 arr
Thomas Weall: bill steel cap
Ric Mores: bow 6 arr
John Alighe:
Ric Alighe: bow 6 arr
Edward Alighe: bill
John Yeare:
Thomas Petheke: bill
Willm Petheke: bow 12 arr
John Oliver: bow 3 arr
Nicolas Bonifant: bow 4 arr
Henrie Worthe: bow 3 arr
Thomas Piper: bill sallet harq.
John Piper: bow 6 arr
Humfry Alighe: sallet bow sh.arr bill
Willm Coke: bill
Gorge Mayne: bow 6 arr
James Trewyne (sen): jack bill
Robt Pethik: bow 6 arr pr.splints
Thomas Pethike: bow 12 arr
Gorge Beafford: bow 16 arr sallet bill
Thomas Beafford: jack sallet bill
John Orchard: bow 6 arrows
Ric Orchard: bill
John Myll de Brendon: bow sh.arr pr.rivets sallet bill
hagabut
John Wickott: bill
Marten Jory: bow 6 arr

Thomas C(ol)wyll: jack sallet bow 12 arrows
Thomas Pawly: bill gorget pr.splints
John Wylls als Heale: bill
John Guscott: sherehoke
Willm Flingger:
Willm Colwyll: bow 6 arr
Davy Heayne: bill
John Jolowe: bill
John Worthe: bow 6 arr
Laurens Worthe: bill
John Juell: corslet bow sh.arr murryn scull
Arthur Mylton: bow 6 arr
John Mehow: bill
Ric Williams: bow 12 arr
John Botters: staff pike
Symone Clifton: bow 6 arr
Willm Smythe:
Willm Savidge: mourich pike
Marten Clifton: bow 6 arr
Robert Richard: bill
Thomas Edye: bill
Mychell Williams: bow 6 arr
Ottes Mayne: bow 6 arr
Walter Bonesall: bill
John Clifton (jun): mourich pike scull
Symon Trewyne: bow 6 arr
John Marten:
John Penvos: bow 4 arrows
Henry Heale: bow 4 arr
John Gibb: bill
Sylvester Cole: bill
Willm Trewyne: bill
Robert Jeffery: bow 6 arr
Thomas Ruffe: bill
John Voler: sherhoke morich pike
John Moole:
John Nowe: bow 6 arrows
John Dogell: bill
John Malber: harqubut
John Prenche: bow 6 arr

The said parishe will find furnishe at theire commen
charges & expences 2 pair of almon Revets.

(Attendance at Muster was compulsory!)

DEFINITION:

doblet	A close fitting body garment
bill	Weapon with spike on the end
jack	Canvas or leather reinforced jacket
halberd	Similar to pole axe
splints	Plates of metal for the forearms
sallet	Short brimmed helmet

And elsewhere....

William Shakespeare 1564: Birth of poet & playwright William Shakespeare at Stratford-upon-Avon, Warwickshire, England. Dies on his 52nd birthday in 1616.

Captain Cook sets sail 1768: English navigator Captain James Cook sets off on his first voyage, to explore the Antipodes.

The Alamo 1836: The Alamo falls to Mexican forces under Santa Anna after a 12 day battle. Frontiersmen Davy Crockett and Jim Bowie are among those killed.

Queen Victoria crowned 1838: Queen Victoria is crowned Queen of England at Westminster Abbey in London at the age of 19.

Crimean War 1853: War starts (1853–56) between Russia and the allied powers of England, France, Turkey, and Sardinia.

Holsworthy to Bude Railway 1898: The Holsworthy to Bude railway opened on 10th August 1898 and closed in 1966 under Dr. Beeching's axe.

First Flight 1903: Wilbur Wright and his brother Orville lived in Dayton, Ohio. They were the first to design and build a flying aircraft. Wilbur was the first to fly in 1903, at Kitty Hawk in America.

Boy Scout movement 1908: Official founding of the Boy Scout Movement by Robert Baden-Powell.

First transmission of Newsreel 1954: Richard Baker is the anchorman of Britain's first daily TV news programme.

Sunday Night at the London Palladium 1955: The highlight of weekend television during the 1950s and early 60s, Val Parnell's show makes stars of Bruce Forsyth, Tommy Trinder and Roy Castle.

Dixon of Dock Green 1955: PC George Dixon (Jack Warner) is the first British copper to appear regularly on TV. Famous for his "Evening all" welcome.

Coronation Street debuts 1960: The soap hits the airwaves for the first time and goes on to become Britain's longest-running TV drama series.

England Win World Cup 1966: England beat Germany 4-2 at Wembley to win the Eighth World Cup tournament. Bobby Moore accepts the solid gold trophy from Queen Elizabeth II.

Fall of Berlin Wall 1989: The Wall comes down five days after the East German government resigned following a massive pro-democracy demonstration. Germany is finally reunited in October 1990.

Operation Desert Storm 1991: The Gulf War allies send hundreds of planes on bombing raids into Iraq at the start of Operation Desert Storm. The move comes after Iraq refuses to comply with a UN ultimatum for its troops to withdraw from Kuwait by 15 January.

The Author

You will have read about the arrival of my grandfather, Philip Herbert Samuel Martin, along with the children evacuated from Croydon during the Second World War.

He was asked to take over the position of Headmaster of the village school upon the departure of Mr. Sincock. The Green Inn, formerly the headmaster's residence 'The Beeches' was duly occupied by the Martin family, gran and grandfather with their three children; my father, Alan, being the eldest, along with his sister Betty and younger brother Michael.

When my mother and father married they moved into 3 Broadclose, one of the first families to occupy the new housing. I was born 29th October, 1948, but not without excitement; an ambulance was called to take my mother, Pauline, off to the maternity home. Dad went round to his father's to borrow the car and duly set off.

For some unknown reason my point of arrival into this world was the Looe Maternity Home! As you can imagine I hate being asked where I was born, to which I reply, "In Looe!", followed by the next question, "....in lieu of what?"

The story is that dad arrived at Looe long before the ambulance, apparently they had got lost. Heavens! I could have been born anywhere!

After my sister Susan was born came a second sister, Janet. Complications set in and she was christened at home before passing away after just two days. Two more girls arrived, Linda and Julie, followed by a brother, Stephen. Our dear mother died suddenly on 22nd December 1978 at the young age of 49 years. We have no record of exactly where Janet was buried in the churchyard so we, as a family, decided to mention her on our mother's headstone.

We all went to the local school and took part in many village events. In those days of schooling and the 11+ exams, I was apparently on the borderline and was told I was to retake the exam. Even with a second chance I didn't make it and upon leaving the Primary School, went to the Bude-Stratton Secondary Modern School. After the casual five-minute walk to and from the village school, it was a rude awakening to be at the school at 8.10 a.m. to wait for the bus, not returning to the village until around 4.50 p.m. - a long day!

I left the Secondary School and went to Camborne Technical College. Because of the distance, like many others, you had to stay in rented accommodation, looked after by 'the landlady!' Camborne was not a particularly friendly place but I found that I had a bit of skill on the snooker table. My second vice was the dreaded weed - tobacco!

At weekends I worked at Goscott Farm, for Joyce and Ken Uglow. They were particularly kind to our family, allowing us to have regular firewood, feeding me and a weekly 1lb jar of real cream!

I received 10/- for my all-day Saturday work and helping with the milking on Sunday mornings. Harvest time and school holidays were mostly all spent on the farm; the healthiest time of my life, upon reflection.

I left Camborne College after one year and continued working at Goscott Farm. The day came when I left Goscott and started work at Cann Medland & Co; the biggest garage in Bude, with not just car sales and repairs but a thriving agricultural business.

My position at the garage was that of Trainee Paint Sprayer; under the guidance of a fantastic character, George Trott. He was well past retirement age and had some marvellous tales about when he was a chauffer for a titled family, driving all over Europe.

It was around this time that I started courting Jean, who also worked at the garage at that time. This employment was quite short-lived really and the garage was bought by a large conglomerate. Their first bold move was to get rid of the agricultural side of the business, followed by the 'Paint Shop' - that meant a long queue at the labour exchange.

A short period of unemployment was spent mostly on the premises of the newly opened 'Treetops Tea Room'. Treetops Leisure Cabins was a new holiday complex under the ownership of retired RAF officer, Squadron Leader 'Jimmy' and Mrs Joy Douglas.

He must have influenced me with his stories of service life and I duly joined the Royal Air Force on 20th February 1967, signing up for a 9-year term.

I married Jean, after a three-year courtship, at Copthorne Methodist Chapel. A very small and quiet wedding, with the reception back at Treetops. In August 1970 I was posted to RAF Akrotiri, Cyprus, where our son Paul was born. I must say I much preferred the climate!

After three years we returned to RAF Chivenor, in north Devon. A nice little camp that allowed us to return to Week St. Mary most weekends, taking both Paul and our cat! He (the cat!) travelled in a box between Jean's feet and after a few weeks of this procedure, Sunday afternoons would find him hanging around the box, waiting to return home.

Then a dramatic change - they announced the closure of RAF Chivenor! All of the camp was off to RAF Brawdy in Pembrokeshire, Wales. I was one of the last to leave the then ghost camp after having packed up most of our workshop equipment for the journey to Wales.

We lived in a flat in Haverfordwest until approaching my last year of service. I decided not to 'sign-on' for another term as the chances were that my next posting would have been a 12-month unaccompanied tour. I certainly didn't want to leave my family.

Employment was not easy to find, nor accommodation, staying with Jean's mother in the village. Eventually we were offered a house in Stratton - we have been here for the best part of thirty-one years!

In 1980 I was 'lucky' to have been accepted for the position of Driving Examiner, undergoing training at the Department of Transport Training Establishment near Bedford. My first year of probation was spent at Chertsey, in Surrey, and this meant a lot of travelling at weekends, all done on my motorcycle, in all sorts of weather, including snowdrifts at Halwill!

My next posting was to Barnstaple where I stayed for eight years before moving to Launceston for a further five. My fifteen years saw nearly 25,000 candidates pass through my hands on a variety of vehicles, ranging from cars, vans and motorcycles to tractors, track laying vehicles and road rollers!

Jean had been working for a local printing and stationery company until the company was about to close, so it seemed natural that we should open a stationery shop.

The Week St. Mary web site was the reason for collecting so much information in the first place and a book just had to be written before all the history is forgotten. As the village becomes occupied by more younger families, many not from this area, the number of 'locals' becomes less and less until one day the old stories and history of the village will have faded completely away.

I hope that this book will help to maintain the excitement and love of the best village in the land - our 'home' - Week St. Mary!

Above: Independence on three wheels

Above Right: My namesake village in the New Forest

Right: My 'Passing Out Parade' at R.A.F. Hemswell, 1967

Bibliography / References

1. Doomsday Book extracts can be found at www.domesdayextracts.co.uk

2. About the Norman Conquest - Britannica Concise Encyclopaedia Copyright © 2006 by Encyclopædia Britannica, Inc.. Published by Encyclopædia Britannica, Inc..

3. English Ecclesiastical Law. The right of presentation of a candidate to a benefice or church office.

4. Map of Cornwall by John Seller, 1694; Taken from Antiquities of England and Wales by Francis Grose, 1787

5. Blanchminster Charity, 12th cent -1949: deeds and accounts; Cornwall Record Office

6. Thomasine Bonventure: "Romance Of Week St. Mary" Published by Frederick Warne & Co Ltd 1930.

7. Matthew Davies; 'Dame Thomasine Percyvale "The Maid of Week" (d. 1512)'

8. C. S. Gilbert 1820; "An Historical Survey of the County of Cornwall to which is added a complete Heraldry of the same, with numerous engravings"

9. Richard Carew (1555-1620); "Survey of Cornwall" published 1602

10. Week St. Mary Magazine

11. Miss D. J. Matthews; "A Year In The Life Of Week St. Mary"

12. Lambley Park Country Hotel - http://www.lambley-park.co

13. From an original sale document by kind permission of Mr & Mrs Coles

14. Bob Booker - Parish Magazine

15. Week St. Mary Parish Council Records

16. J Cocks (1888-1988) Centenary of Week St. Mary Methodist Chapel; and numerous Members of the Week St. Mary Methodist Circuit

17. Richard Guest; "A Loving Father", Tredenham Publishing ISBN 0952430118

18. "Narrative of the Adventures and Escape of Moses Roper, from American Slavery", published in 1848 at Berwick-upon-Tweed, Printed at the Warder Office

19. 'The Complete Parish Officer' 1772, Printed by W. Strahan & M Woodfall

20. Josef Sedlich and Francis Hirst, "A History of Local Government in England" 2nd Edition 1970

21. 'The Office of Constables' Sir Francis Bacon 1610; contained within 'The Complete Parish Officer' 1772, Printed by W. Strahan & M Woodfall

22. 'The Office of Constables' Sir Francis Bacon 1610; contained within 'The Complete Parish Officer' 1772, Printed by W. Strahan & M Woodfall

23. Recommended Reading Peter London; U-Boat Hunters Cornwall's Air War 1916-19

24. Bob Booker; for communications with the ROC Association and Lawrence Holmes (Truro Branch ROC) for providing the information from which this article references

25. As reported by The Cornish & Devon Post

26. Philip Herbert Samuel Martin; War Time Correspondent, Headmaster & Grandfather!

27. Week St. Mary Magazine - Contact Lesley Booker

28. The Blizzard In The West On the Night of March 9th, 1891; Simpkin, Marshall, Hamilton, Kent & Co., Limited, Paternoster Row, London

29. Week St. Mary bids farewell: Market moving to Hallworthy. Reproduced by kind permission of the Cornish & Devon Post

30. Mrs Linda Cobbledick - "Week St. Mary over the past 50 years"

31. Bench Mark Database: www.bench-marks.org.uk

32. Bob Booker & John Clifton (Palm Beach Florida) for their endless research and contributions

Whilst many examples of the above can be found on the Internet, in the main, any such references have been made only to those items found in the public domain. Assorted references have been made to a wide variety of brief but important web references to which all extracts are acknowledged.

In some cases it has been impossible to confirm the exact details regarding the origin and therefore copyright of photographs and/or documents, despite extensive enquiries. Frequently similar, but slightly differing, copies of an article or image exists in the hands of several people, thus confusing the situation even more. Every effort has been made to trace the copyright holders and they will be duly acknowledged if they come forward. Should this be the case their understanding and support is therefore appreciated in the preservation of this example of local history.

Definitions / Explanations

d1. Greena Moor (Greenamoor) Grid Ref: SX 234 963: lies south of the village by nearly 1 mile and is an area now classified as a Site of Special Scientific Interest (SSSI). It covers an area of some 30 hectares (79 acres) and is classed as type 'Fen, marsh and swamp'

d2. Before decimalisation in 1970, the monetary system in use was as follows: a pound (£) contained 20 shillings (1s or 1/-), and 1 shilling consisted of 12 pence (1d). Therefore an amount of money may be expressed as '£1/12/7' or '£1 12s 7d' (both being defined as 1 pound, 12 shillings and 7 pence). A guinea was £1/1/0 (1 pound and 1 shilling) - a unit still used today in horse racing circles

d3. 'feoffee' Middle-English: One to whom a feoffment is granted. The historical method of granting a freehold estate in land by actual delivery of possession originally by livery of seisin

d4. Dunheved College, later Launceston College, was founded in 1873. Originally housed in Westgate Street, because of its popularity and increasing roll, the school moved in 1874 to the site it now occupies. In 1931 Dunheved College was purchased by Cornwall County Council. At the same time it was amalgamated with the Horwell Grammar School for Boys and was re-named Launceston College. There were just 122 pupils with their Headmaster H. Spencer Toy. Launceston College became a co-educational grammar school when the Horwell Grammar School for Girls joined it in 1962. This merger accompanied a building programme enabling improved coverage of the curriculum. Two years later the Launceston College again increased greatly in buildings and pupil numbers when the Pennygillam County Secondary School was phased out. Since January 1965 Launceston College has received all children of the town and from a very large catchment area

d5. Polyphant stone, which is worked near Lewannick, Cornwall, is a very distinctive rock of limited occurrence. It has been used for ornamental carvings since the 11th century and is currently worked on a small scale, for sculptural, monumental, decorative and dimensional purposes

d6. Ornamental facing or screen behind an altar in a church, free-standing or forming part of the retable. In larger churches it separates the choir from the retrochoir, Ladychapel, and other parts to the liturgical east, and is often found enriched with statues in niches, pinnacles, etc.

d7. Landmark Trust: a charity founded in 1965 that rescues and restores historic buildings at risk and gives them a new life by offering them for holidays. For more information please visit: www.landmarktrust.org.uk

d8. Bude Grammar School, Bramble Hill, Bude, was amalgamated with Bude-Stratton Secondary Modern School in 1973, to form the Budehaven Community School. The Grammar School building was demolished soon afterwards

d9. The Cunard liner 'Carpathia', so instrumental in rescuing survivors from Titanic - was torpedoed by a German U-Boat in 1918 and sunk with the loss of just 5 men, whilst 215 survived

d10. 'Cann Medland & Co' Was a British Leyland garage, situated opposite the railway station, in Bude, now the site of a busy filling station

d11. Church Army: Wilson Carlile founded the Church Army society in 1882. As an unconventional Church of England curate his vision was to encourage and enable ordinary Christian people to live the good news of Jesus Christ in such a way that others would be attracted to follow Him. Carlile believed very much that the Christian message had to be shared through words and action and he encouraged grooms, coachmen and other working people to witness to their faith in the open air and at packed indoor gatherings. For more information please visit: www.churcharmy.org.uk

d12. Stratton Workhouse - on the site of the A W Bent factory, by the A39

Index

Week St. Mary Village

Village

a community at large

Old College - built 1506

"Be judged by the sum of your deeds"